UNIVERSITY OF SOUTHERN MAINE

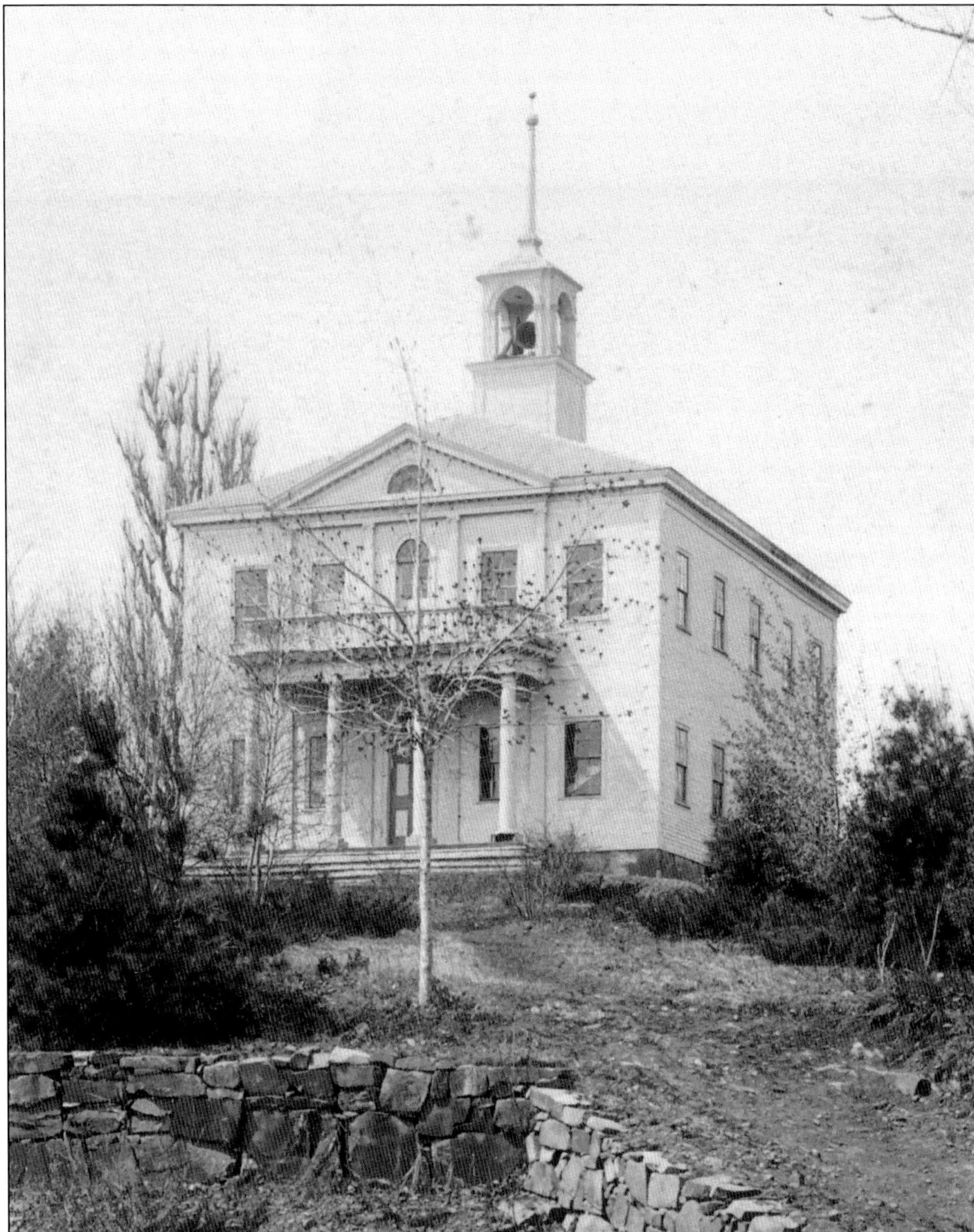

Academy Hall is not only the oldest classroom building on campus but is also one of the best examples of Federal school architecture in Maine. The building was a precursor to the university. After the closing of Gorham Academy, its trustees searched for a good use for its buildings, leading to the founding of the Western State Normal School in Gorham. Ironically, the hall was insufficient for the newer institution and, although used occasionally, it was not leased to the normal school until 1910. That year, the trustees wisely stipulated in a 999-year lease that the exterior could not be changed and that the building must be restored exactly if it became damaged or destroyed. (Detail.)

The College History Series

UNIVERSITY OF SOUTHERN MAINE

JOYCE K. BIBBER

ARCADIA PUBLISHING

ISBN 978-0-7385-0537-4

Published by Arcadia Publishing
Charleston, South Carolina

Printed in the United States of America

Library of Congress Catalog Card Number: 2001086985.

For all general information contact Arcadia Publishing at:
Telephone 843-853-2070
Fax 843-853-0044
E-mail sales@arcadiapublishing.com
For customer service and orders:
Toll-Free 1-888-313-2665

Visit us on the Internet at www.arcadiapublishing.com

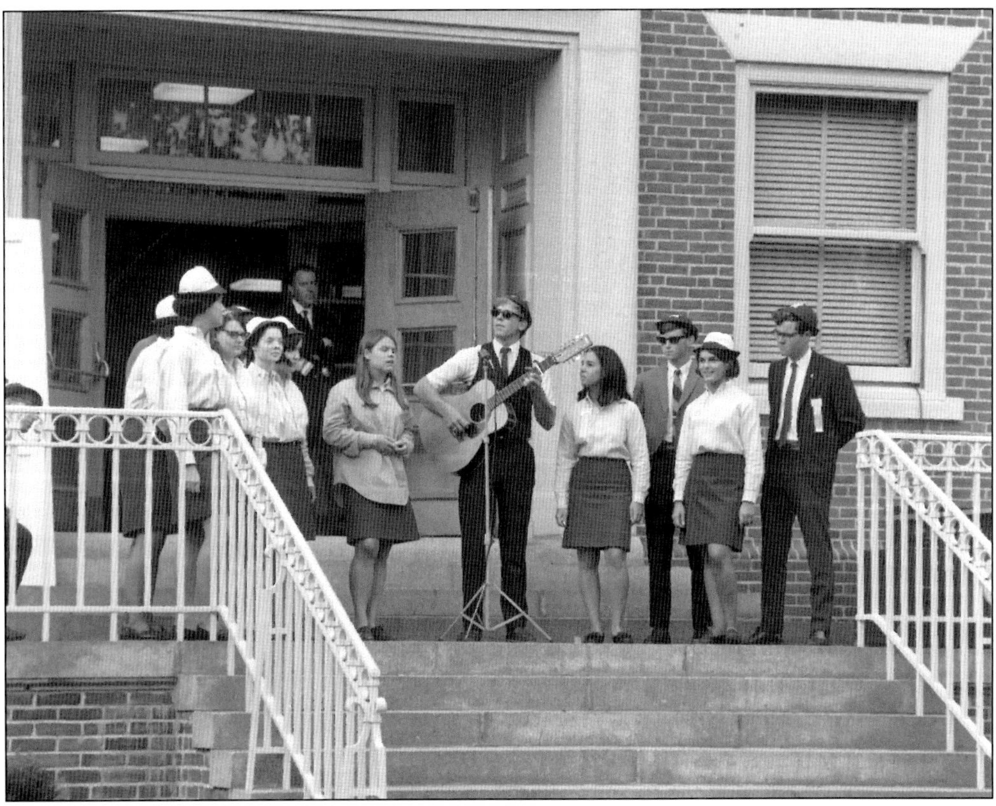

Standing on the south porch of Payson Smith Hall, sophomores offer a musical greeting to incoming freshmen in the 1960s.

Contents

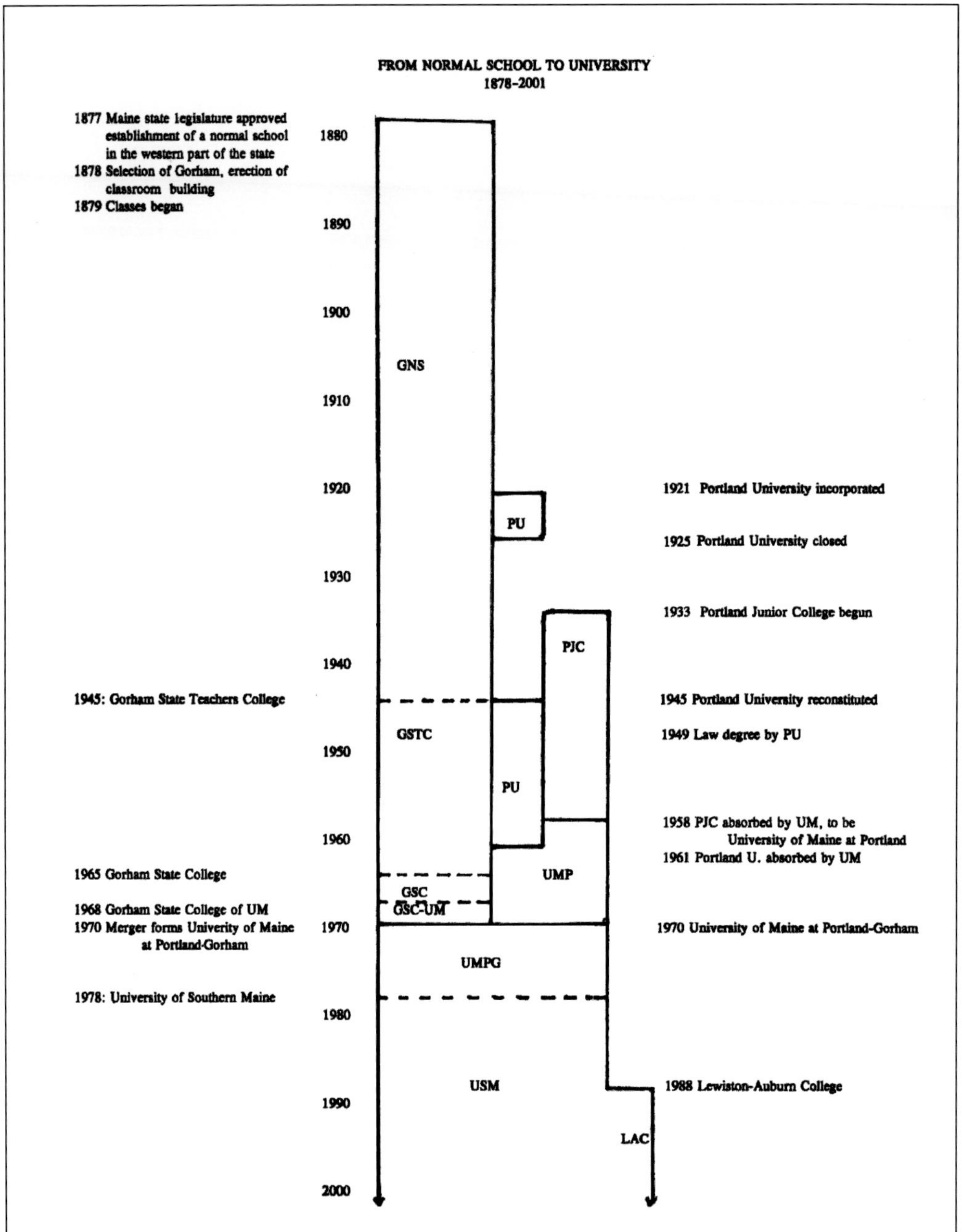

This diagram shows how the university evolved, with an emphasis on the dates of important developments, but without reference to numbers of students or to the variety of courses and programs offered.

Introduction

The University of Southern Maine had existed under that name for less than a year when it staged a centennial celebration. As can be seen by the accompanying chart, the present institution had many contributing predecessors. It was formed (under the name University of Maine at Portland-Gorham) by the merger of a state college and a branch campus of the state university—a branch that had its own varied background. The present alumni magazine, *Mainestream*, includes nine college seals across its news pages, representing either separate schools or name changes. This book is an attempt to give some shape to those confusing early years and to illustrate through images both the obscure and the well-known developments.

The content of any book of pictures is largely shaped by the availability of illustrations. While it is usually possible to find images relevant to major developments, it is often necessary to neglect an interesting occurrence because no one took or preserved good photographs. Conversely, stacks of publicity shots of an event may give it undue importance.

Even as one attempts to strike a balance, personal preferences must play a role in selection. People come and go, but physical aspects of a campus remain and serve to jog the memories of alumni from different classes. Thus, one will find here more emphasis on buildings and campus facilities than on individual students, faculty, or staff. Images that illustrated a development gained precedence over smiling portraits. Identified and dated photographs were chosen over anonymous ones, and sharp prints were chosen over less clear ones. Any of these criteria, however, may have been ignored for an unusual glimpse of a special activity.

Some situations have been nearly impossible to illustrate—among them the impacts of wars on the colleges, a subject worth pursuing. We have little to tell how the Spanish-American War affected the Gorham campus (the only one extant at the time), but the effect was probably slight, as it was in the rest of Maine. World War I was different and had its impact even on a largely female student body. (Only about two dozen students, prewar and postwar, had military service in that war.) Students kept up with events in classroom discussions, substituted money-raising events and Red Cross classes for the usual social activities, observed "meatless" and "wheatless" days in the dining room, and saved money by gathering wild flowers to decorate the stage for graduation exercises. They wrote about such matters (early yearbooks were more informative than later ones) but apparently left no illustrations of them.

World War II shut down Portland Junior College in 1943, but did not close the Gorham institution, as males then constituted only about a third of the graduating classes. Nevertheless, with men away in the services and many women leaving school to help alleviate teacher shortages, student enrollments shrank between 1942 and 1945. A small graduating class of 1944 shows this reduction, but there are few photographs to illustrate how government night-school classes helped fill classrooms during the first year of the war. Furthermore, it is difficult to find photographs of the well-attended Red Cross first-aid classes, the blackout drills held by "defense committees," and the commuters who, because of fuel shortages, moved to campus. For the first time, men lived in a Gorham college dormitory, semesters were shortened by holding Saturday classes, and all intercollegiate sports were suspended. Without the supporting images, it is difficult to illustrate these major changes and effects.

The Korean War also brought unphotographed change. A summer supplement to Gorham's 1953 yearbook was dedicated to the college's men and women in the service. Portland Junior College's dean spoke of "unsettled world conditions" when he explained to newsmen why enrollment had fallen in late 1950. Vietnam, on the other hand, caused protests, which protesters made sure were photographed.

Veterans of the wars made contributions. The GI Bill helped a few men and women attend the Gorham Normal School, but swelled the enrollments at Portland Junior College. The numbers of men returning from the war and desiring an education served as an excuse to make the college all male. Trustees must have felt that female veterans did not need the same opportunities. As women were invited to social events, where pictures were taken, one has to consider the Portland Junior College photographs with care to see the change.

Also not illustrated here are the early years of Portland University, either in the 1920s or in its postwar reincarnation, because no photographs have surfaced. Even the pictures of buildings used by that school before it became part of the larger university had to be found elsewhere.

Mergers and the reactions to them do not lend themselves to illustration. How did Portland University's College of Business Administration faculty and students react to losing "college" status and becoming merely a department of a university branch? Informal comments suggest that improved finances compensated for the loss of independence, but there are no pictures to illustrate this, and the question remains if one could show such reactions in pictorial form. Equally problematic is how one might depict the struggle between Portland and Orono over campus autonomy after the Portland campus was taken over by the University of Maine.

It is also difficult to depict the friction caused later by the Portland-Gorham merger. Students clung to their campus traditions and some complained about the tuition differential that existed at first. Faculty and staff, in endless committees and meetings, attempted to find common ground for working together, each group fearing domination by the other. It was not easy—as can be seen by the rapid turnover of administrators in the first decade. The arguments were not photographed, but pictures of some of the numerous presidents, acting presidents, and interim presidents are included, if without their changing staffs.

One common bond on the two campuses was wry amusement that the merger was supposed to save money and reduce administrators. This did not happen, partly because the new university tried to accomplish more than the separate parts had. New posts and new programs were regularly formed, all needing funding. Another campus was added and was given more autonomy. Only by reducing pictorial emphasis on classes and student activities has it been possible even to hint at the proliferation of adjunct groups through which the University of Southern Maine serves the community, thus lessening the percentage of attention to undergraduate—or even graduate—education.

The University of Southern Maine is now an undeniably complex institution with multiple missions—impossible to depict accurately in so few pages and challenging to understand. This volume should, however, help explain its past.

One

Gorham Normal School, 1878–1945

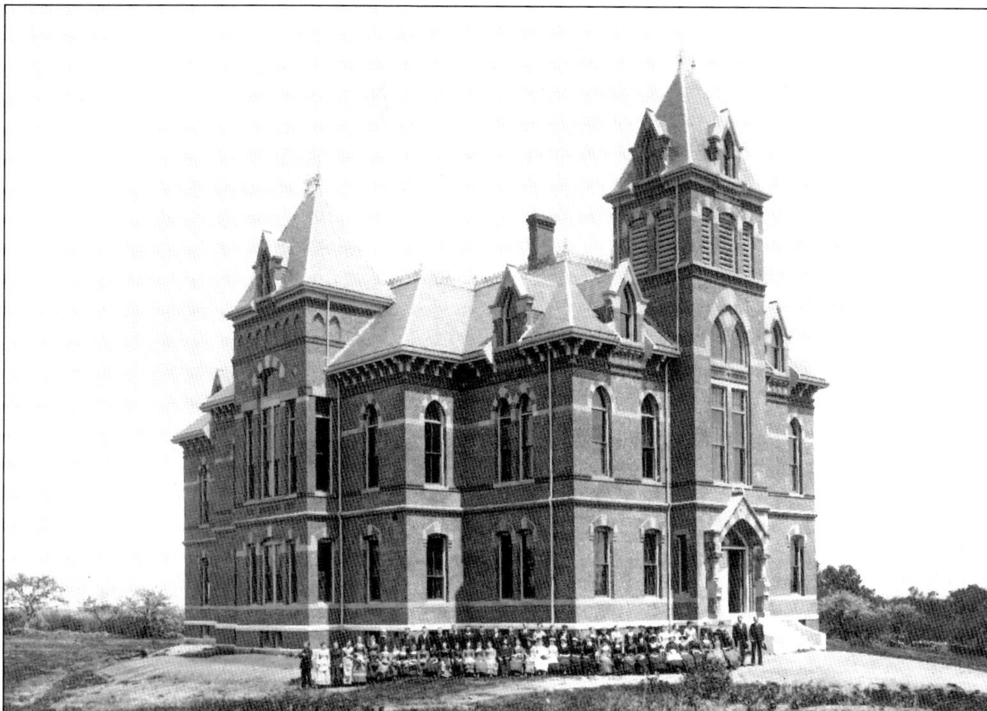

The first new building constructed "on the hill" was designed by Francis H. Fassett of Portland to hold both classrooms and administrative offices and was dedicated in December 1878. This photograph may well be of the first graduating class with the faculty. The 7 men and 37 women completed a 20-week course in the spring of 1879. From that time through 1904, two classes were graduated each year, although some two-year programs were begun in 1890 and three-year ones (for language teachers) by 1895. In 1926, the year that three-year junior high programs were instituted, the "recitation building" was named for William Corthell, who served from 1878 to 1905 as the first principal of the normal school.

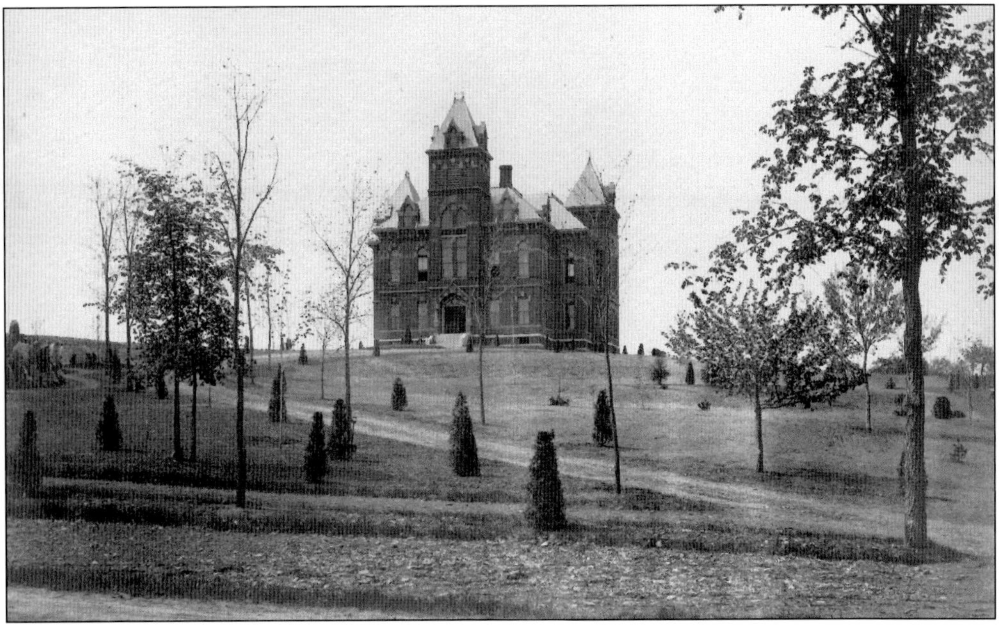

A somewhat later view of the normal school building shows early landscaping. Some of the arborvitae trees along the carriage drive remained in place until the windstorms of the 1990s.

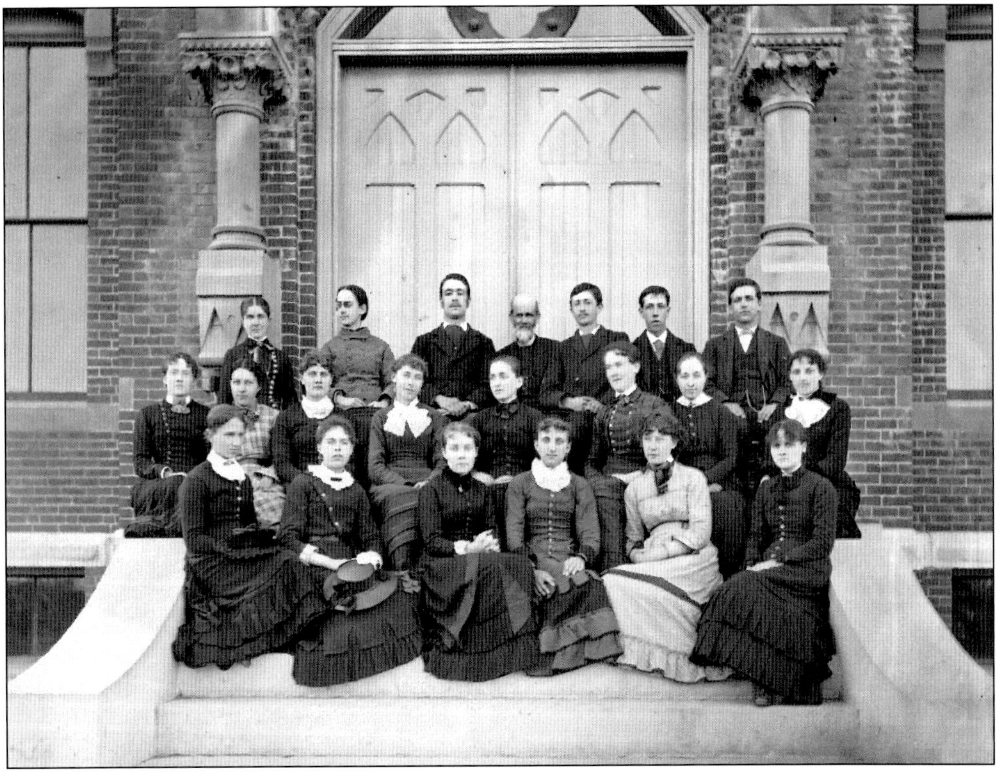

An 1882 class is shown outside the south doors of the main building, together with Principal Corthell (center, back row). This spot became a favorite location for taking pictures.

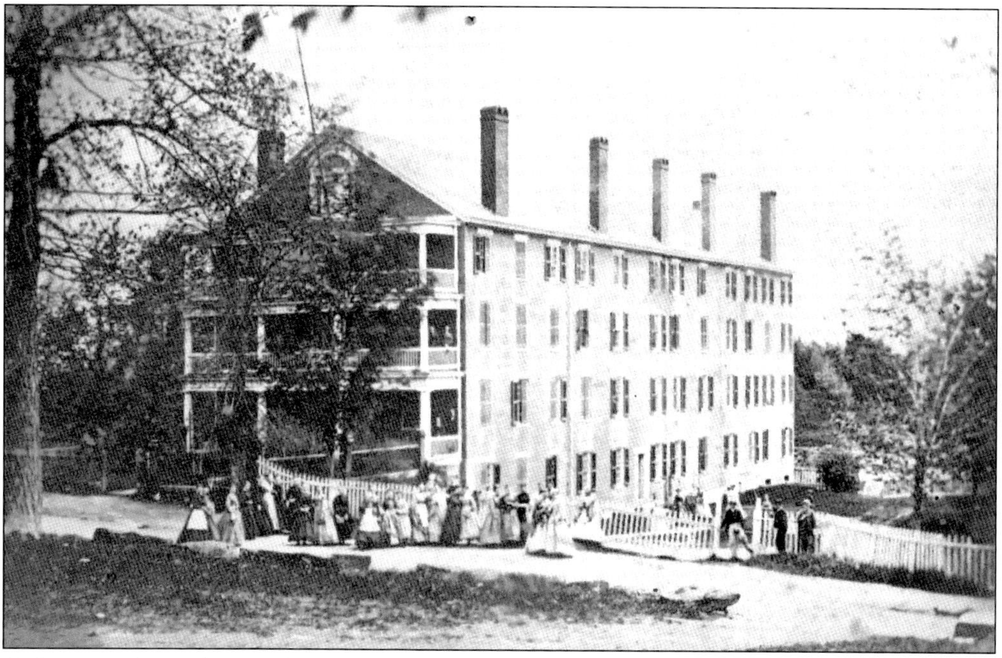

Girls were admitted to Gorham Academy in 1806, the year after it opened. By 1834, however, a separation of sexes had begun. Three years later, the Female Seminary (shown here) was erected. It served as a women's dormitory for the normal school from 1878 until it burned in October 1894, at which time all students were taken in by townspeople.

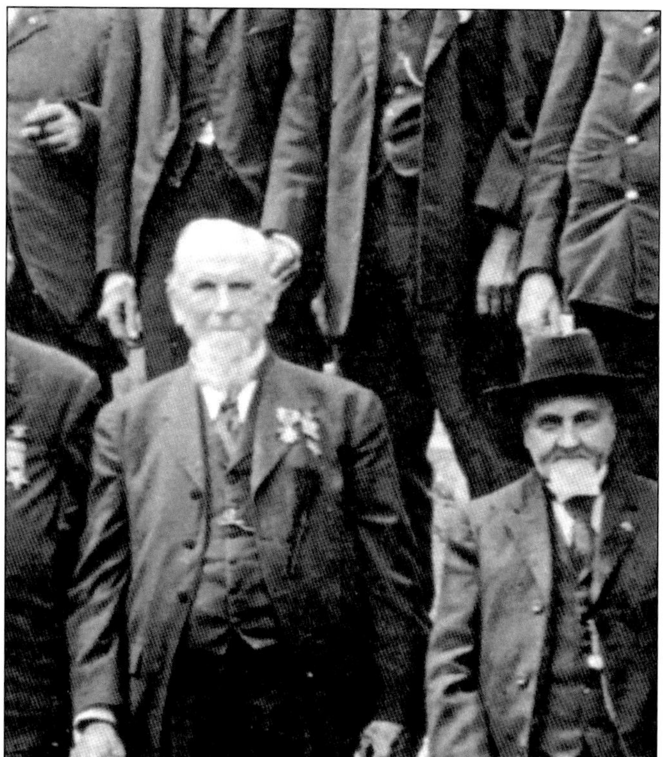

Frederick Robie (left), a native of Gorham, served as a trustee of the academy. While he was a state legislator, Robie introduced the bill establishing the new normal school and was active in its being located in Gorham. Later, as governor, Robie signed a bill to construct a new dormitory and donated a sum of his own money for its construction. He is shown here in 1910 at his GAR (Grand Army of the Republic) reunion, held in Gorham.

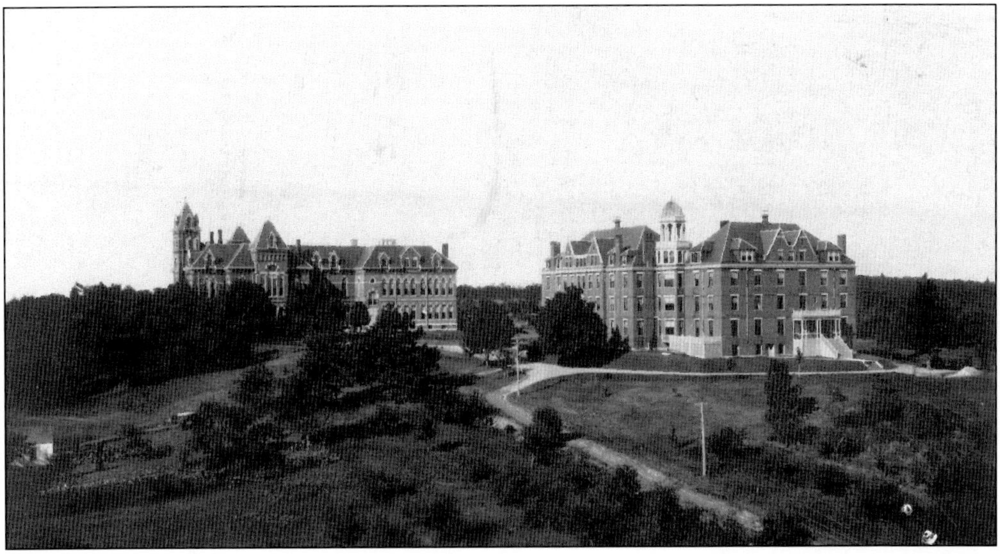

Frederick Robie Hall (right) first opened in 1898, with lounges, dining facilities, and rooms for female students. Men continued to find housing off campus. The recitation building (left) received a wing that doubled its size in 1905, at which time the third floor of the older part was finished off, increasing classroom space considerably.

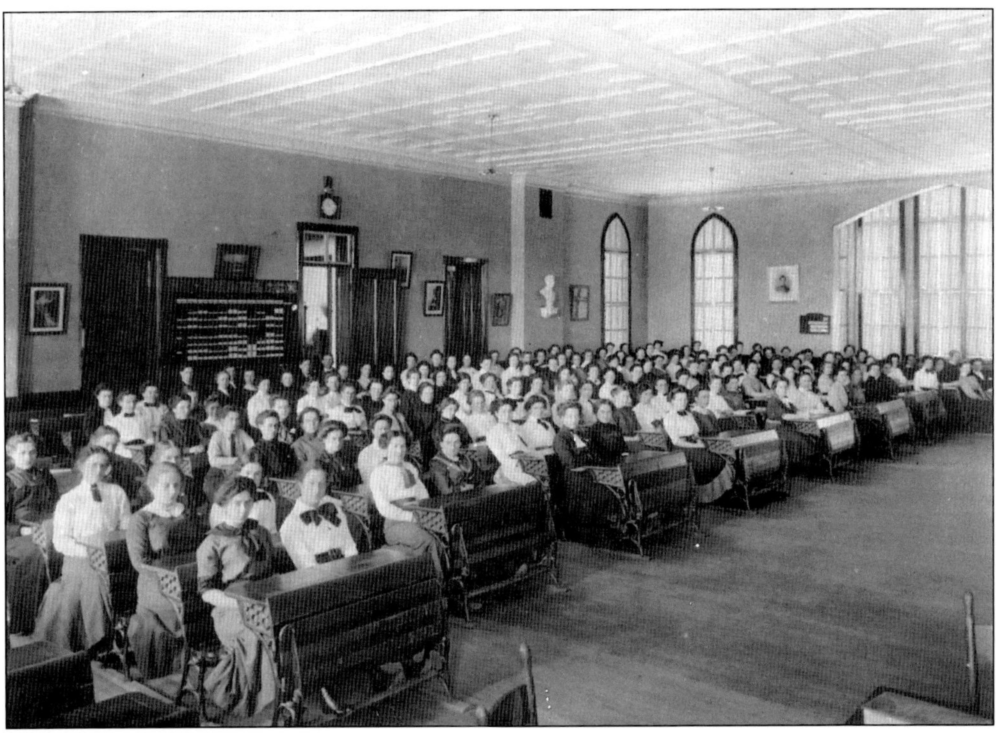

Before it was divided, the south room in the classroom building was large enough to hold the entire student body. Shown here are the Classes of 1911 and 1912. Much later, this area was remodeled into a small auditorium for musical performances.

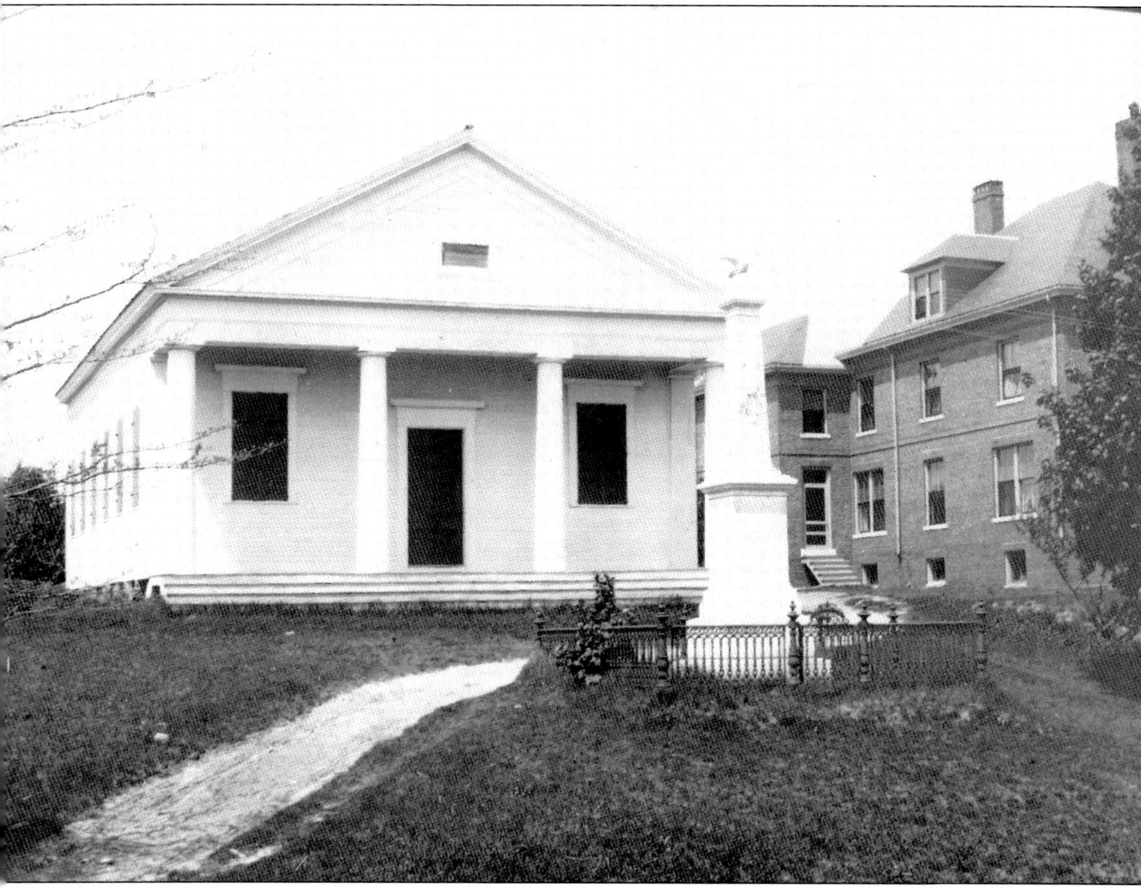

The first principal, William Corthell, had a home off campus. Corthell's successor, Walter Russell, lived in a new residence (right) built in 1906 through the generosity of Frederick Robie, who contributed 70 percent of its cost. It was located beside the building constructed in 1821 as a free meetinghouse and then remodeled for use as the Gorham Town Hall. In front of that building stood the Civil War monument, which contained the names and pertinent data for the 56 Gorham men lost in the war. Erected in 1866 and paid for by Toppan Robie (Frederick Robie's father), it was one of the earliest such monuments. Frederick Robie had the cast-iron fence installed later. (The front of the president's residence is shown on page 114.)

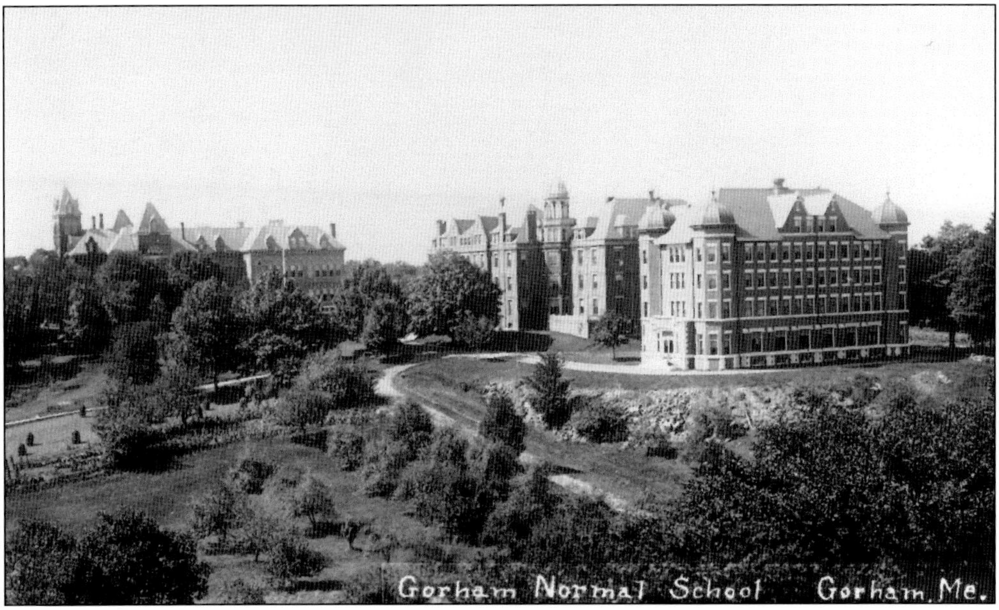

When, by 1910, residents were too numerous for Robie Hall to house them, the academy building was remodeled to house 30 women until East Hall, attached to the east side of Robie Hall (and nearest the camera), was opened in January 1916. East Hall was renamed Andrews Hall in 1956 to honor Miriam Andrews (page 21).

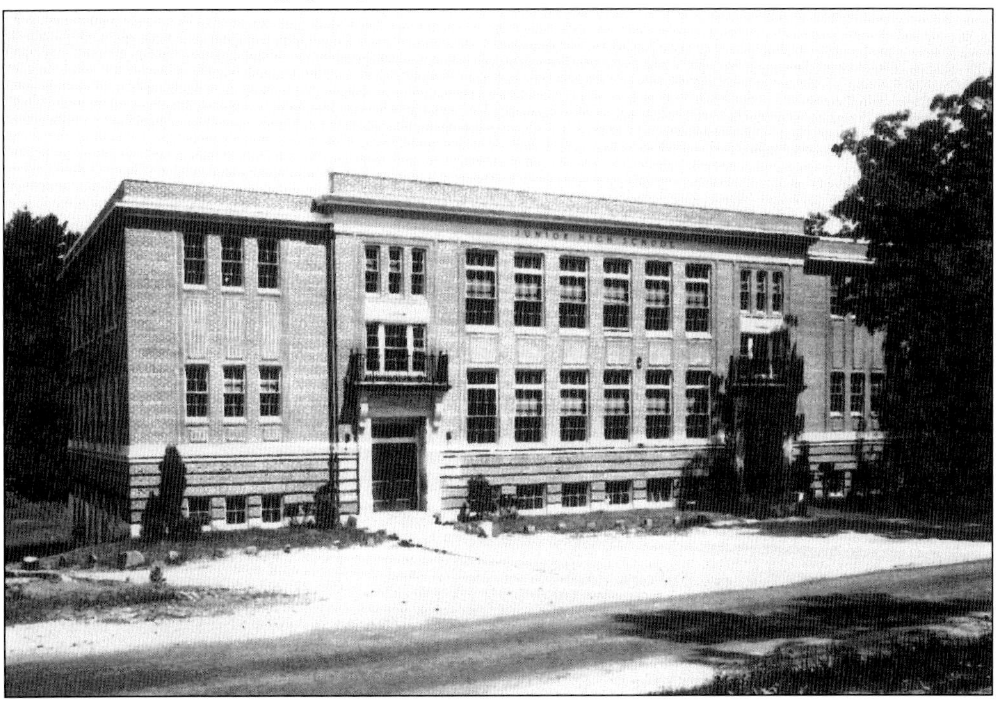

Dormitory rooms were not needed for students living close enough to commute. In the late 19th century, students arrived by trains but, by 1901, a trolley system had reached Gorham. For the next 30 years, students from Portland or Westbrook could ride to the end of the line (shown here) and then walk up the hill to classes.

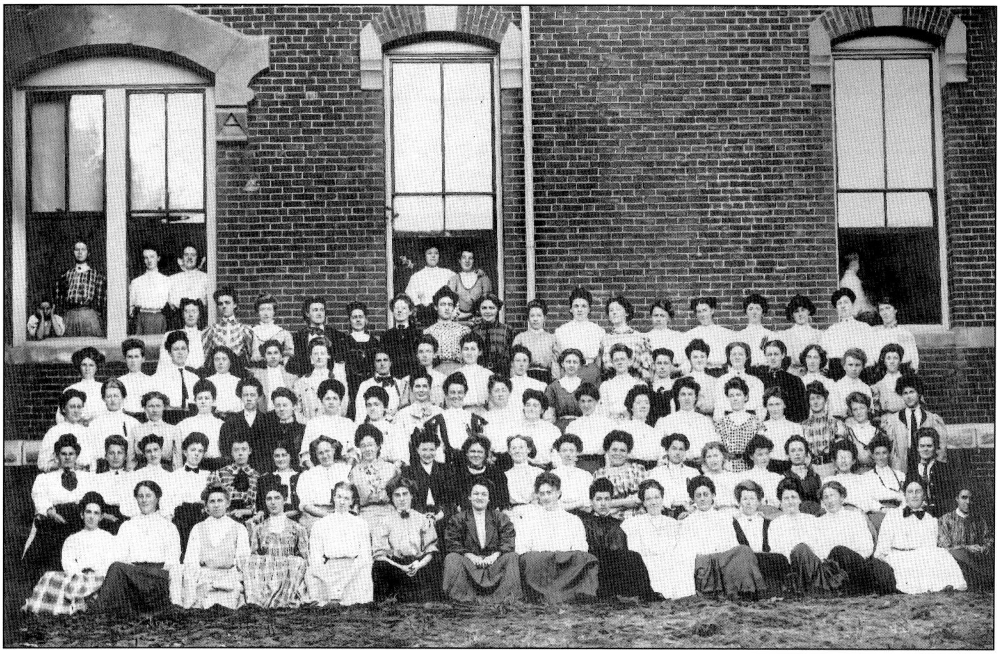

One reason women's dormitories were built is evident in this 1907 photograph of the student body. The Classes of 1907 and 1908 were both larger than those preceding and were all female. Elementary school teaching was clearly considered women's work.

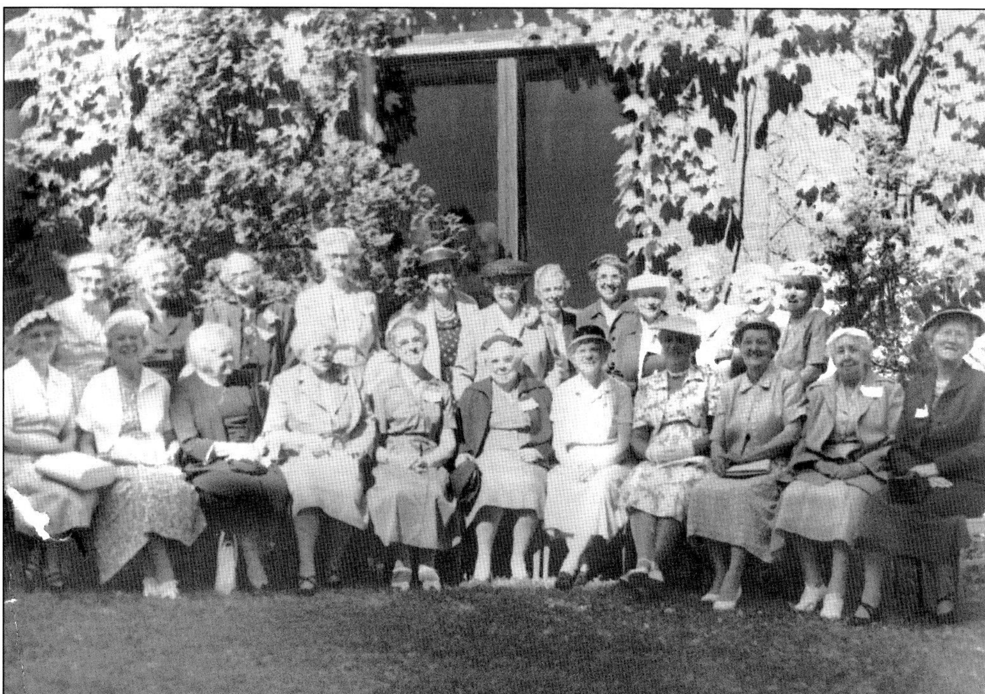

The Gorham Alumni Association began to meet as early as 1890 and was chartered in 1893. Its members maintained a healthy interest in their college, for many years being accorded a section in the yearbook. These 23 women from the 1907 class all attended their 50th reunion.

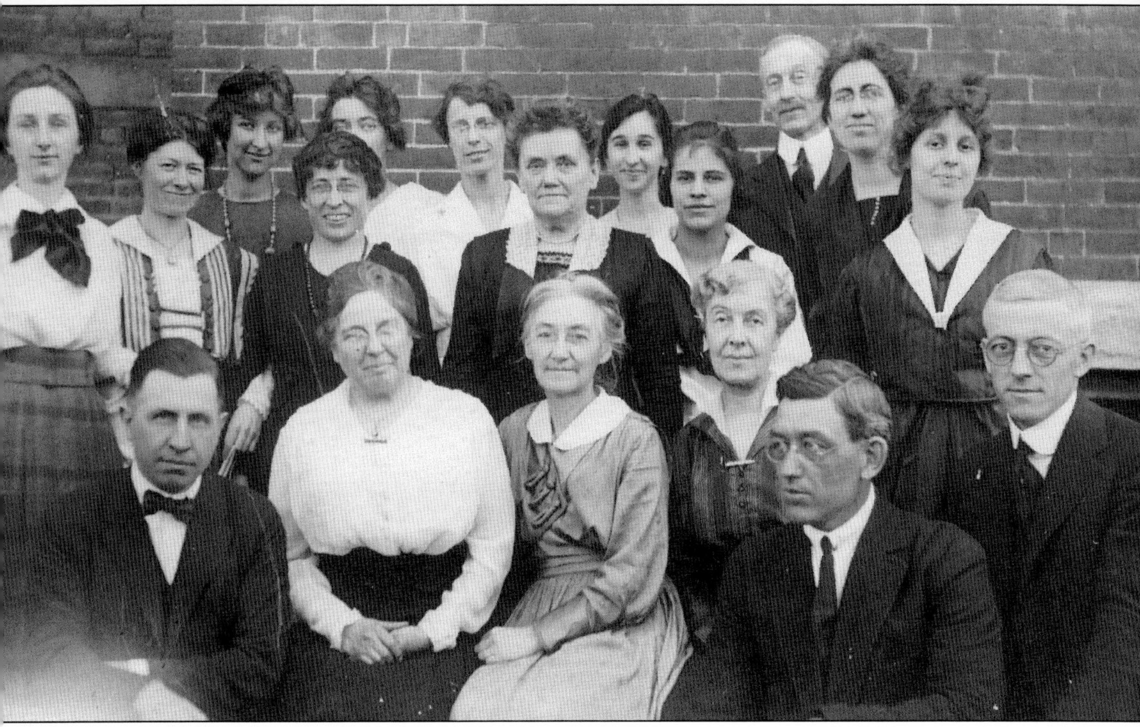

The 1917–1918 faculty included, from left to right, the following: (front row, sitting) George Hutcherson (manual training), Mary Oliver (English, psychology), Katharine Halliday (history, literature), Gertrude Stone (psychology, rural sociology), George Brown (manual training), and Louis Woodward (natural and social sciences); (back row, standing) Nathalie Moulton (student teaching), Emily Parsons (music, reading), Marion Cutts (student teaching, rural), unidentified, Emma Daggett (drawing), Faye Bartlett (sewing, cooking), Helen Bartlett (physiology, gymnastics), Viola White (botany, drawing, geography), Hildah Appel (physiology, gymnastics), Principal Walter Russell (science), Jessie Keene (industrial arts and science), and Vera Davidson (student teaching).

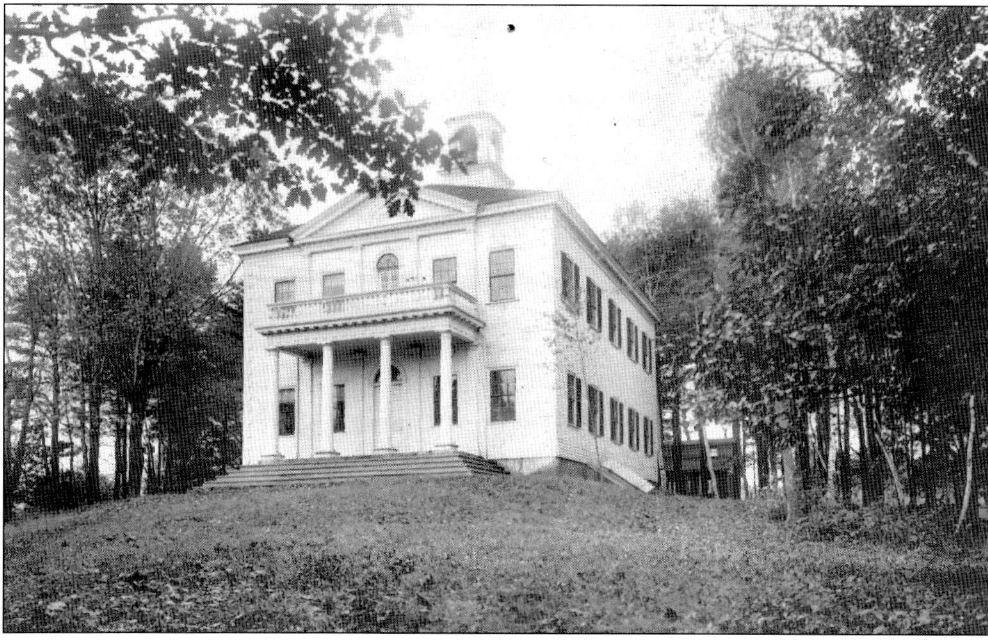

In 1911, a program for industrial arts teachers was instituted, the only one in the state. A low brick building, erected in 1913, held a forge and machine shop. In 1916, the old Academy Hall (shown here as Gorham Manual Training School) was converted for drafting and cabinetry classes. The new program took three years to complete. With a few exceptions, its students were male, contributing to increased numbers of men on campus.

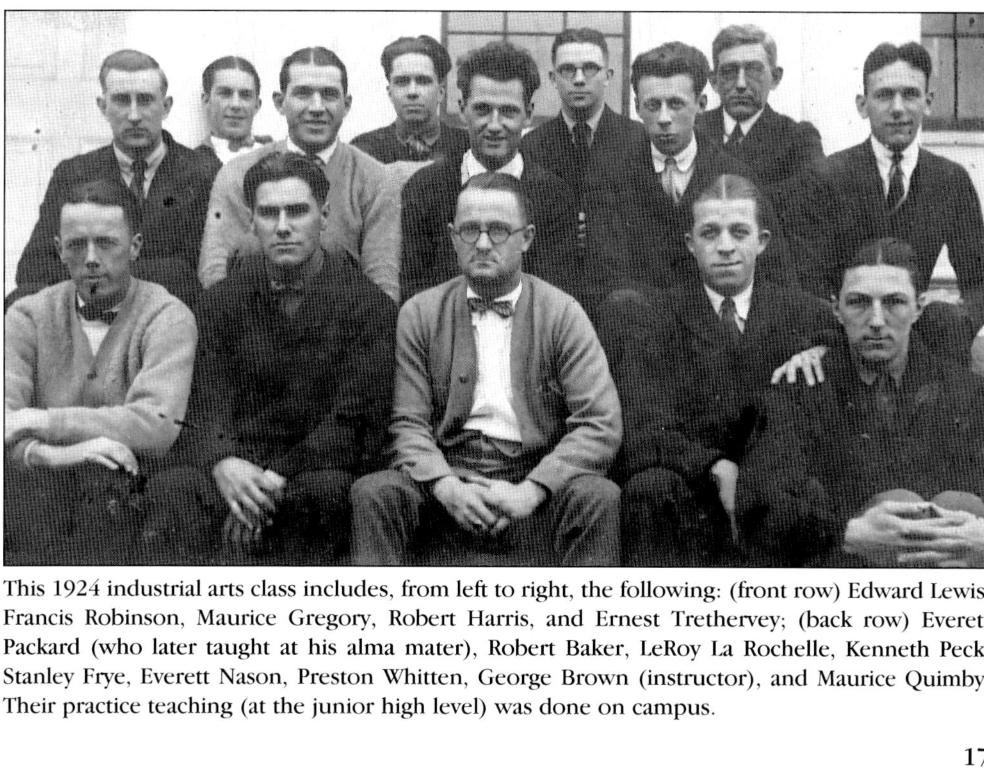

This 1924 industrial arts class includes, from left to right, the following: (front row) Edward Lewis, Francis Robinson, Maurice Gregory, Robert Harris, and Ernest Trethervey; (back row) Everett Packard (who later taught at his alma mater), Robert Baker, LeRoy La Rochelle, Kenneth Peck, Stanley Frye, Everett Nason, Preston Whitten, George Brown (instructor), and Maurice Quimby. Their practice teaching (at the junior high level) was done on campus.

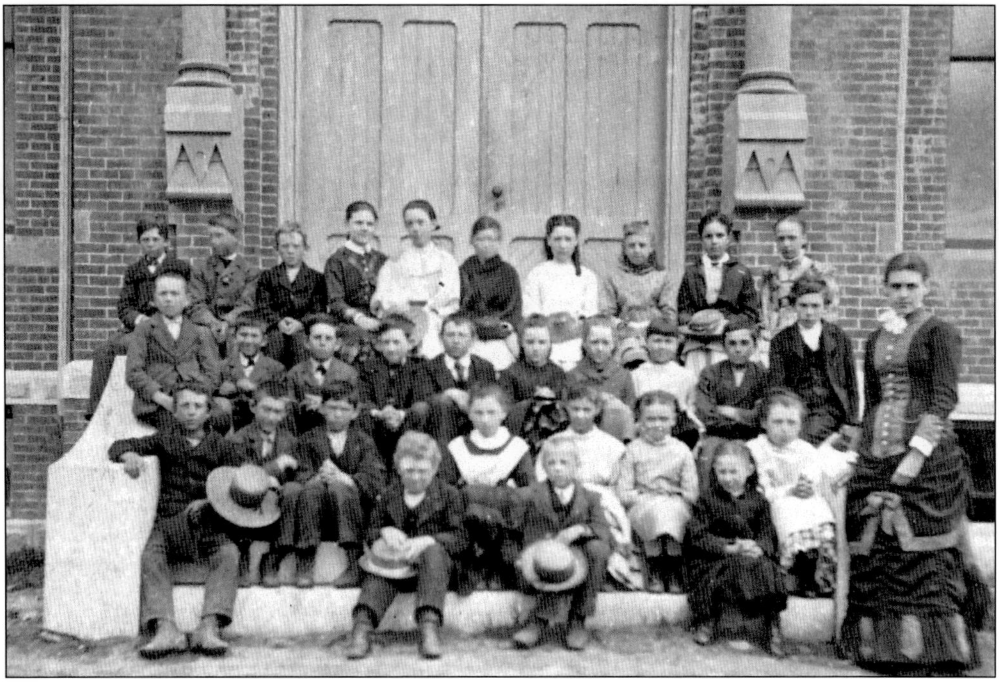

No matter what else was being offered (and course requirements did change), practice teaching was required of all students, although the time involved and the location varied. At first, rooms were set aside in campus classrooms for children brought in from nearby. In this 1888 photograph, children of the Gorham Model School pose with their teacher, Mary Haskell.

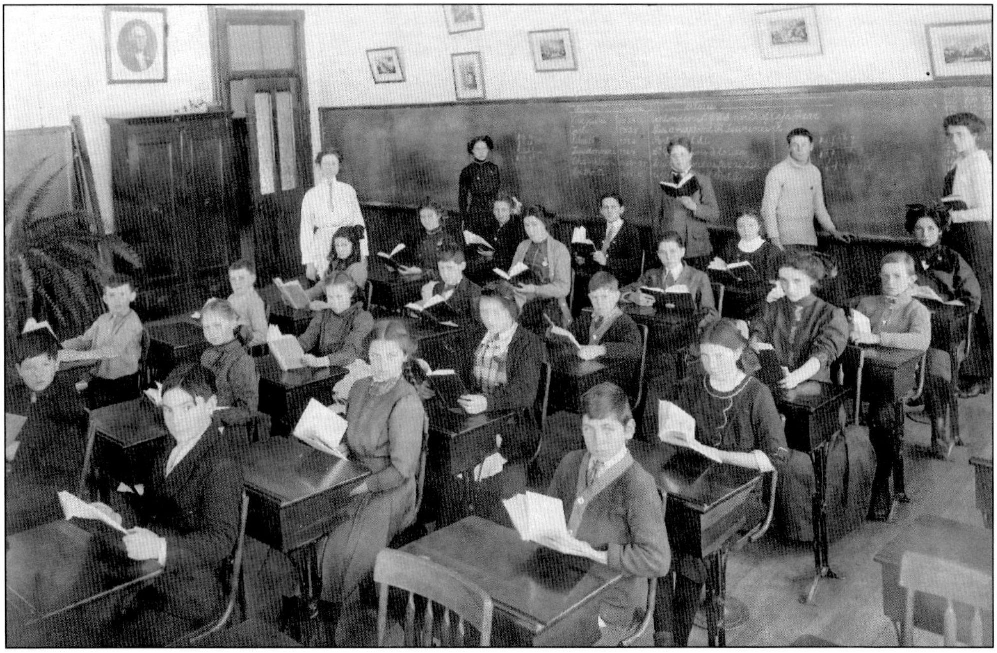

Although increased use was made of local schools after 1890, this 1912 seventh-grade practice class was held in the campus classroom building. Student teachers were Maud McKusick and Florence Hildreth.

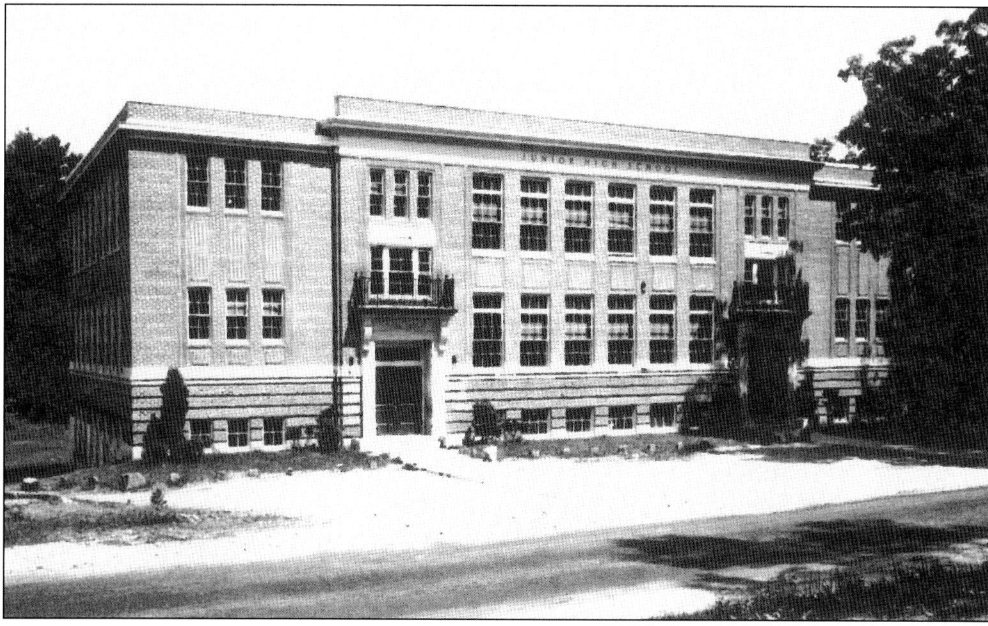

A new school—built in 1924 jointly by the town and the state on the property once occupied by the Female Seminary—was variously known as the Laboratory School, Training School, or Campus School between 1926 and 1967. It was officially named the Charlotte Millett School in 1961, honoring a local woman who was active with Camp Fire groups in town and with group leaders at the normal school. The building was razed in 1983.

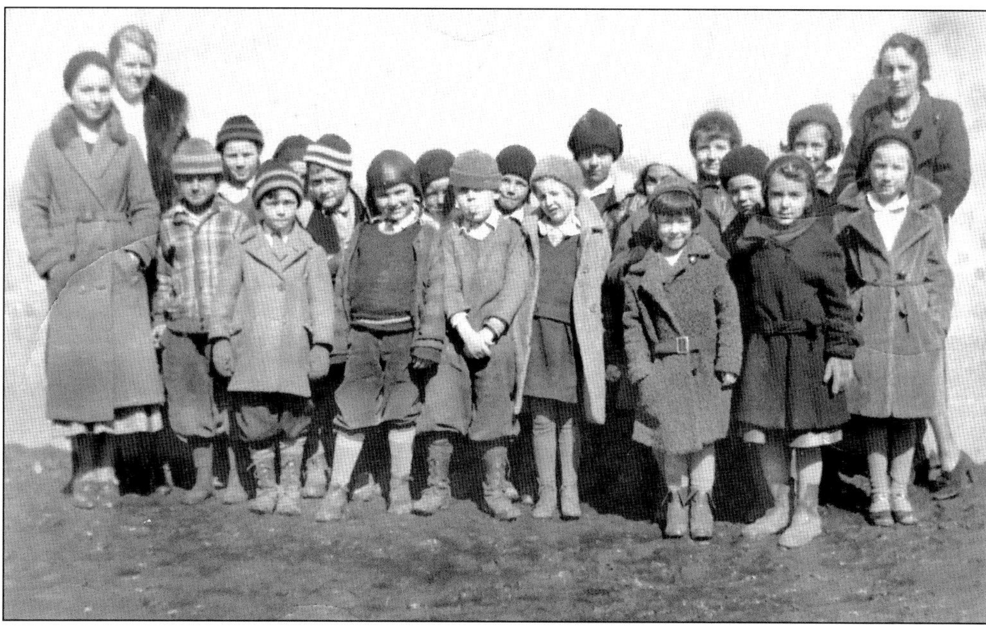

Madelyn Swett '33 (left, front row) and Mary Hall '33 (left, back row) had as pupils, from left to right, the following: (front row) Clinton Doucette, Douglas Baker, Arthur Harrison, Everett Bean, Phyllis Clark, Sylvia Woodward, Esther Cole, and Pauline Fogg; (back row) Robert Bean, Richard Burgess, William Rioux, Arthur Davis, Carroll Young, Ernest Cressey, Edith Hatt, Carolyn Weiden, Elinor Clark, and Jeannette Mittsmenn. Helen Whitcomb (right, back row) was the supervising teacher.

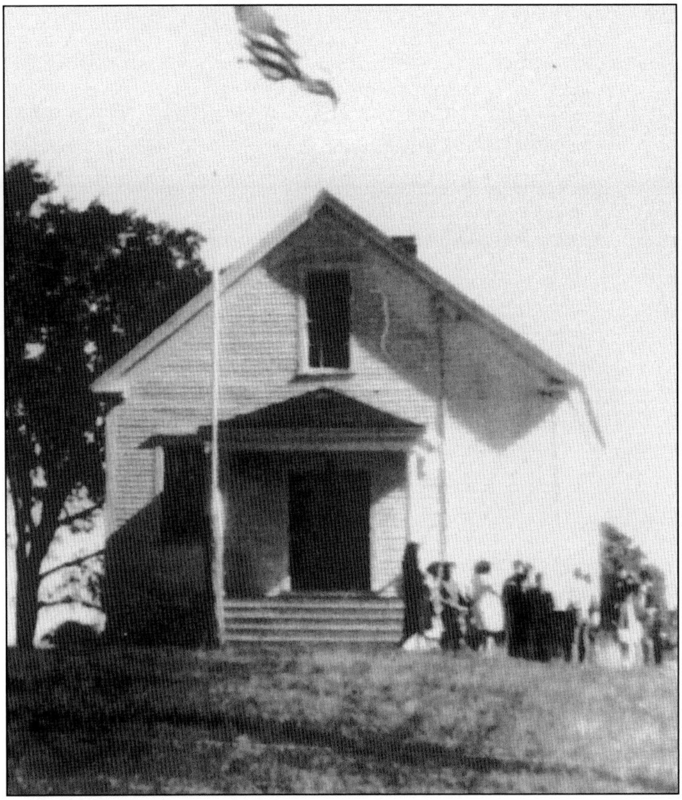

Students from a Rural Sociology class made visits to the one-room West Gorham schoolhouse, which soon became a model rural school. From *c.* 1918 until 1951, its teachers supervised the practice teaching of students from the normal school who wished to prepare for work in multigrade settings.

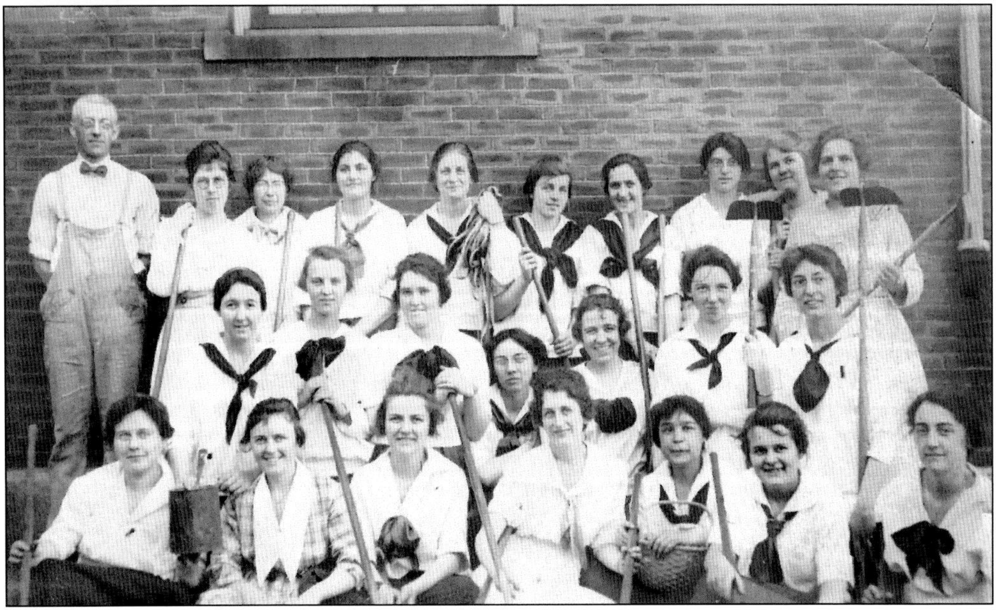

For a period after World War I, freshmen were expected to take a course in agriculture, where they not only studied topics such as the composition of soils but also planted a garden each spring. In this 1922 photograph, Louis Woodward, teacher of natural sciences, poses with a group of "farmerettes."

Katharine Halliday taught literature and history at the Gorham Normal School from 1894 to 1932. For many years, her classes formed clubs with names like the Halliday Club or Yadillah Erutaretil. These clubs sought to familiarize members with parliamentary law and to improve writing and speaking skills.

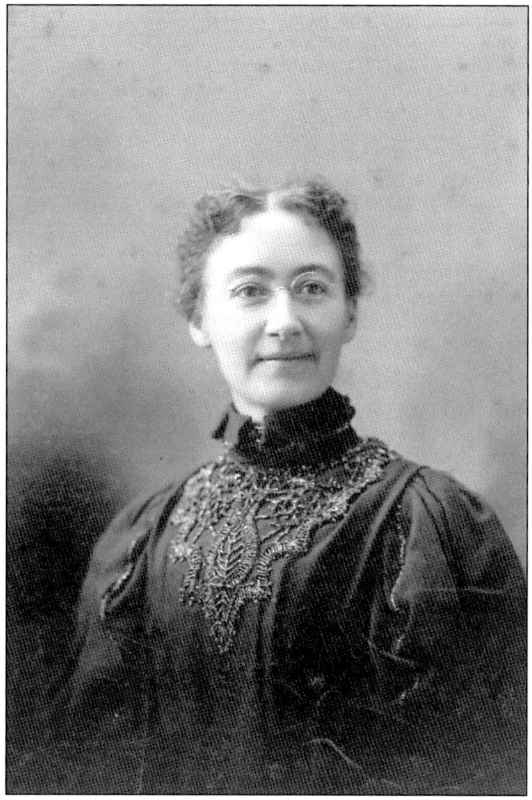

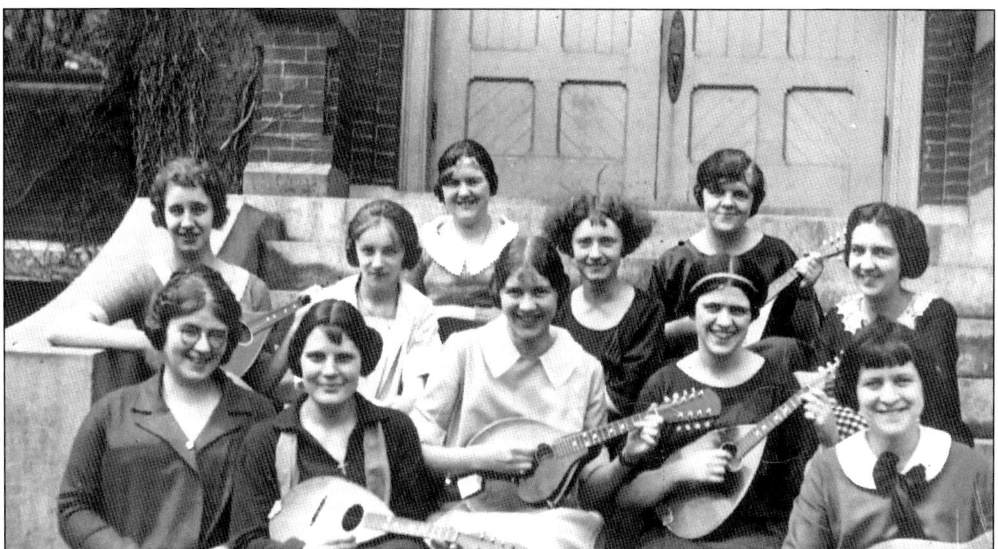

Miriam Andrews (left, front row) taught from 1922 to 1960. Like Katharine Halliday, Andrews inspired the formation of clubs. Shown here is the 1923–1924 Music Club, which became the Mandolin Club the next year, reflecting the popularity of that instrument in the 1920s.

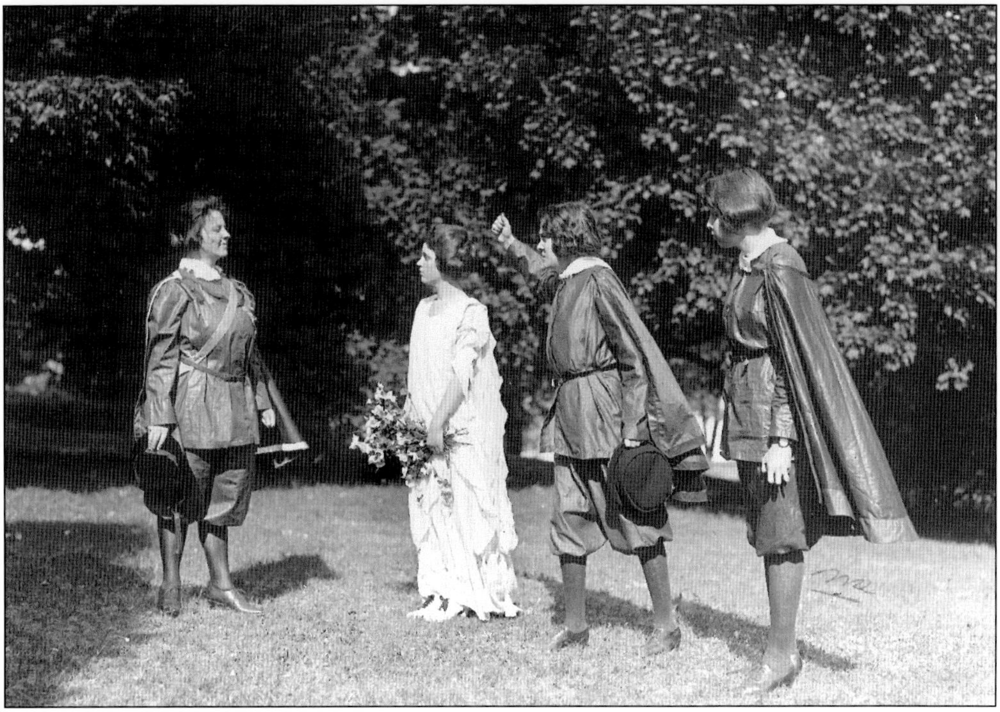

Whether musical or not, staged presentations were common, including the traditional out-of-doors performance by each year's seniors at commencement. The class play of 1921, called *The Steadfast Princess*, included Arlene Moulton, Vera Doherty, Leonore Fraser, and Thena Allen.

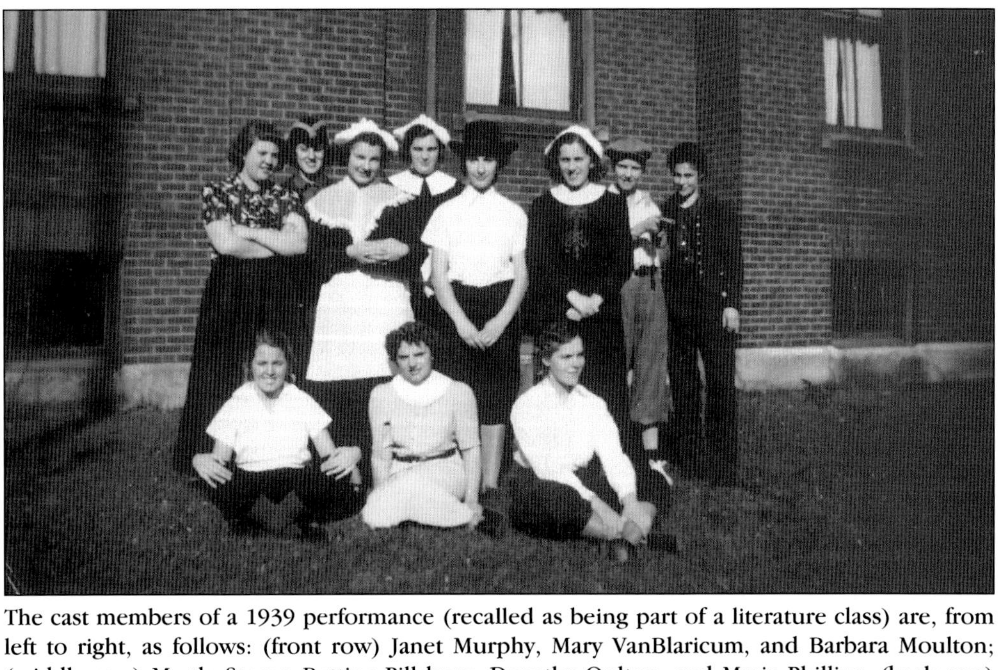

The cast members of a 1939 performance (recalled as being part of a literature class) are, from left to right, as follows: (front row) Janet Murphy, Mary VanBlaricum, and Barbara Moulton; (middle row) Myrtle Storer, Bettina Pillsbury, Dorothy Oulton, and Maria Phillips; (back row) unidentified, Lucille Winslow, Doris Meserve, and Kitty Lewis.

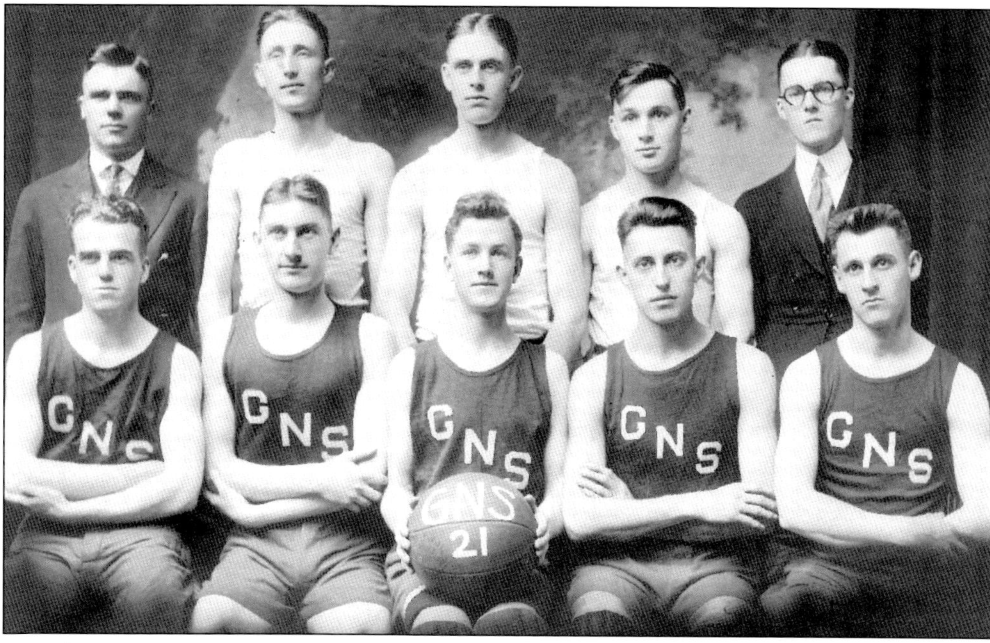

A small gymnasium/assembly room on the third floor of the 1906 addition relieved pressures on the classroom, which had been used for gymnastics before then. The members of the first men's basketball team (1920–1921) are, from left to right, as follows: (front row) Stephen Brown, Andrew Carstensen, Clayton Fossett, Lawrence Bush, and Guy Davenport; (back row) Urban Chase, Marion Packard, Leon Weymouth, Harold Jones, and Ralph Stevens.

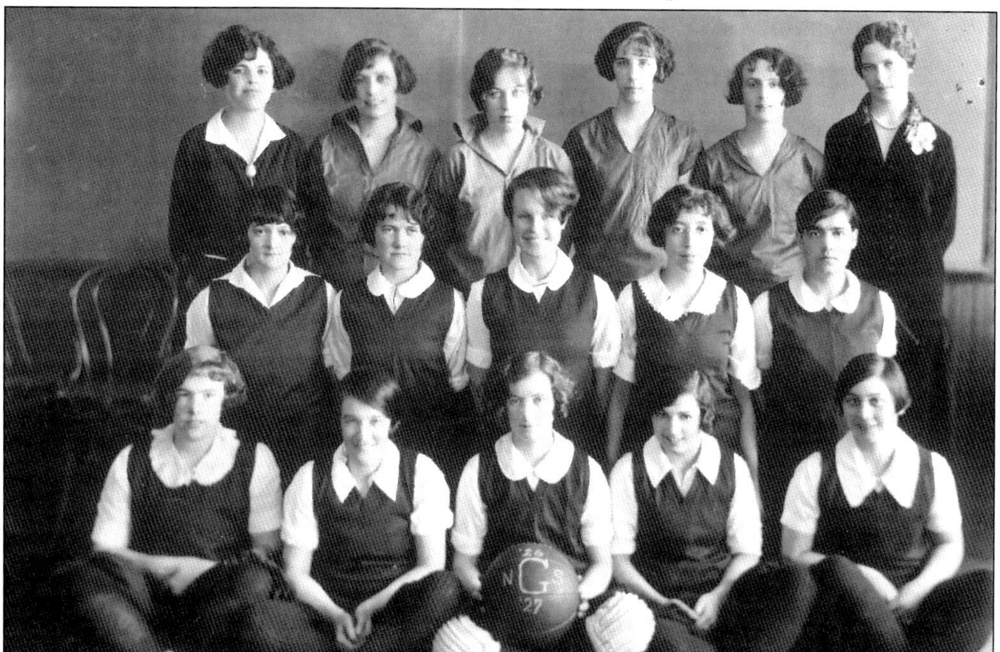

The 1926–1927 women's basketball team won seven of its eight games with other schools. After that, until the 1950s, women's sports were confined to interclass competitions in the belief that this situation better reflected the environment in which the women would later teach.

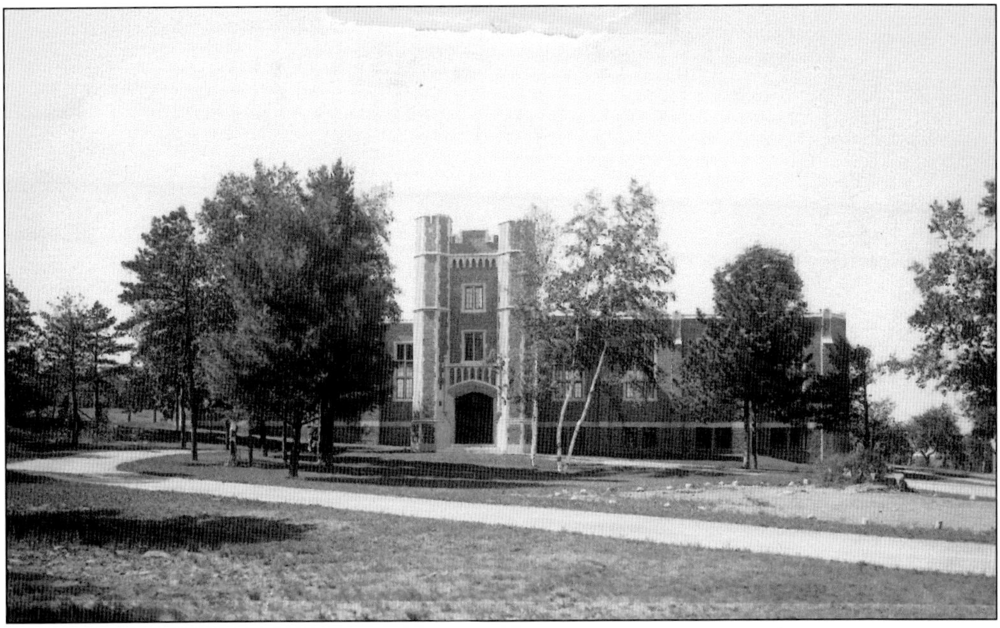

Facilities for sports and dramatics improved after 1931, when a new building was constructed. Named after Walter Russell, principal from 1905 to 1940, the building held a gym (sized to junior high basketball requirements) on one side and a theater on the other, with smaller classrooms below. Tennis courts were built nearby.

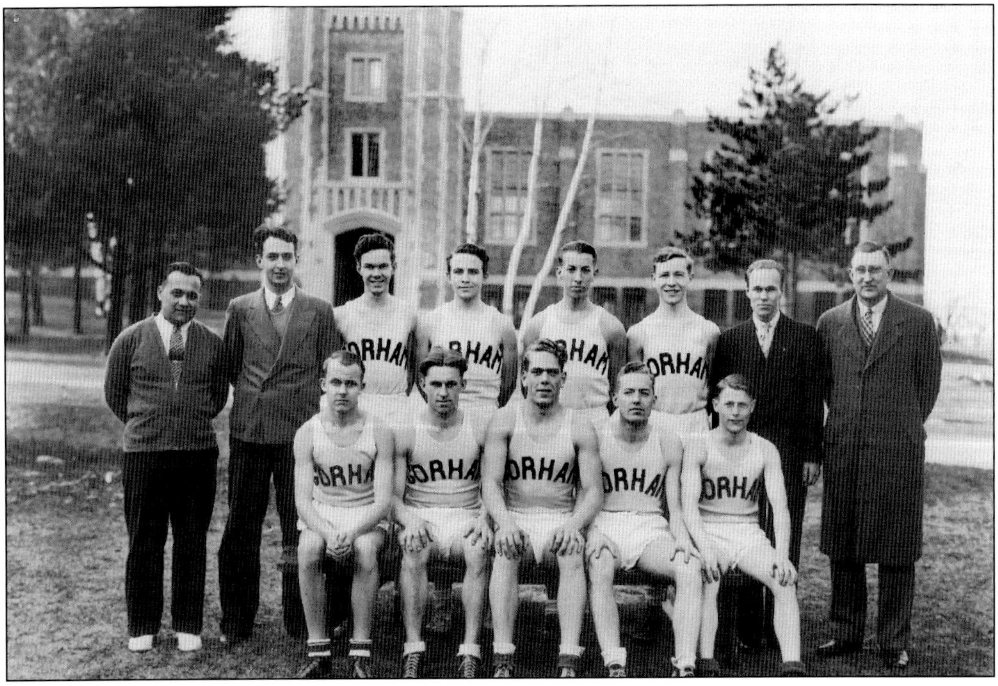

The cross-country team of 1935–1936 poses in front of the new gym. Shown from left to right are the following: (front row) Edward Jess, Ralph Willis, Philip Grover, Kervin Ellis, and Vernon Stapleford; (back row) Norman Provencal, Kenneth Webber, Charles Loomis, Stanley Reed, Wilbert Hayes, Arthur Boswell, John Norton, and Everett Packard (coach).

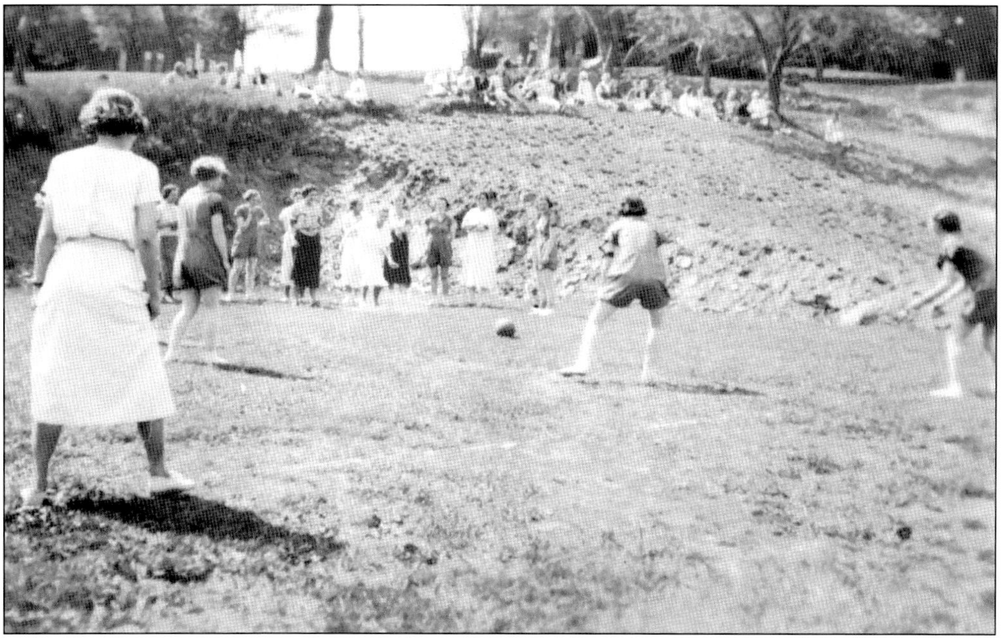

The campus in the 1930s was so small that soccer was played on the sloping front lawn below the dormitories.

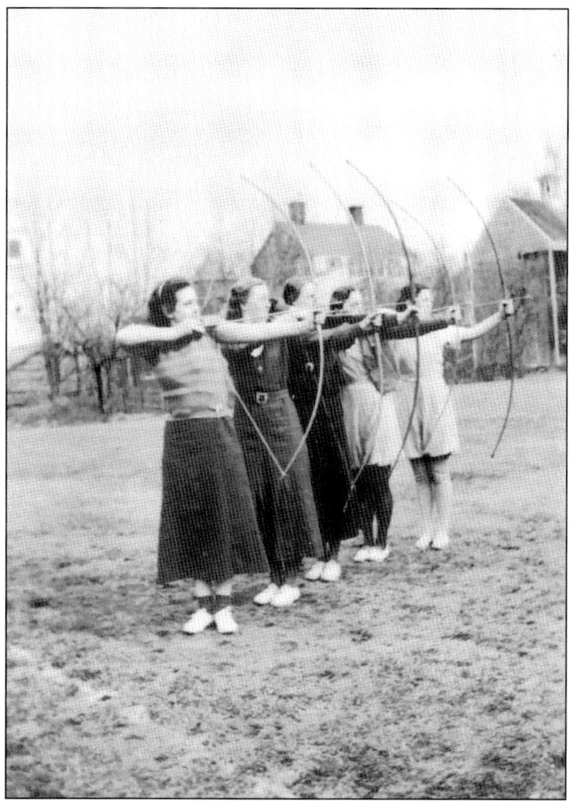

An archery class practices on the front lawn *c.* 1935. Private homes in the background are on College Street. (The barn and house on the right were purchased much later to hold university offices.)

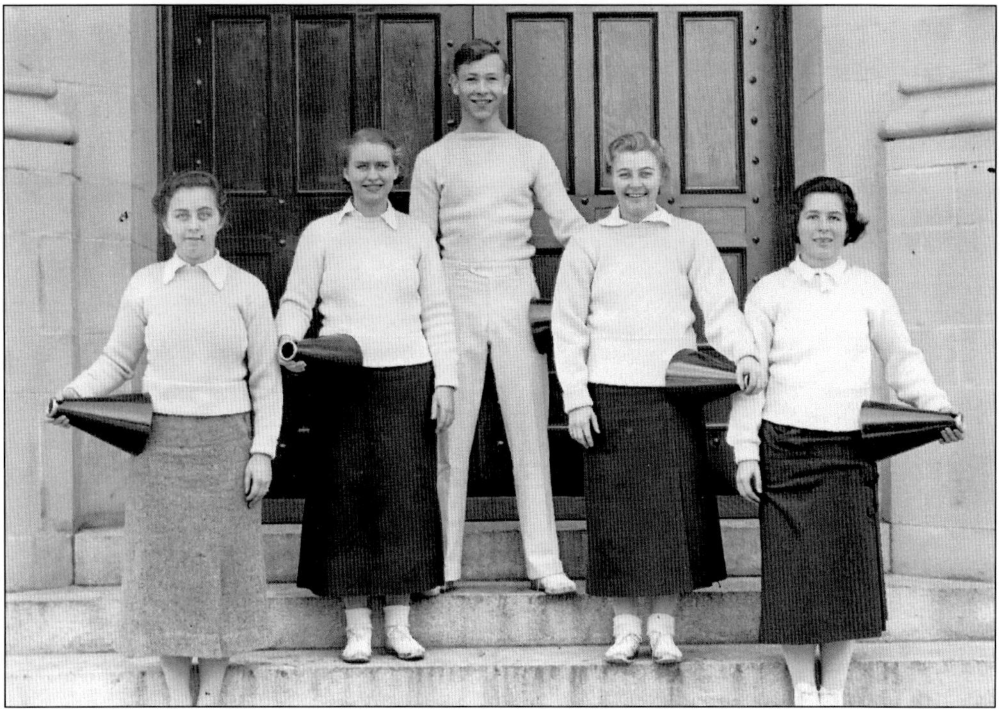

Cheerleaders first organized in 1935–1936. Those shown here, from left to right, are Mary Shepard '37, Margaret Johnson '38, Arthur Boswell '39, Eleanor Parker '36, and Lorraine Fitzpatrick '39.

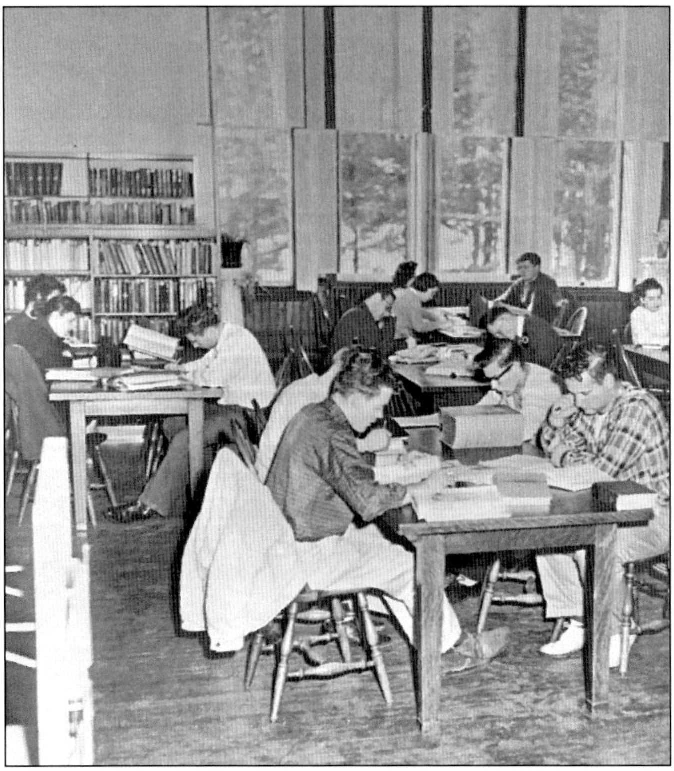

Moving the gym out of Corthell Hall created space for a library (shown here in the 1950s). A librarian was hired and the Library Club was formed, composed largely of students who worked there. In earlier years, a small collection of books had been kept at Robie Hall.

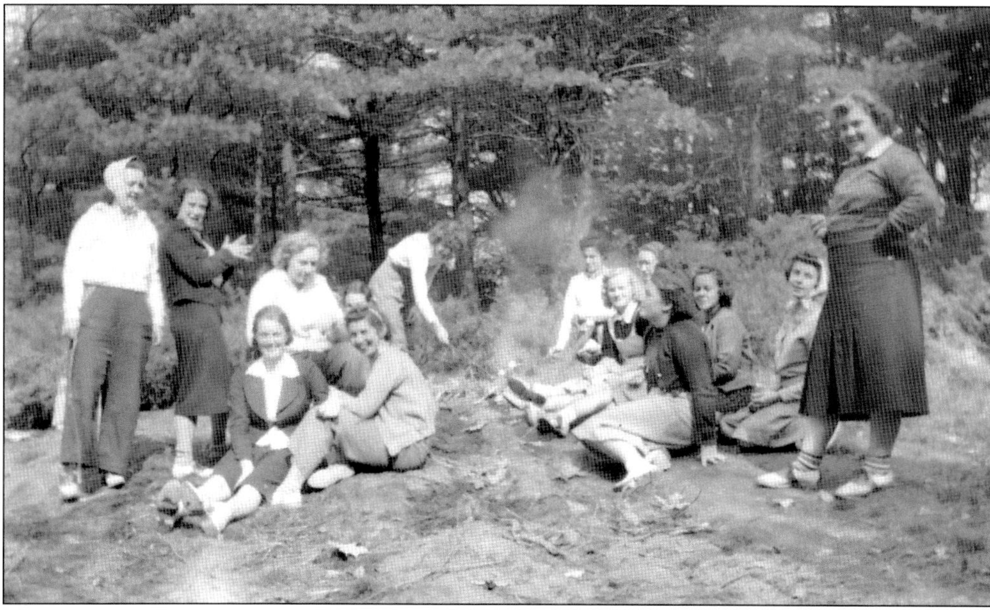

The Poetry Club, formed in 1935–1936, was fairly exclusive, choosing its members from a waiting list. Obviously, they did more than read and write poetry—this is one of their picnics in 1939.

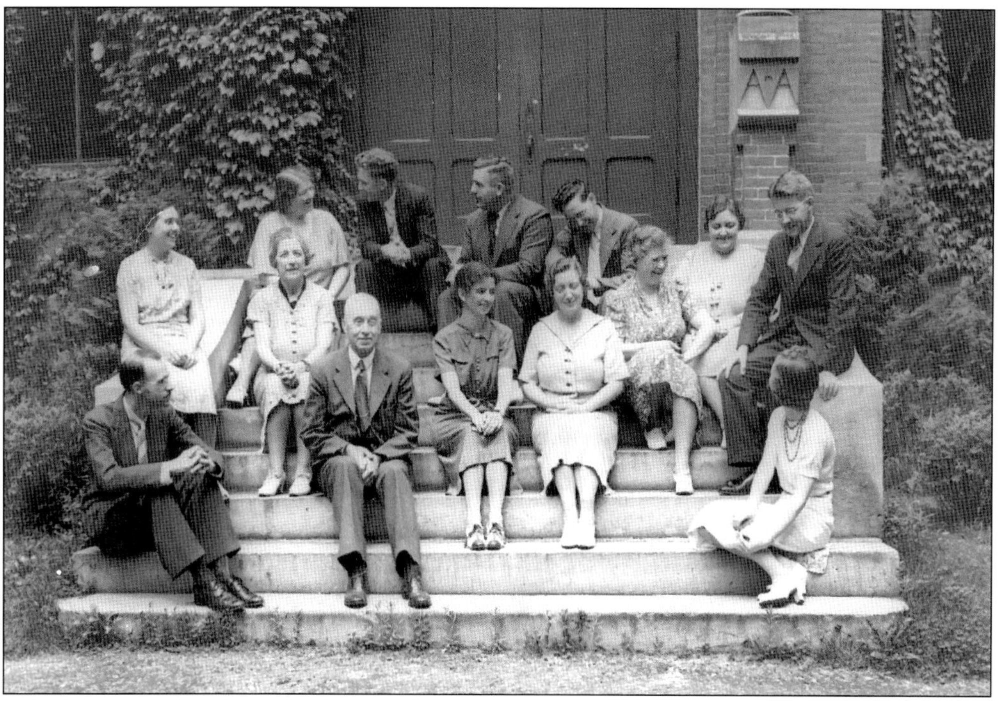

Summer sessions were held from 1908 on, although Gorham and Farmington Normal Schools operated in alternate summers during the 1930s and 1940s. Summer faculty and staff members in 1938 included from left to right, the following: (front row) unidentified, Walter Russell, Marjorie Eames, unidentified, and Gwen Sawtelle; (middle row) Phyllis Lord Treworgy, Bess Lewis, Florence Black, unidentified, and Clifford Weiden; (back row) Miriam Andrews, Louis Jensen, Everett Strout, and Chester Sloat.

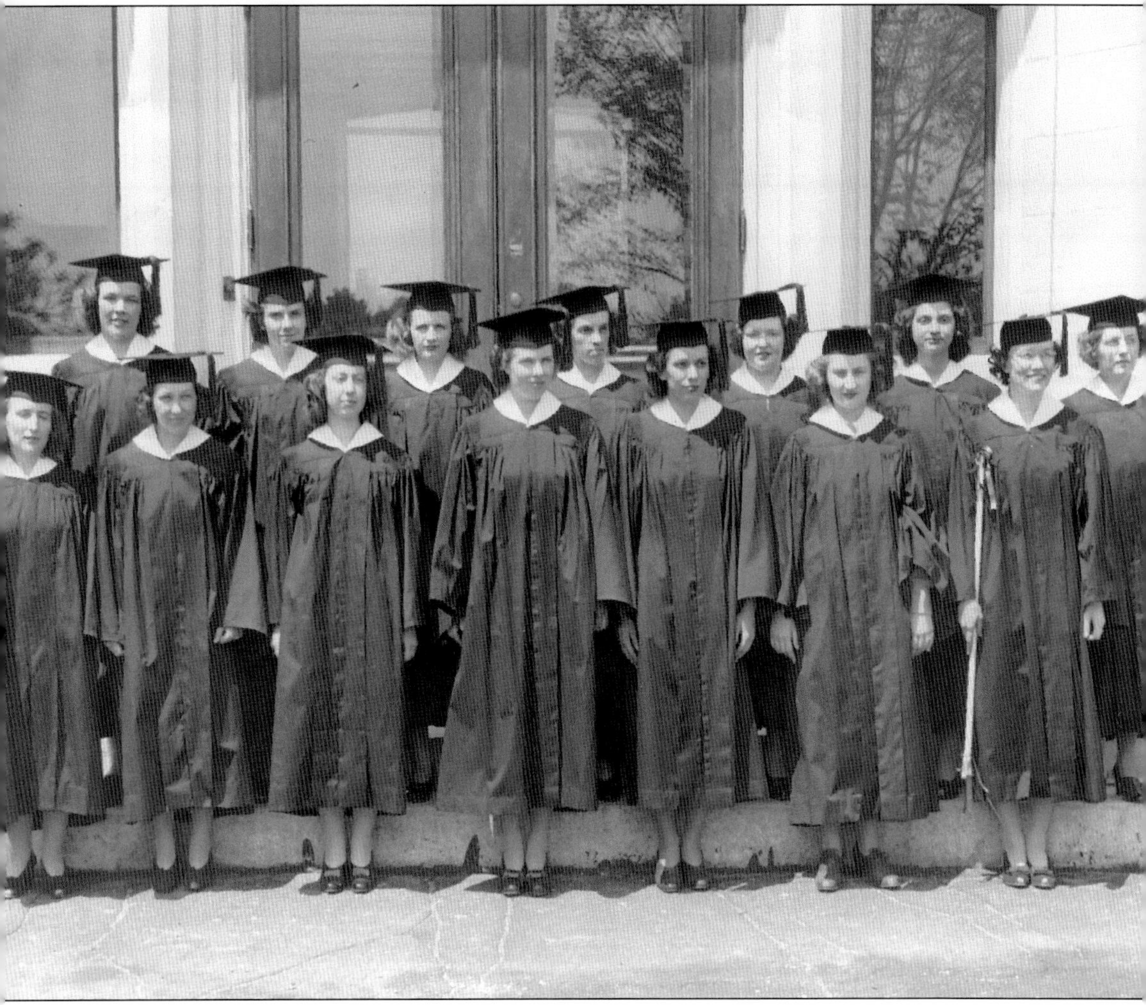

When four-year programs were instituted in the late 1930s, nearly half of their students were male. World War II, however, brought upheaval. The Class of 1944 (shown here) originally included 70 freshmen. Men joined the services, and women (lured by a temporary lowering of teaching requirements) left school to meet the wartime teacher shortage. The members of the class, from left to right, are shown as follows: (front row) Maybelle Leach, Louise McLain, Alice Lowell, Mildred Jackson, Helen Brown, Pauline Supple, and Nancy Goodwin; (back row) Helen Cox, Marion Harvey, Alice McCarthy, Margaret Swett, Joscelyn Tozier, Adeline Montebello, and Della Willey.

Two

Portland University, 1921–1925, 1945–1961

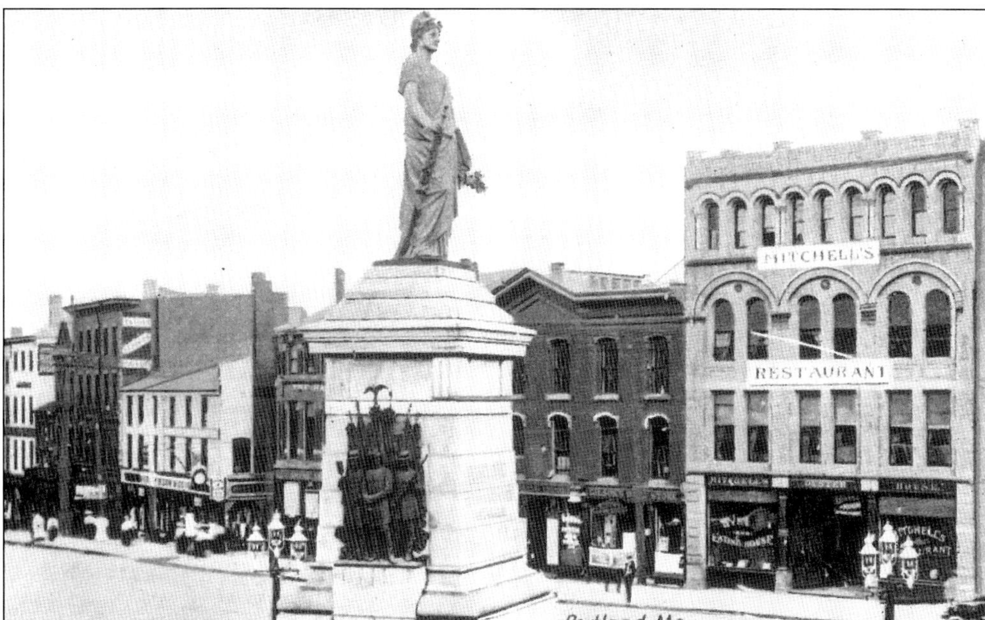

The first home of Portland University was on Monument Square, dominated by the 1891 memorial to Portland's "Sons Who Died for the Union." The new school used the upper floor of the Benoit Building, the light-colored structure to the left of the monument. Organized in August 1921, the institution was the project of Earle H. Cunningham, a local businessman who decried Maine's lack of training for accountants and who had been giving private tutoring in his field. With two other men, Cunningham planned the new nonresidential university. That fall, 25 students enrolled.

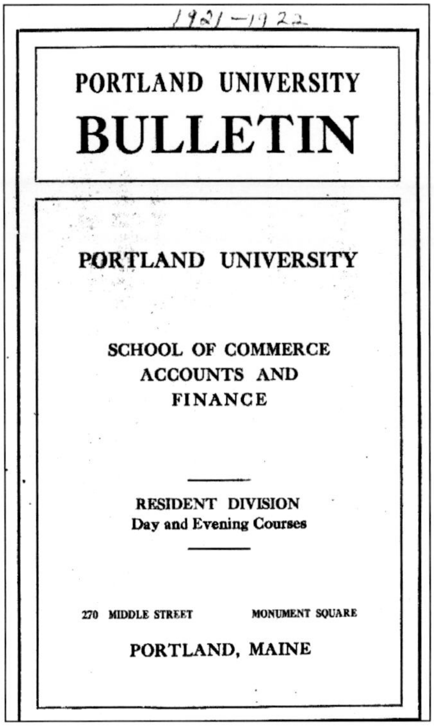

1921–1922

PORTLAND UNIVERSITY

BULLETIN

PORTLAND UNIVERSITY

SCHOOL OF COMMERCE
ACCOUNTS AND
FINANCE

RESIDENT DIVISION
Day and Evening Courses

270 MIDDLE STREET MONUMENT SQUARE

PORTLAND, MAINE

The first catalog offered two programs, a three-year course in accounting and a two-year secretarial course. Noting that "Women Are in Business to Stay," it welcomed both men and women into its classes and offered the use of a library of several hundred accounting books.

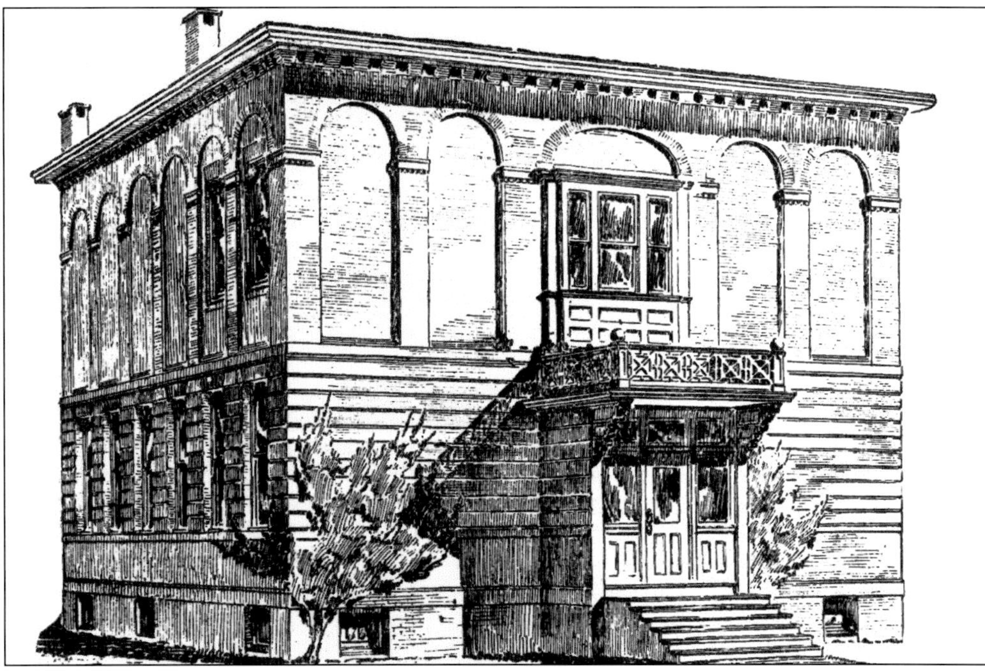

A year later, the new school was relocated at 135 Chadwick Street, in the building originally constructed for the Maine Medical School. The students (numbering 100 in early 1925) organized a debate club, took part in sports, and published a school paper and a small yearbook, *Puvian*. Bachelor's degrees in secretarial science and commercial science were proposed for 1926, but the school closed instead.

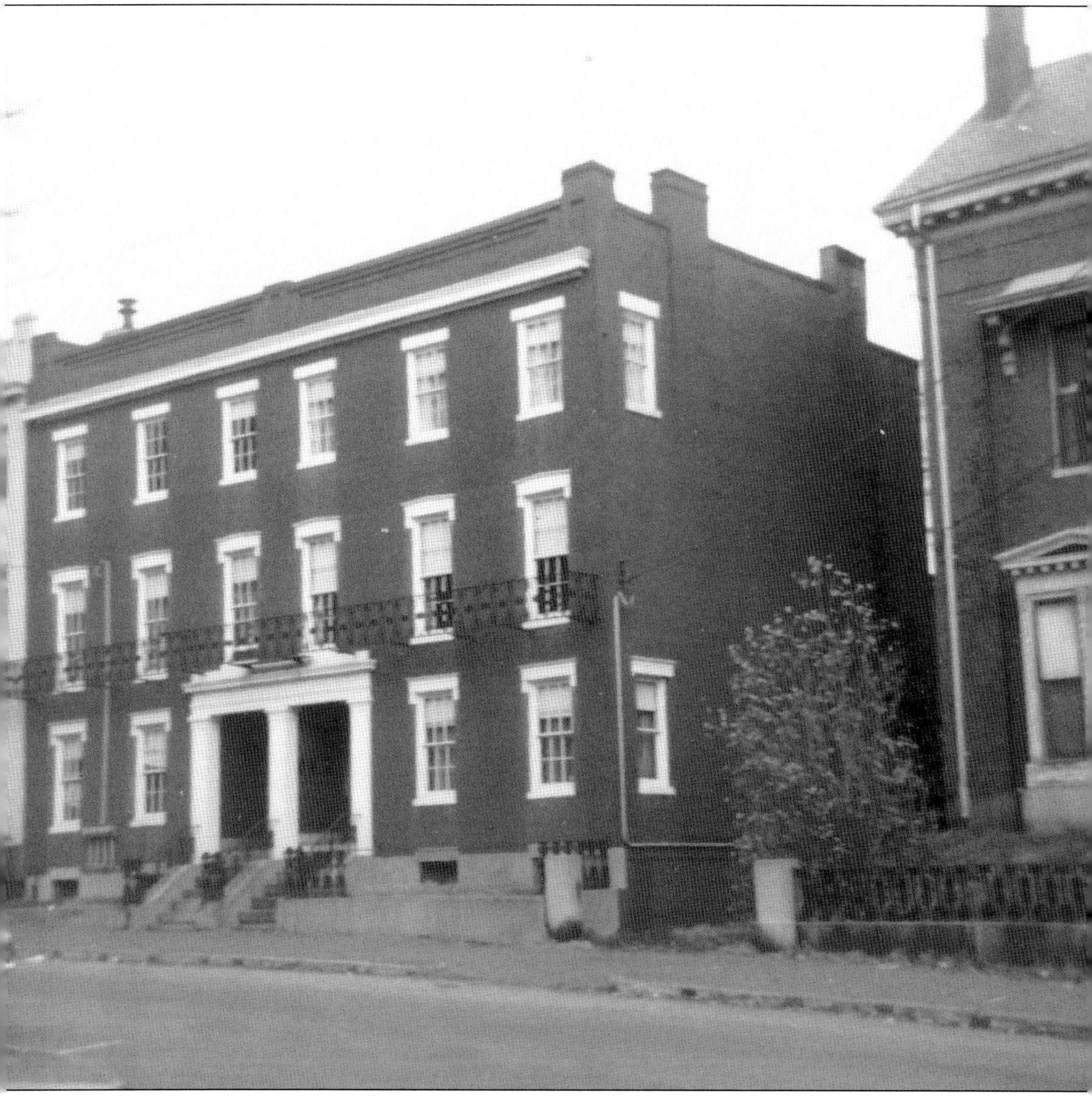

After World War II, the old charter of Portland University was revived (and revised) due to the insistence of lawyers who were disturbed by the state's lack of legal training. (An earlier University of Maine law school in Bangor had shut down in 1920; a private one with Judge Peabody in Portland closed during the war.) By 1947, the reorganized Portland University began giving pre-law courses, first at Northeastern School of Business and then at the YMCA (page 33). Later, the legislature granted the institution the right to give the bachelor of laws degree. In 1953, other degrees were permitted, a business college was added, and Portland University set up in these Park Street houses, with the Law School at No. 89 and the College of Business Administration at No. 91.

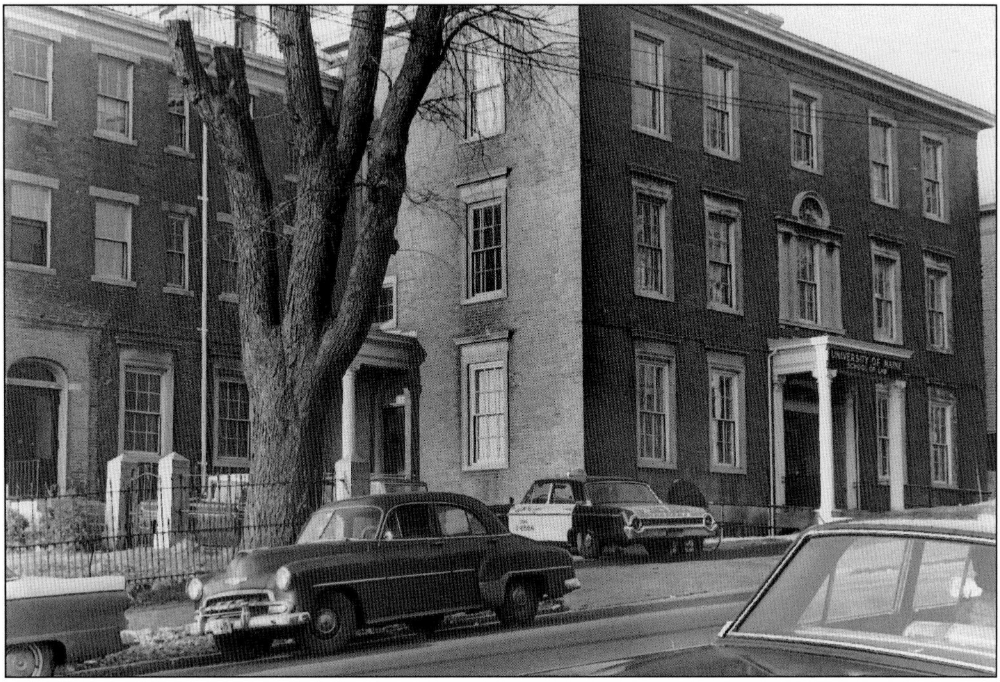

Another move occurred in 1960, when 68 High Street (previously housing the Children's Hospital, then the Salvation Army) and the adjacent Muzzey Mansion were purchased. A year later, Portland University was absorbed by the University of Maine, and the business program was relocated on the latter's Portland campus. The mansion next door was razed.

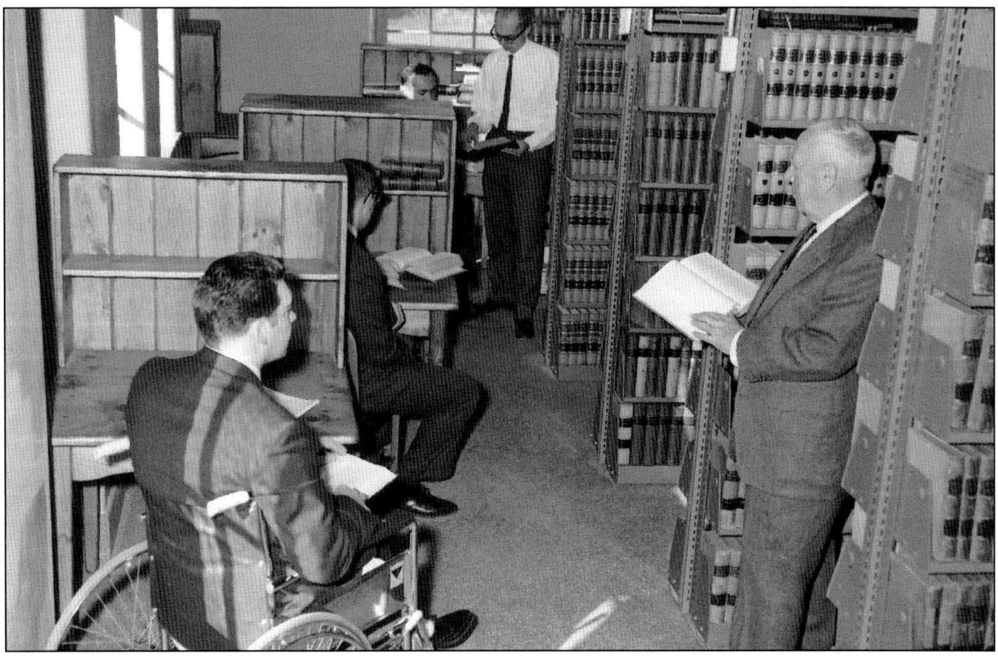

An important feature of the school was the law library, with carrels for concentrated study and librarians (Donald Garbrecht, top center, and Arthur Pulling, right) who were regularly available to help students.

Three

Portland Junior College, 1933–1957

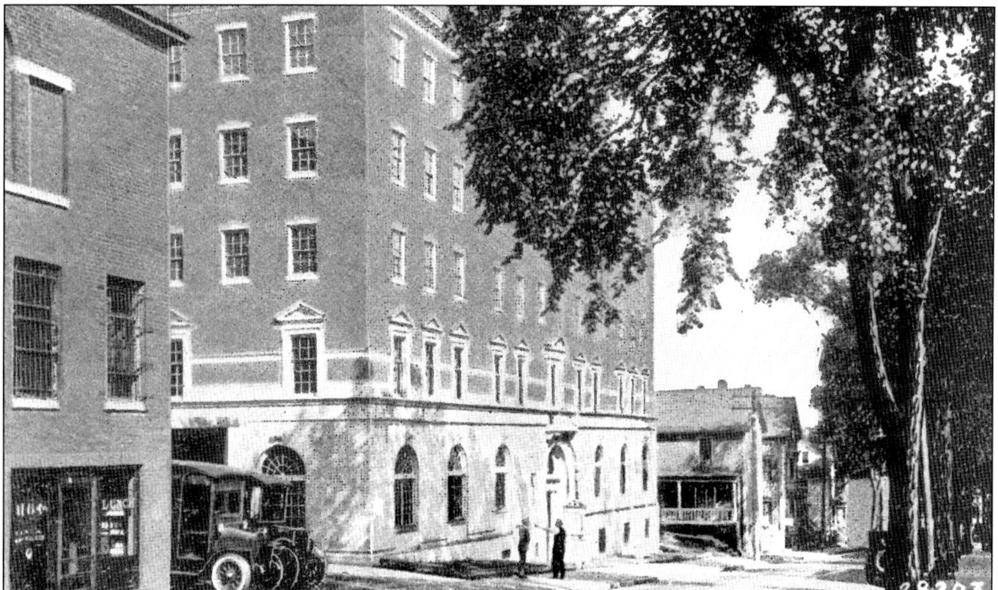

In 1933, officials of the Portland YMCA and local educators proposed to make college-level classes available to young people who were unable (because of the Depression) to go elsewhere to study. From this, Portland Junior College evolved. In return for the students (men and women) becoming Y members, that organization offered space for classes and even for sports in its facility, built in 1927 on Forest Avenue to designs by local architect John P. Thomas. First-year course offerings in liberal arts and business were patterned on those of Boston University, and a second year in business was soon added at student request.

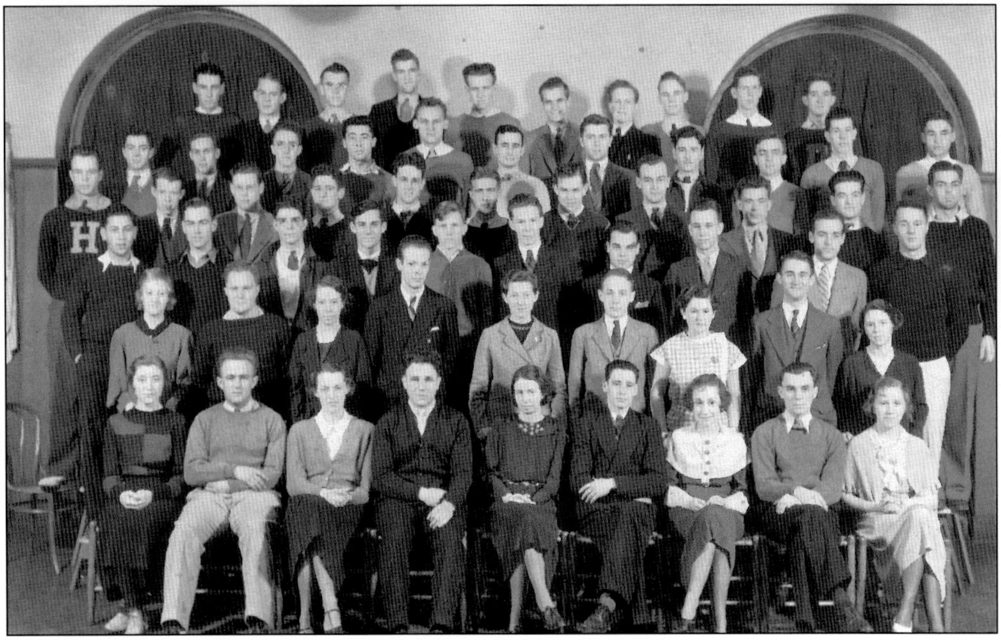

The student body poses at the YMCA in 1933. This picture indicates not only how small the enrollment was at the time but also how few of its students were women.

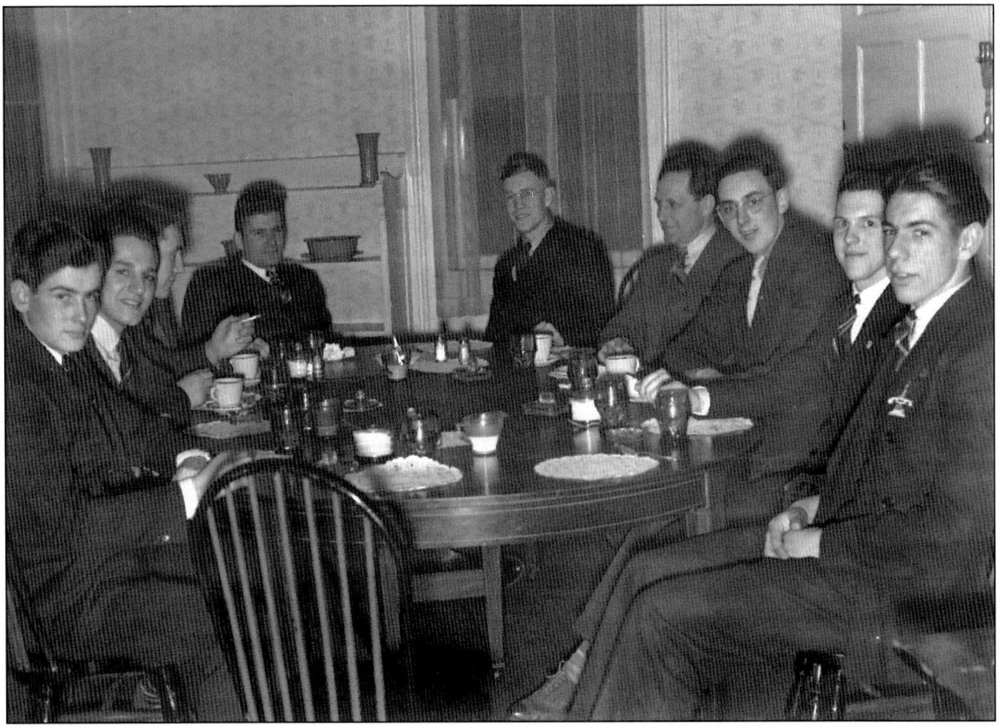

The limited numbers of students and faculty (five full-time, some part-time) permitted good interaction. Holding a discussion after a shared meal in 1938 are, from left to right, Otis Graham, Samuel Giftos, William Wender, Robert P. Ashley (English), Dorman J. Hayes (economics), Dean Luther I. Bonney (mathematics), Dana Cook, Robert Dodge, and Charles Harding.

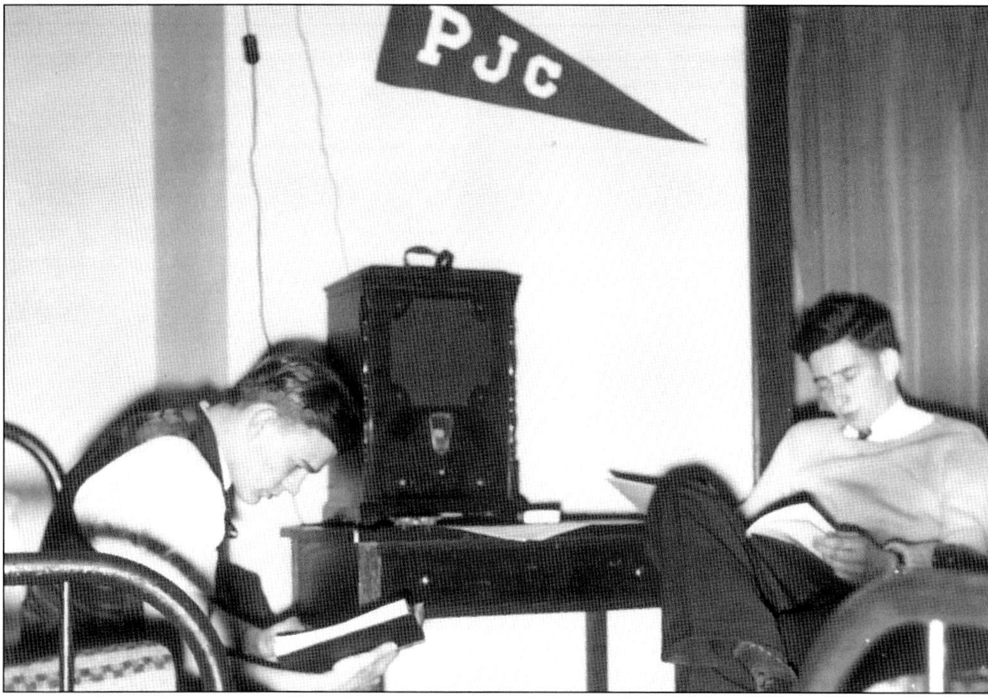

The YMCA offered housing for young men who did not live nearby. The rooms resembled those in many college dormitories of the era, 1938.

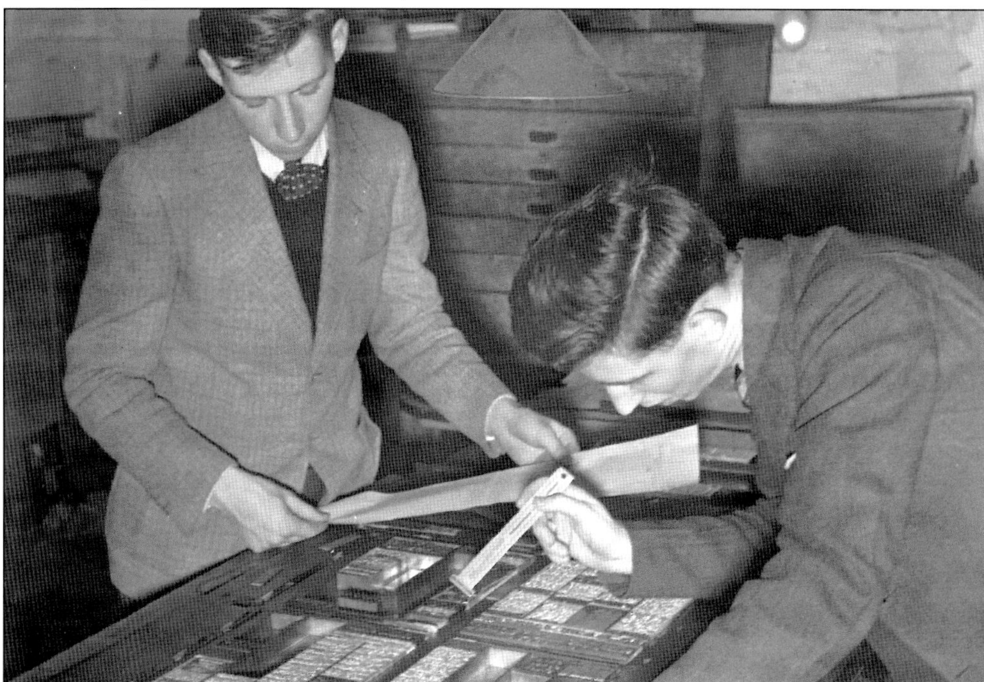

Among organized activities was a college paper, the *PJC News*, begun in 1937. Its assistant editor, Thomas Fox (left), and editor, George I. Lawley, pose while setting up a page of that newspaper in the spring of 1939.

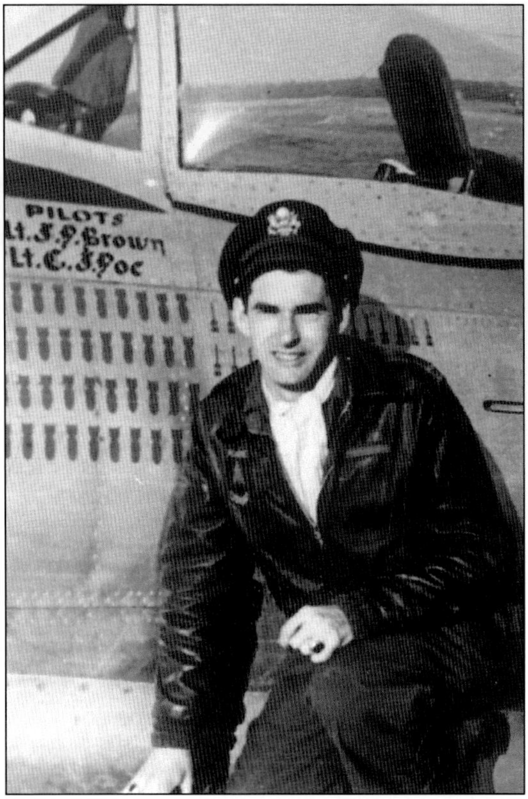

In spite of a program for training pilots, World War II drew off all but 14 of its students by 1943, and Portland Junior College closed down for the duration. Dean Luther I. Bonney attempted to hold the institution together by sending his own *PJC News* to former students, including news of former faculty and of men and women in service. In mid-1945 he discussed plans for the future and printed pictures sent him by alumni, including Lt. John P. Brown, U.S. Air Force.

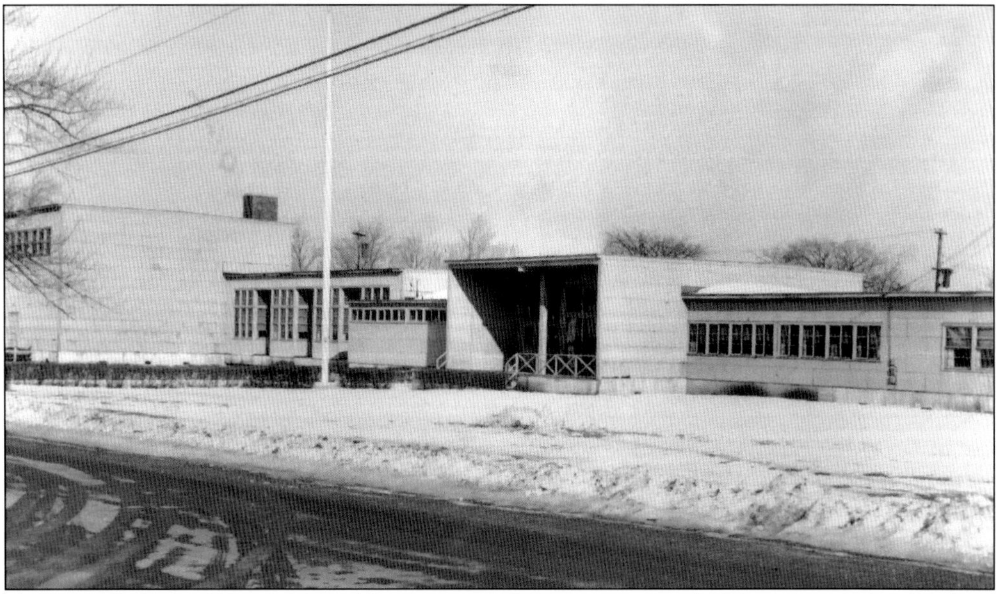

The response to Portland Junior College's announced reopening in 1946 was so great (ex-servicemen by then had the GI Bill to help pay for an education) that the YMCA could not handle the numbers. Mountainview Recreation Building in South Portland, built during the war as the community building for a housing project, was leased while the search for a permanent campus was launched.

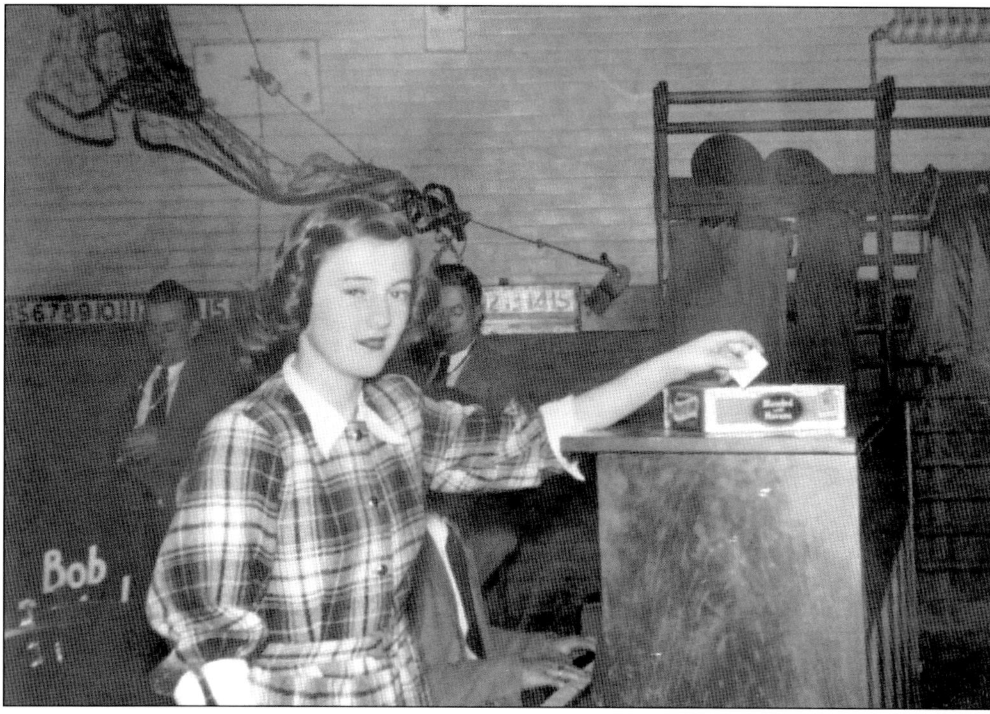

Citing the many ex-servicemen who needed an education, the board of trustees reopened Portland Junior College for males only. Women, however, were invited to social events. Deering High School student Anne Libby is shown drawing a ticket for a door prize at a PJC dance in the YMCA in November 1947.

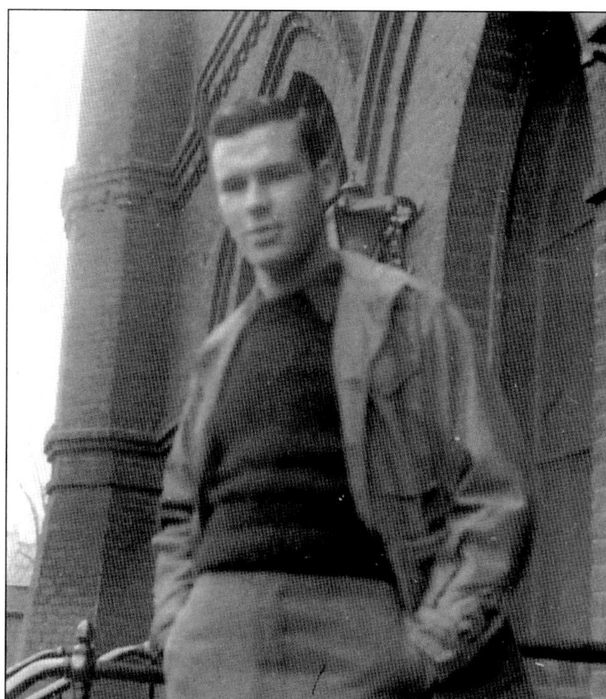

Adding to postwar enrollments was a pre-college program designed to accommodate men who had joined the service before completing high school or who needed extra study to get ready for college. The program was at first housed in the Granville Lee Memorial Recreation Building at India and Congress Streets, where this student was photographed.

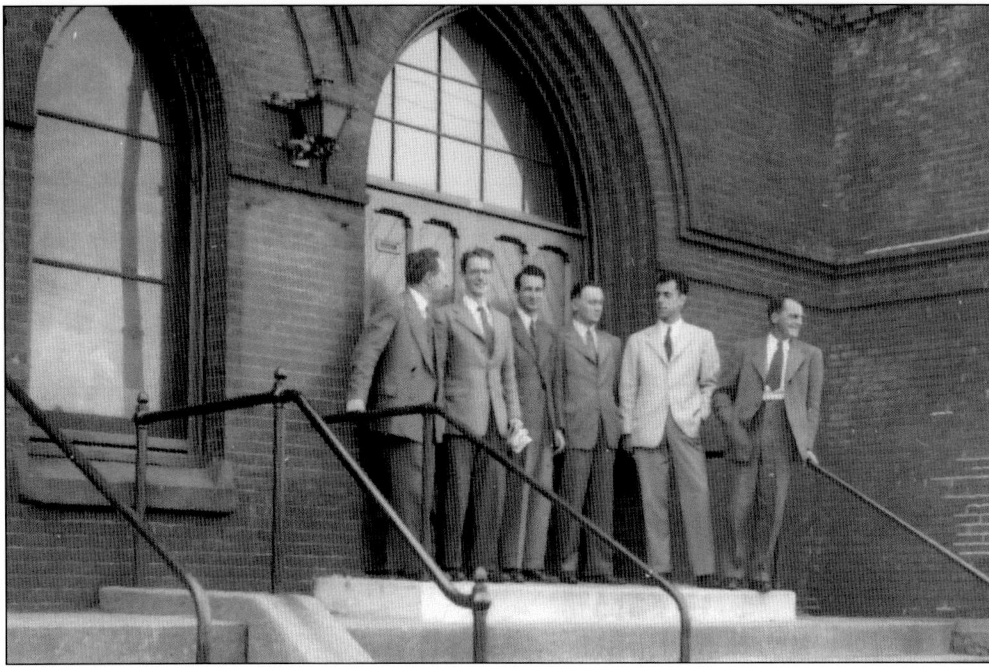

Faculty members posing on the steps of the Granville Lee Memorial Recreation Building are, from left to right, John Jaques (English), Clayton Smith, Robert B. Carr, Luther Bonney (dean, mathematics), John E. Marsh, and Arthur R. Sprague (geometry, psychology). Sprague had attended Portland University in the early 1920s.

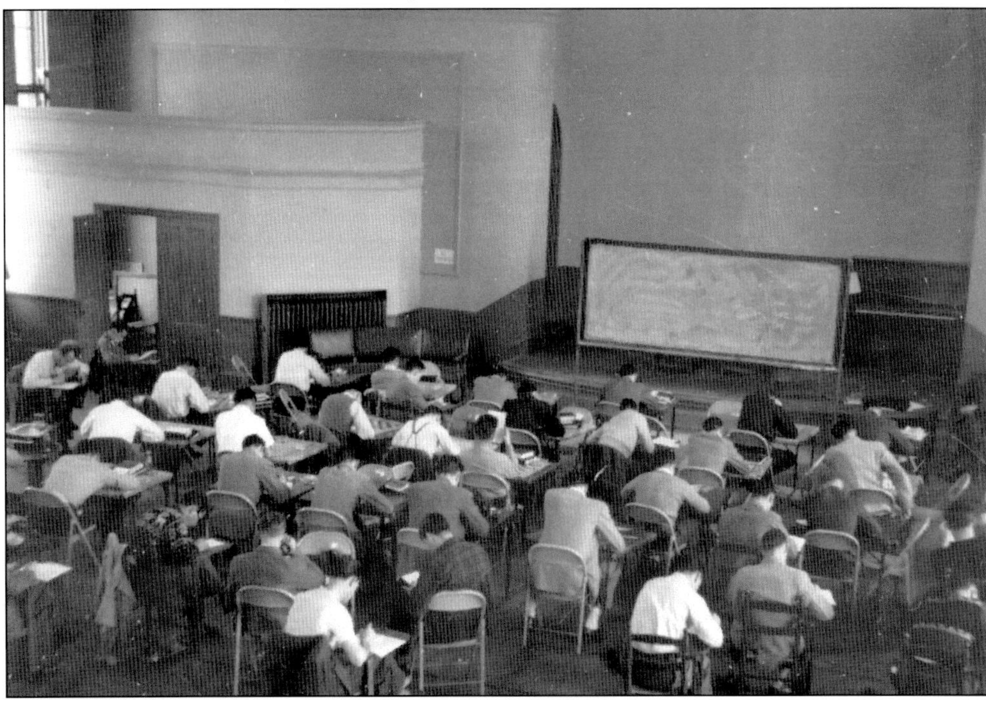

Built in 1865 as the Second Universalist Church, the Lee Memorial Building had an open interior, which, with the addition of suitable seating, could serve as a classroom.

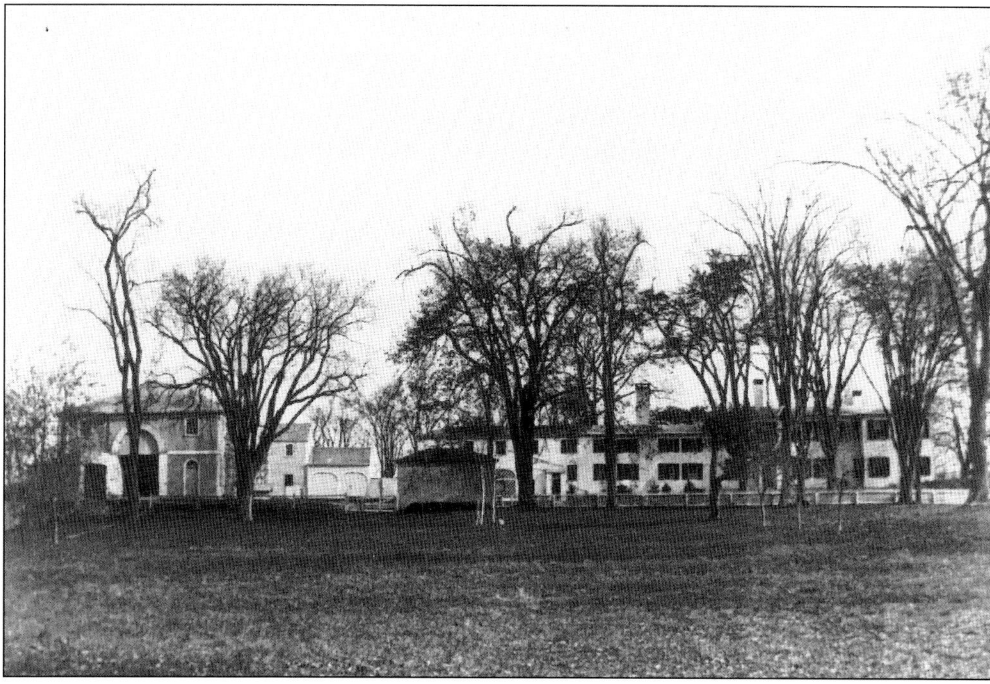

Late in 1946, the search for a permanent location culminated in the purchase of about six acres of the old Deering Estate, shown here. The purchase included the stable on the left and the shed to the right of it, but not the mansion on the far right. Also part of the purchase was a small farmhouse, located to the left of this picture.

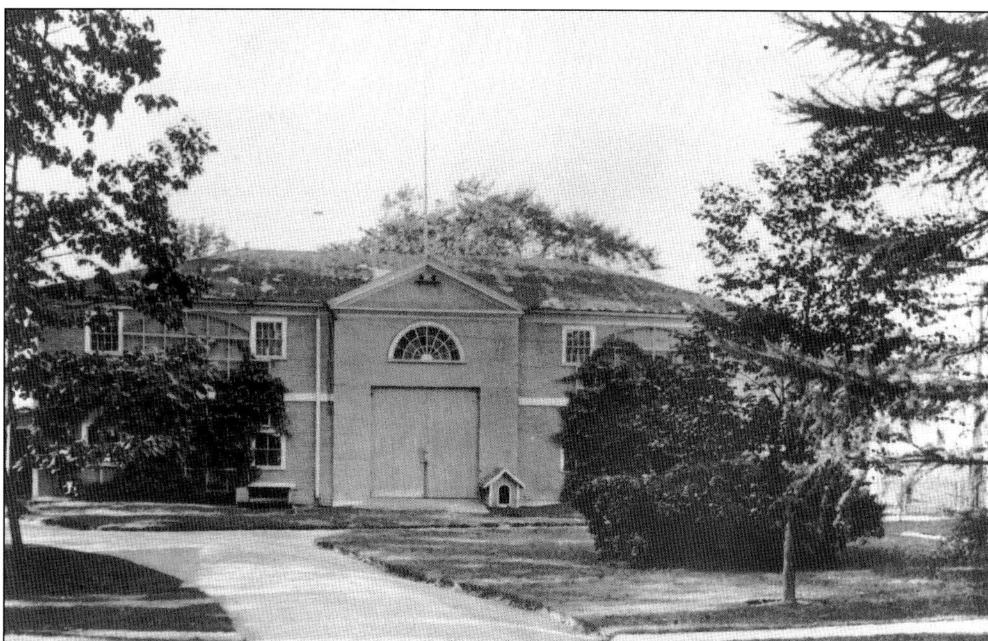

The unusual stable, designed in 1805 by Alexander Parris, would be sensitively remodeled to have a gymnasium/assembly hall on the main floor, with showers, a lounge, and a snack bar in the lower "daylight basement" opening to Falmouth Street.

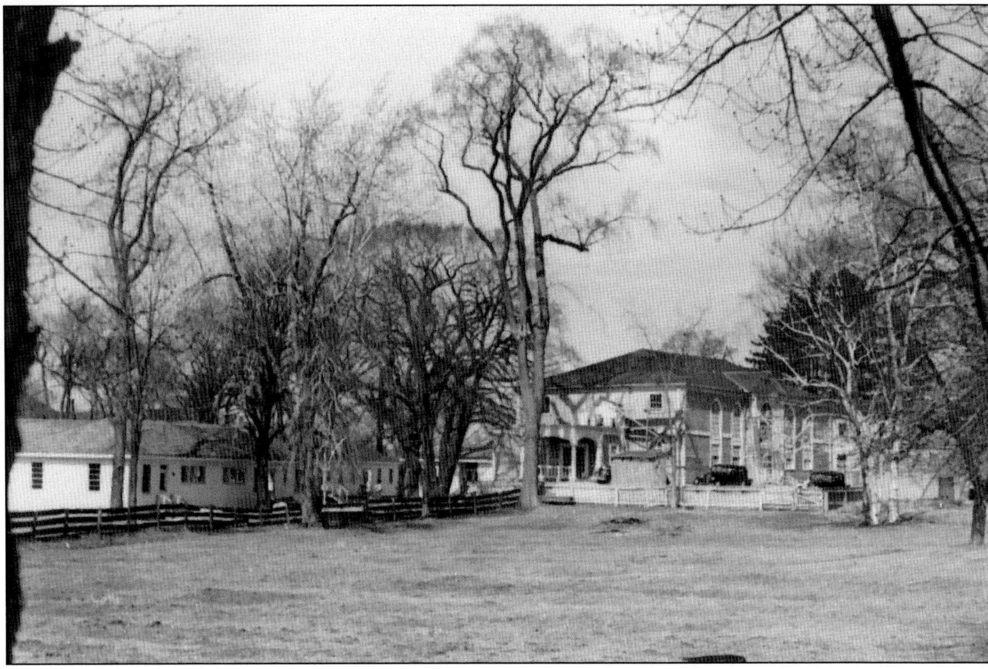

For classrooms, surplus military barracks from Great Diamond Island were rebuilt as three low structures (left) around "the Barn." The new campus was not ready for occupancy in the fall of 1947, and classes once again met at the YMCA, with the pre-college men at the Boys' Club. By February 1948, everyone moved to the new campus. The pre-college courses continued, albeit with dwindling numbers, as long as did Portland Junior College.

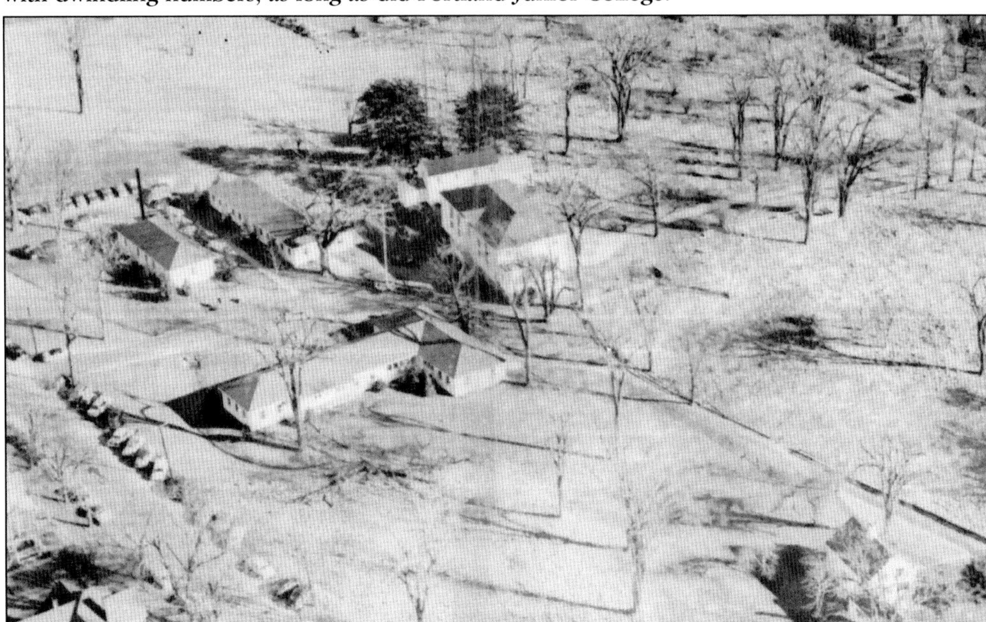

This aerial view shows the campus in the mid-1950s, after the old Deering Mansion had been razed. Classroom buildings are in the upper left, on either side of the path from Falmouth Street to the Barn. The old farmhouse is at the lower right.

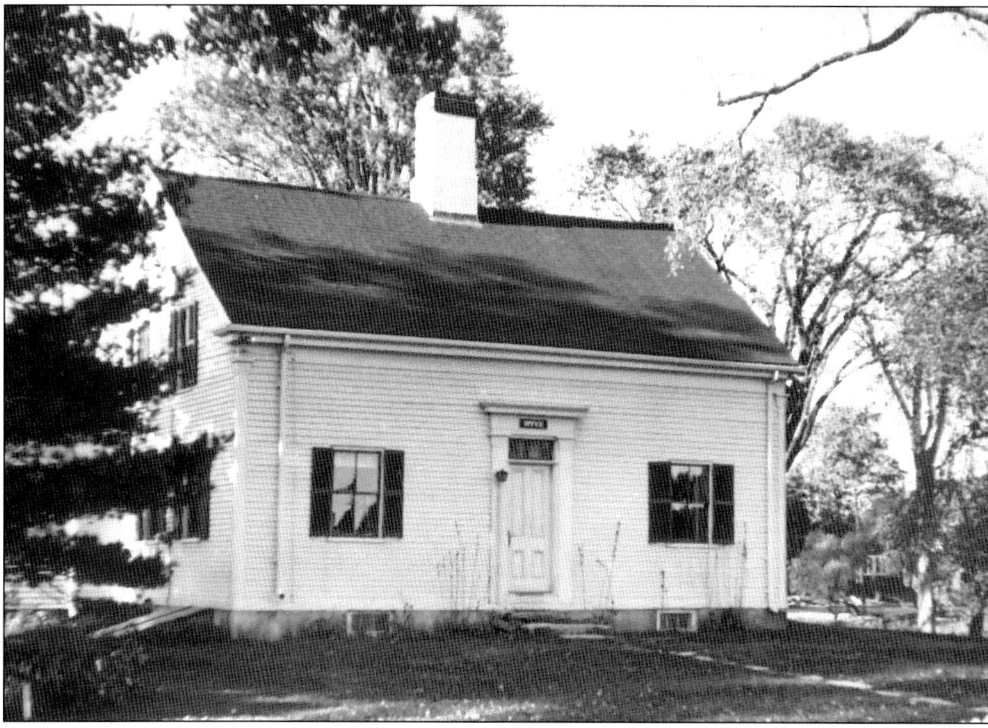

The Deering farmhouse provided room for the administrative offices of the Junior College.

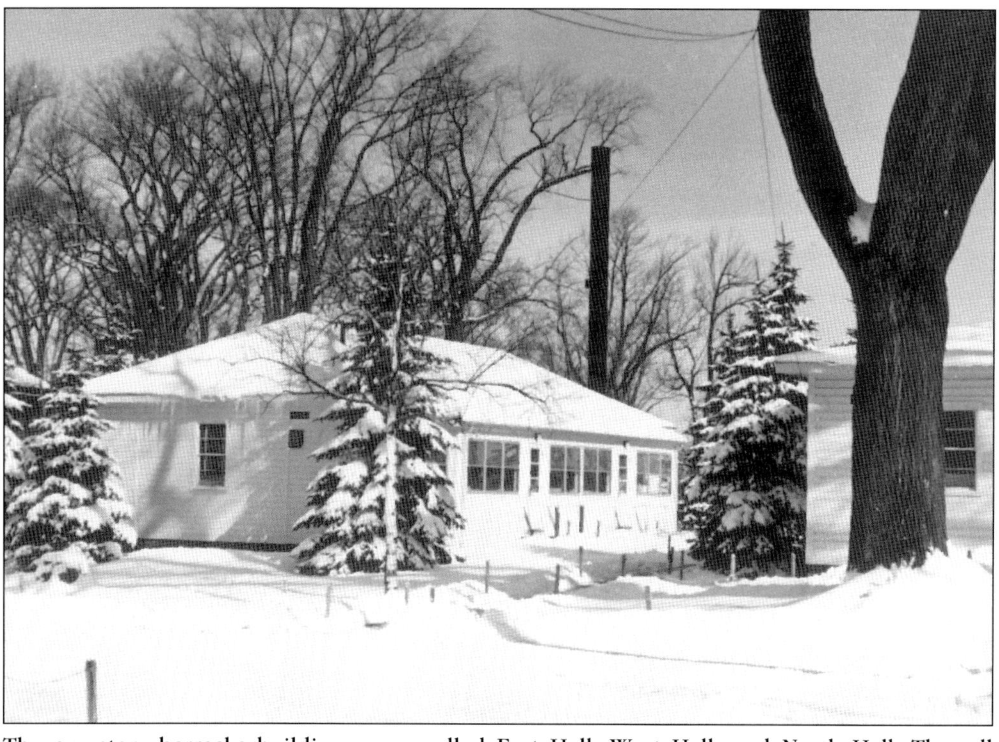

The one-story barracks buildings were called East Hall, West Hall, and North Hall. The tall chimney of North Hall marks it as the location of the heating plant. East Hall is on the right.

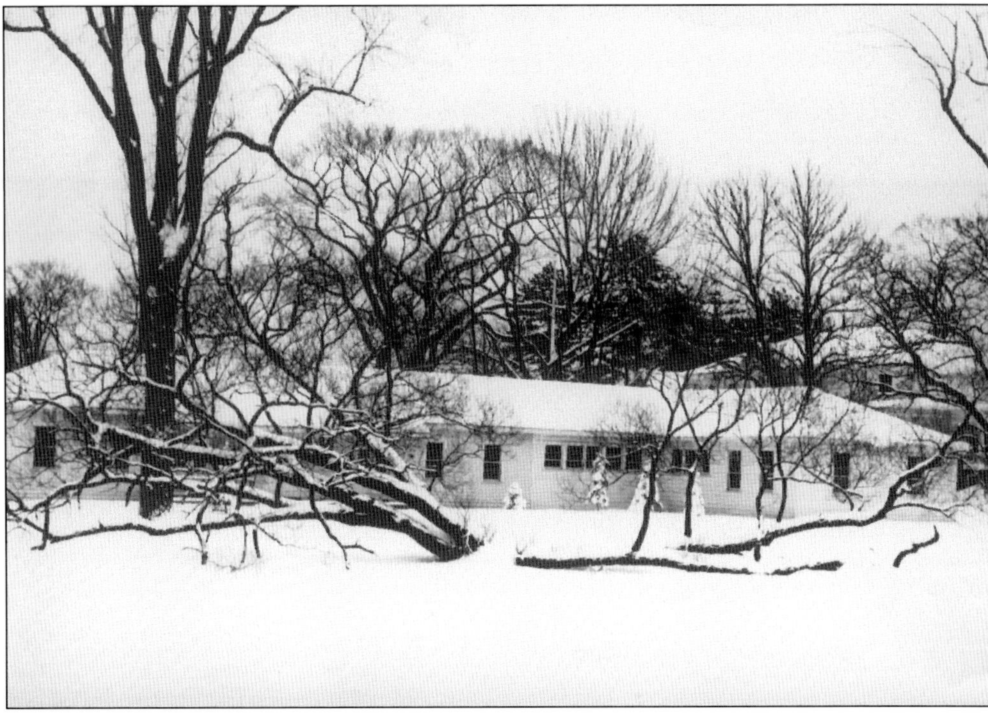

West Hall was the largest and had space for most of the 10 classrooms, the offices, and the college's first library.

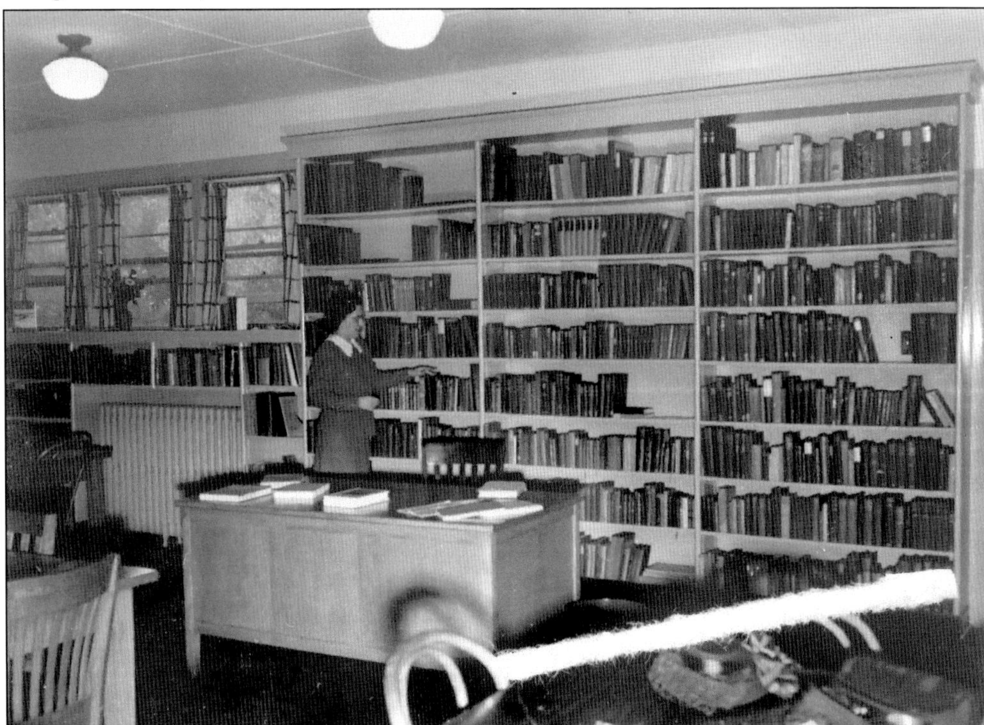

For the first time, a librarian was needed, and Muriel Leighton joined the staff.

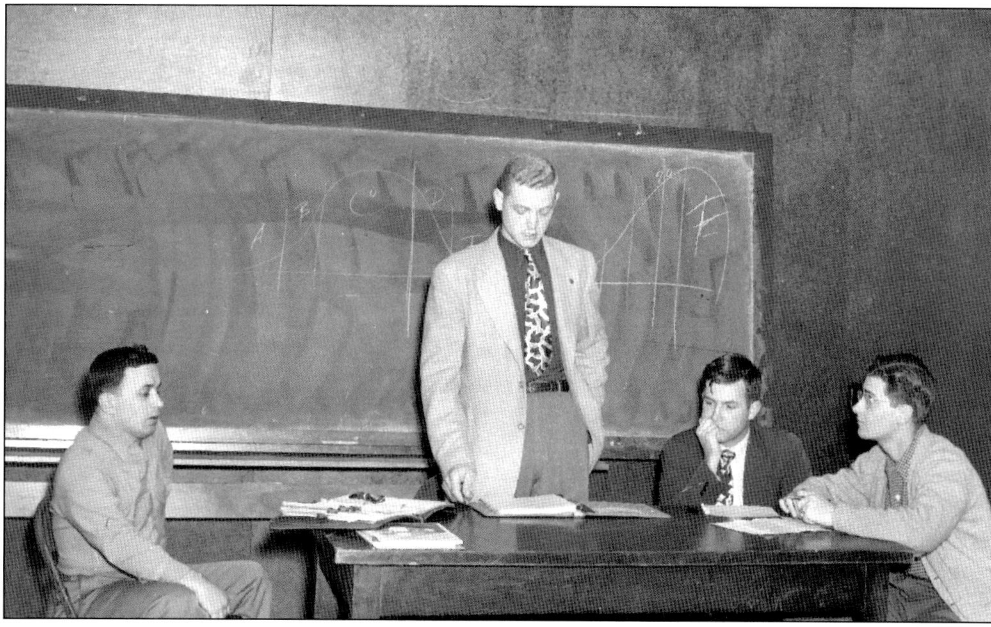

Pictures of organizations serve to show the interior finish of the buildings. This group, identified only as a "student forum," met in one of the classrooms. Note the inexpensive fiberboard walls and the rather small blackboard. Even the furniture was more serviceable than expensive.

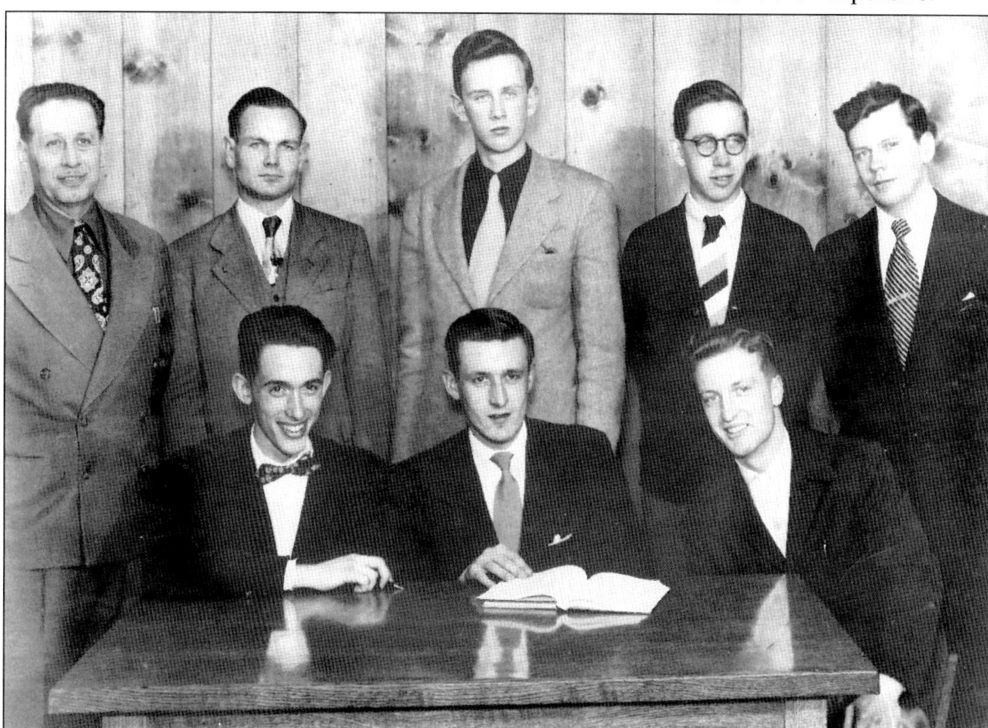

Vertical boards covered other walls. The staff of the 1949 *Student Review* is shown, from left to right, as follows: (front row) Tolford Young, Harold Kyte, and Dan Sullivan; (back row) Carl French (advisor), Kenneth Giddings, John Pettengill, Vernon Kelly, and Paul Nichols.

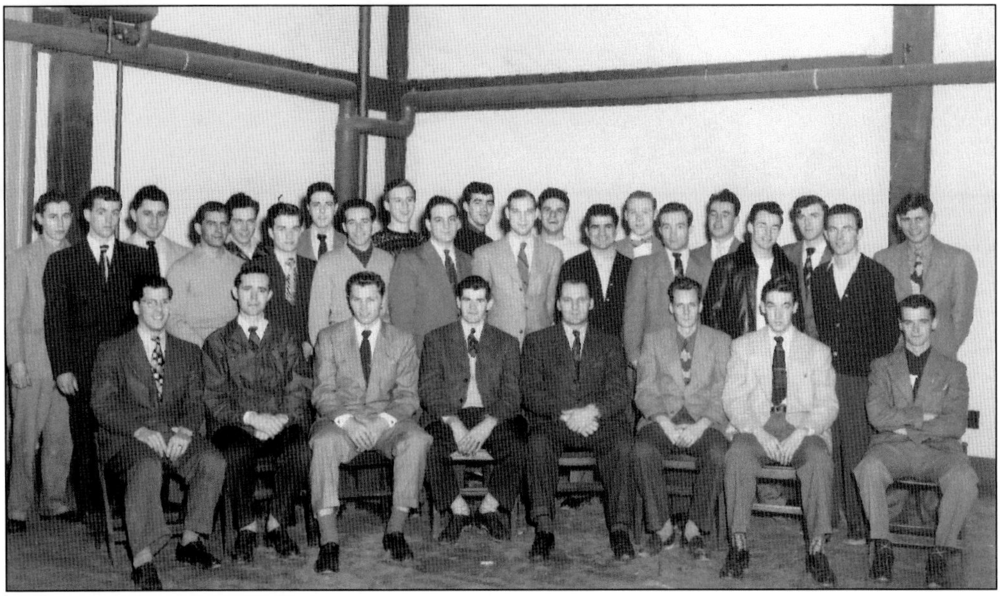

The Harvard Reading Film Class, founded in 1948, poses that year in the gymnasium. Their goal was self-improvement. In order to increase their reading speed and better their comprehension, student members contributed funds to buy the special films, which they then donated to the college for the benefit of later students.

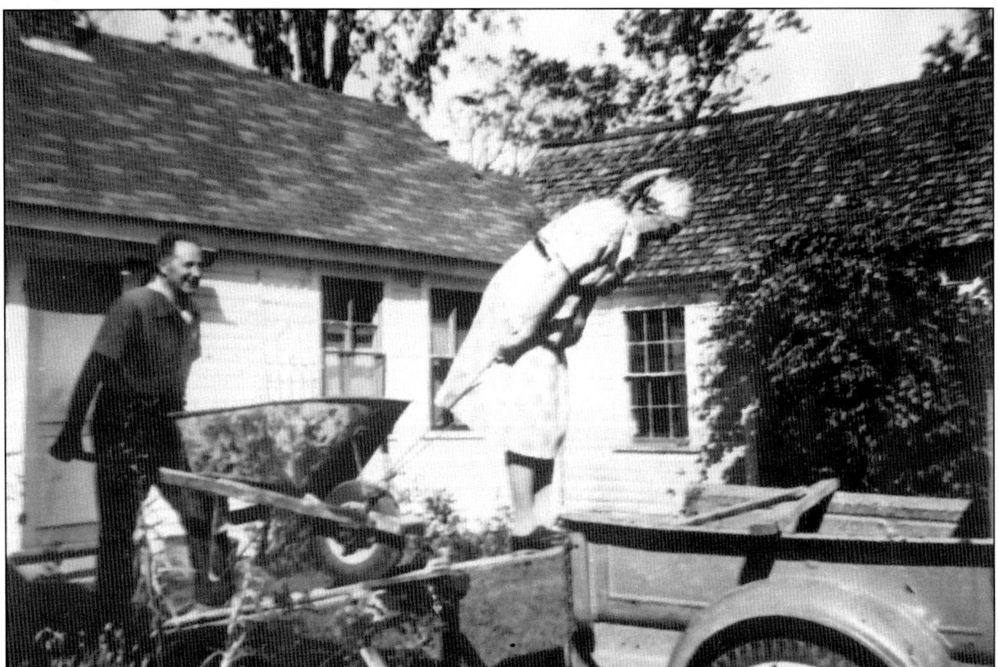

A new campus demanded work, and students and staff pitched in for a cleanup day. Here, Dean Luther Bonney, with Mrs. Bonney pulling the wheelbarrow, moves unwanted material to their truck. The 1929 truck was well known by students, who dedicated their yearbook to "Oscar" in 1954, saying it had served the college since 1938, not only carrying the dean to work, but also attending every Portland Junior College Mountain Day.

Mountain Day began in the mid-1930s when students, faculty, and guests took advantage of the Columbus Day holiday to climb Mount Chocorua, in New Hampshire. In 1939, they also tried Maine's Mount Blue. When the practice was revived in 1946, Bradbury Mountain was selected. A field day, on a Casco Bay island or at Sebago Lake, was also held in the spring.

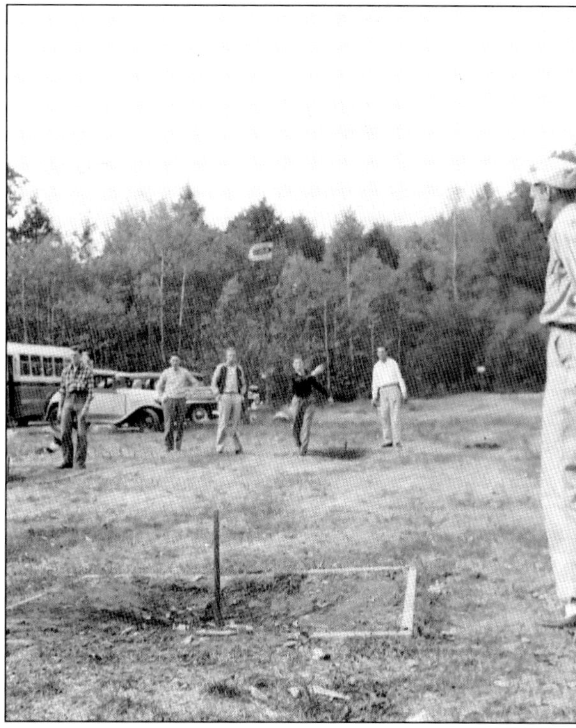

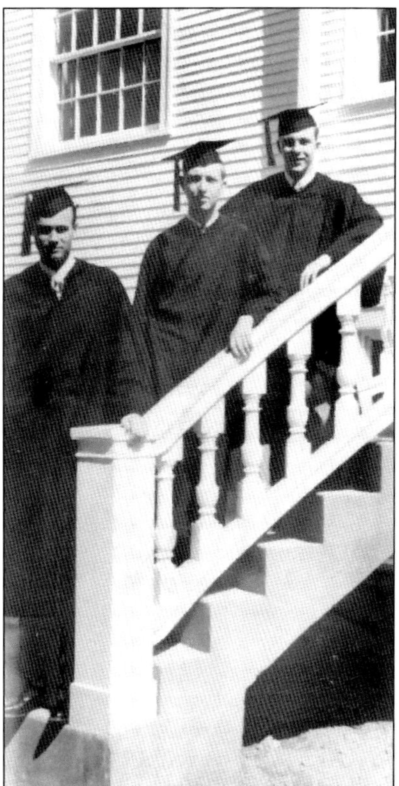

The Class of 1948 boasted that they were the first class on the new campus and issued the institution's first yearbook, *The Stag*. They also designed the school seal, selected the school colors (green and white), and held the first commencement ceremony. Among the speakers at that 1948 commencement were graduates Edward E. Dudley (left), Michael J. O'Toole (center), and John H. Curran (right).

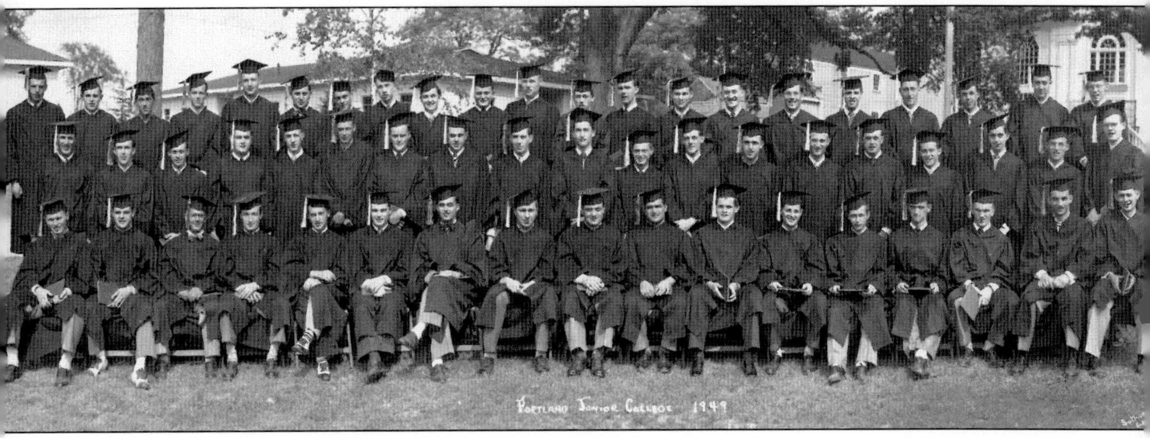

The Portland Junior College graduates from the Class of 1949 are shown, from left to right, as follows: (front row) Thomas Roche, Jerry Howard, Donald Cockburn, Daniel Fowler, Richard Goodie, Richard Groves, Richard Chaplin, Frank Nanos, Henry Latini, Pete Barris, Cedric Williams, Philip Kates, Mark Andrews, Richard Noyes, Robert Southworth, James Nicholas, and Russell Yates; (middle row) Pierre Harnois, John Coune, Giles Beaulac, James Skeehan, Robert Slipp, Bradford Bonney, John Jordan, Harold Martin, Edward Feeney, Richard Palmer, Percy Durost, Clyde Hatch, Richard Boothby, Charles Ammann, Louis Waugh, Orlando Dipaolo, James Nanos, Elliott Mitchell, and Frank Asnault; (back row) Wilfred Reid, James Dawson, Charles Scontras, Frank Ross, Richard Gaisford, Leonard Margolin, Larry Brydon, John McCallum, Philip Michaud, Charles Jortberg, Ronald Smith, Donald Libby, Robert Rankin, Larry Campbell, Donald Hoyt, Eli Kroot, Irving Marcus, Bradley Mack, Ralph Roberts, Raymond Leeman, and Scott Hoar

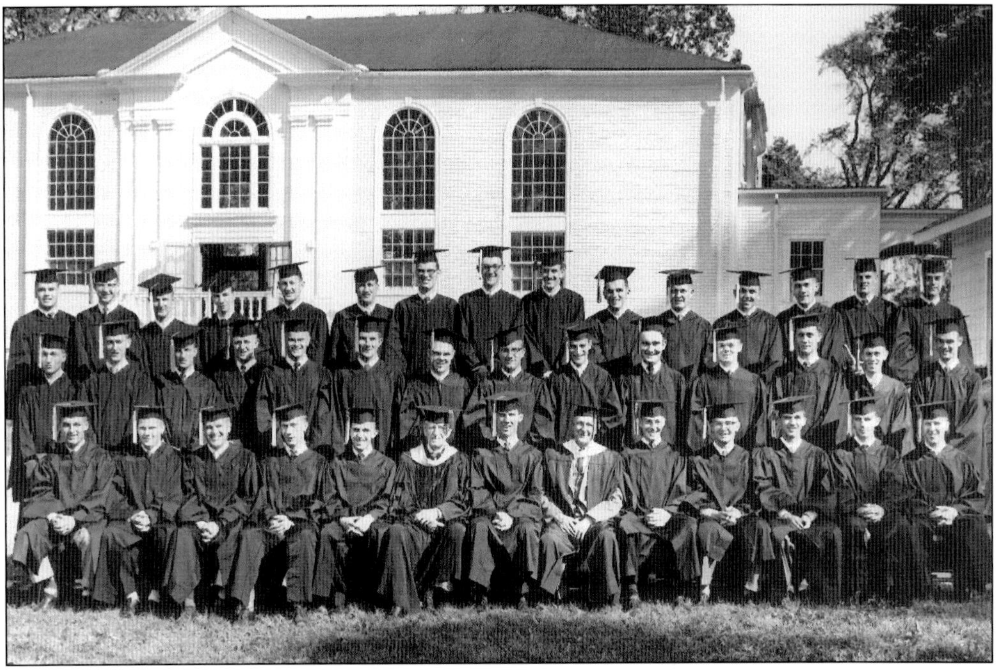

Raymond Oakes, president of the board (sixth from left in front) and Dean Luther Bonney (eighth from left in front) pose in 1957 with the final Portland Junior College graduation class. Behind them is the Barn. Note its massive arched windows, which echoed an older structure and helped retain a Federal appearance.

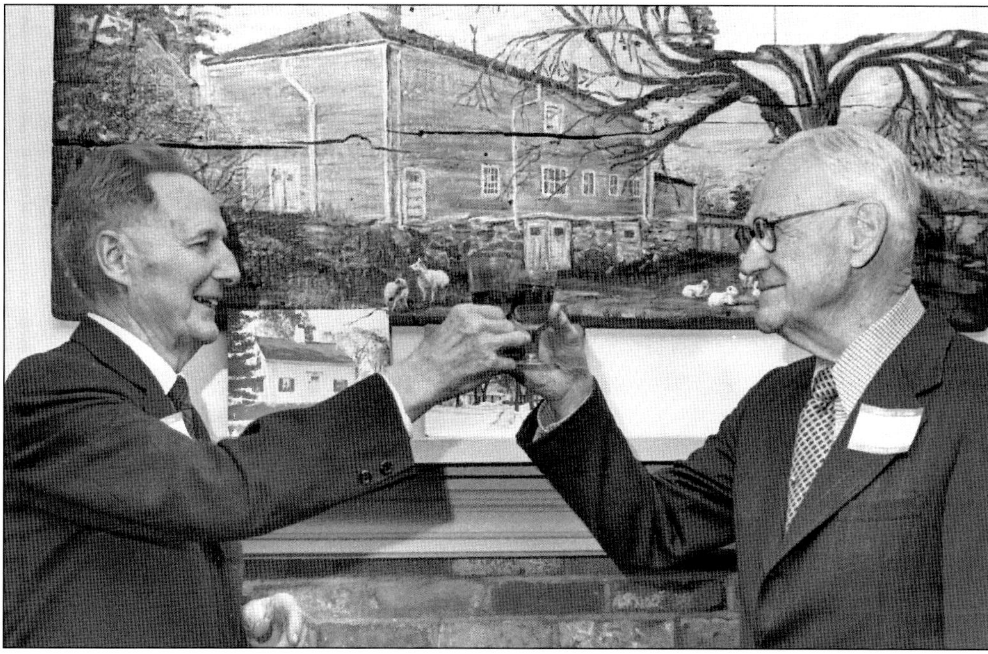

Luther Bonney and Raymond Oakes were reunited nearly two decades later in what had been the administrative office of Portland Junior College. The painting, based on an old photograph, shows the old Deering barn, north side, when it was a barn.

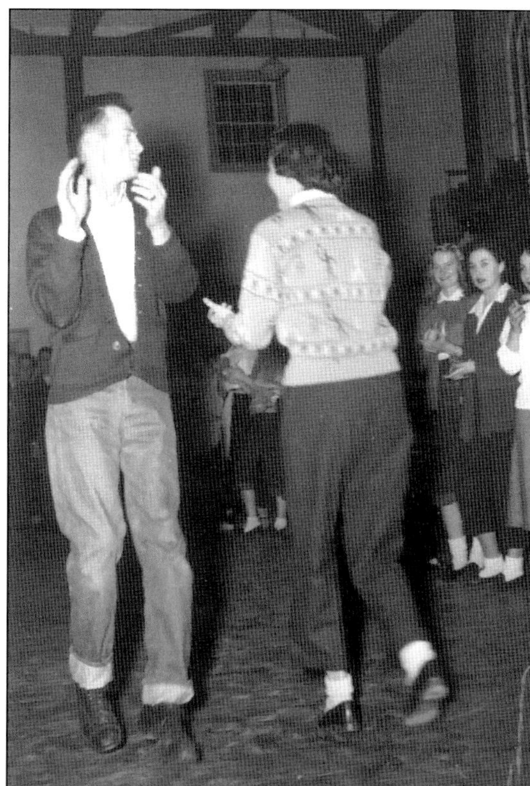

The Barn's interior served many functions, including regular dances, such as this one sponsored by the Outing Club.

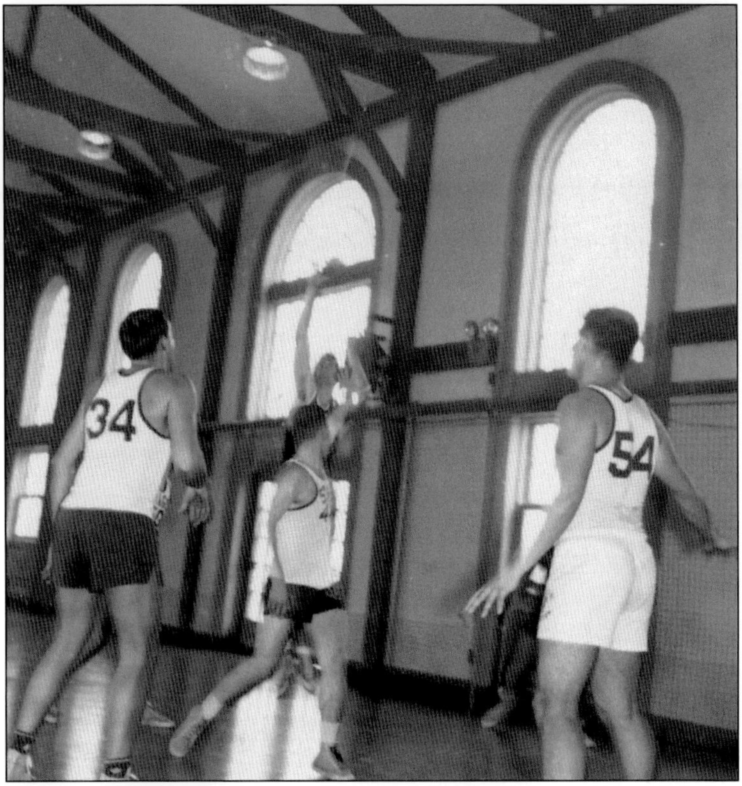

With netting to protect the windows, the space was well suited to use for basketball practices and games. The team was called the Stags.

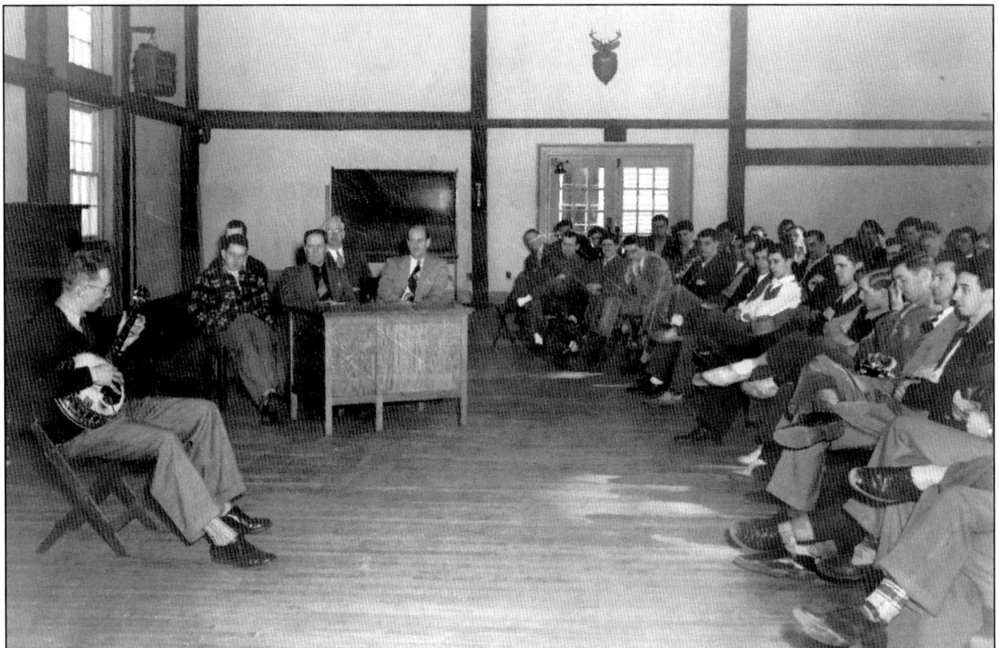

Although no music program was offered, individuals from the community were brought in to direct special groups, and musical moments flourished. An assembly in the gym might be led in song by a student or faculty member with a guitar or banjo.

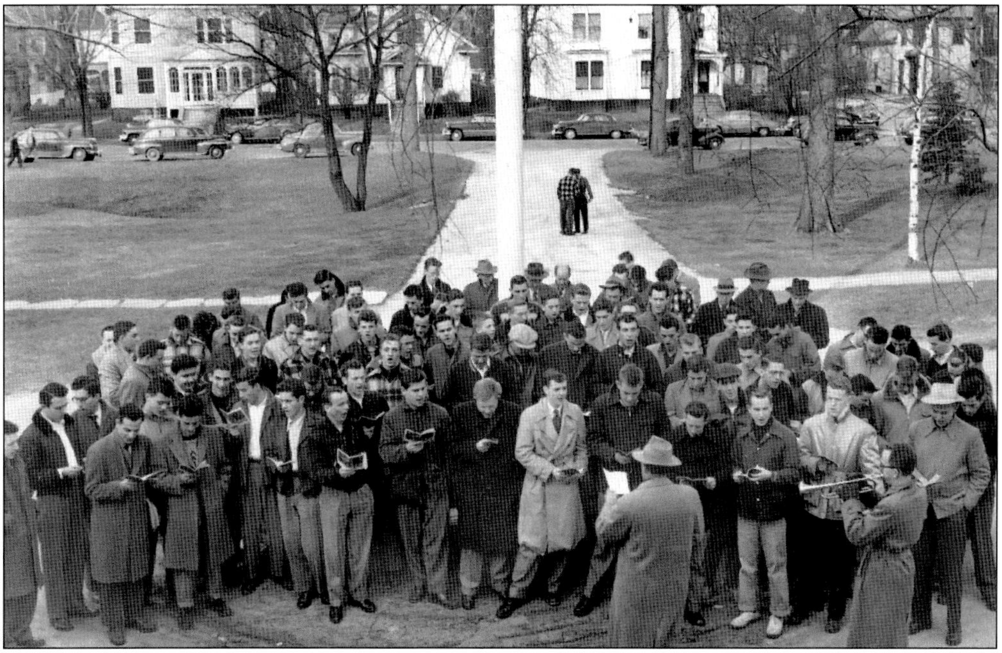

In this photograph, taken just before Christmas in 1949, students sing carols outside the Barn, standing where sheep had grazed earlier.

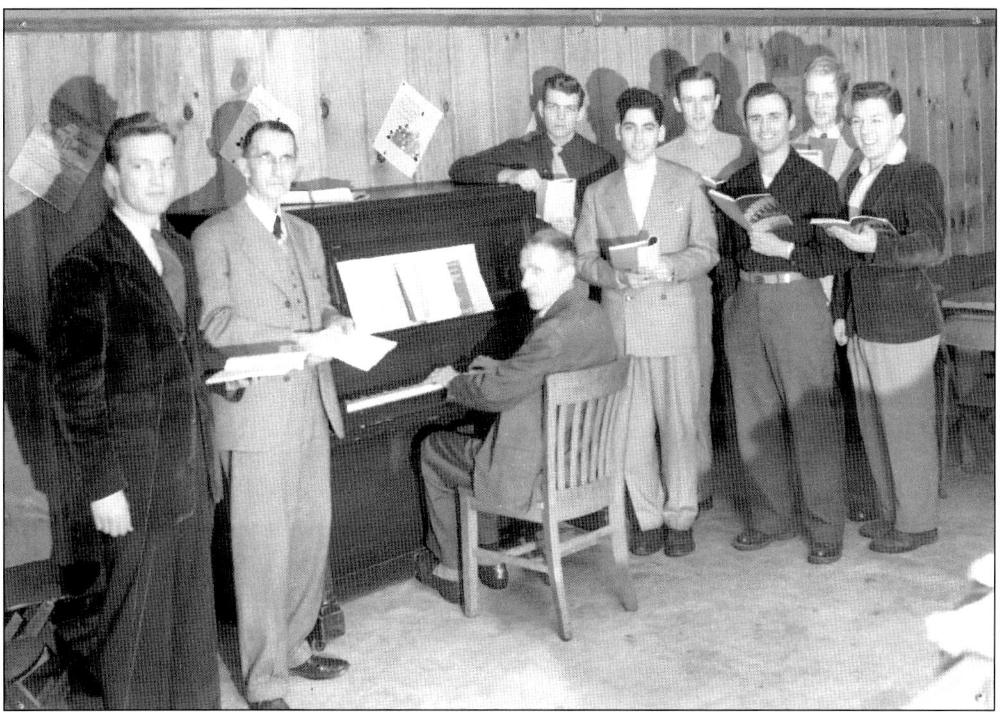

The members of the 1950 Glee Club are shown standing, from left to right, as follows: Dan Sullivan (president), Howard Stevens (director), Larry Stinchfield, Al Levine, Harold Kyte, George Dunn, Dudley Hughes, and Charles Liponis. Robert Goff—who taught English, German, and mathematics—is at the piano.

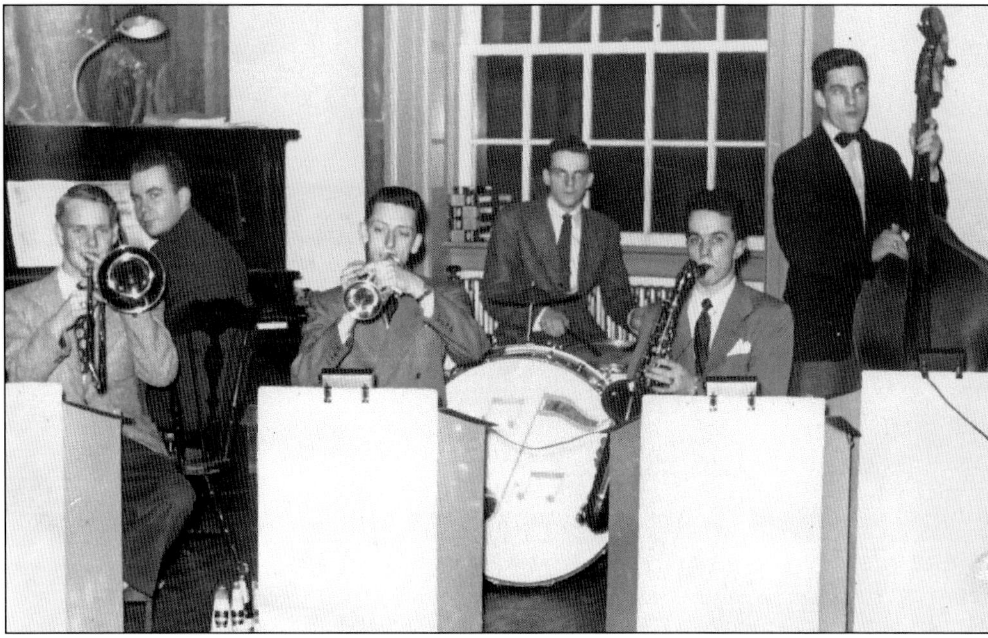

Students on occasion operated their own dance band. This group, however, seems to have been part of a Dramatics Club presentation.

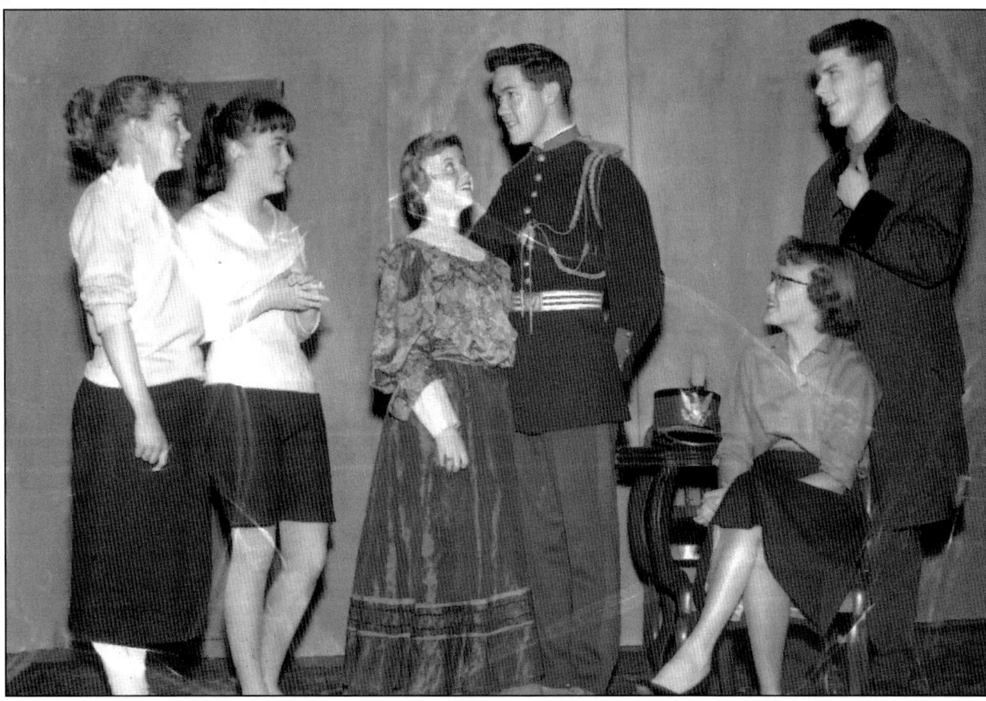

Because resources were limited on campus, chemistry classes were taught by faculty at nearby Westbrook Junior College (for women), utilizing that college's labs at night. The two drama clubs frequently combined forces, using the WJC's theater. Shown in a 1957 performance of *The Gay Lord Quex* are, from left to right, Diane Libby, Mary Alice Chandler, Polly Peterson, Chester Keefe, Cynthia Nevers, and Robert G. Moseley.

Four

Gorham State Teachers College, 1945–1965

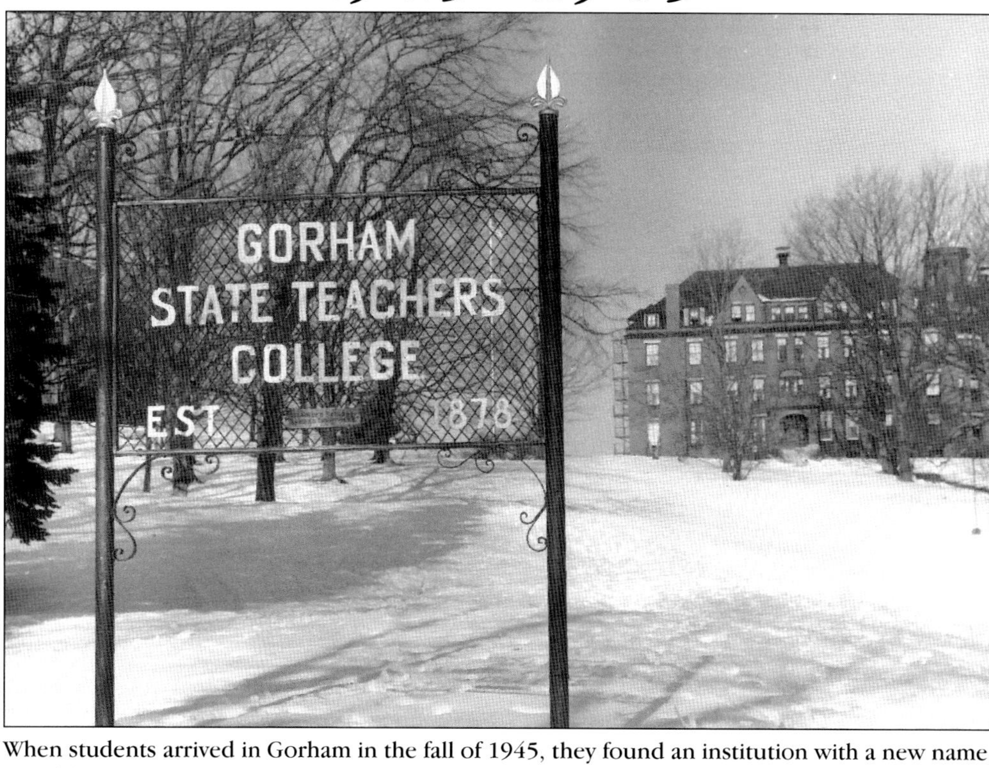

When students arrived in Gorham in the fall of 1945, they found an institution with a new name. Possibly the name and the sign were the greatest immediate changes. But classes also expanded as veterans (nine male and two female veterans received degrees in 1946) and women who had been teaching returned to complete their degrees. It would be three more years (to live up to agreements with those already enrolled) before the three-year programs were completely phased out so that everyone took four-year degrees. The "principal" became a "president," and campus activity increased.

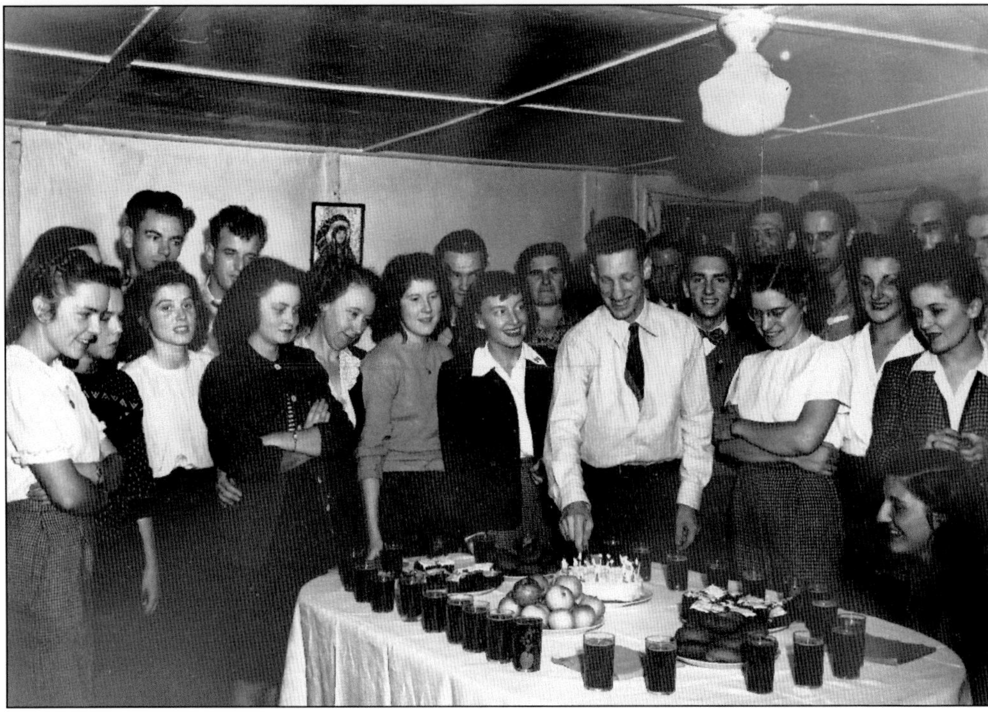

With the end of gasoline rationing, commuting once more became a way of life for some, and the Commuters' Club evolved. Here the group celebrates the birthday of Horton Briggs on October 30, 1946. The hostess, Amanda Martin, stands behind Briggs' right shoulder. The group's faculty advisor, Esther Wood, is just below the picture on the wall.

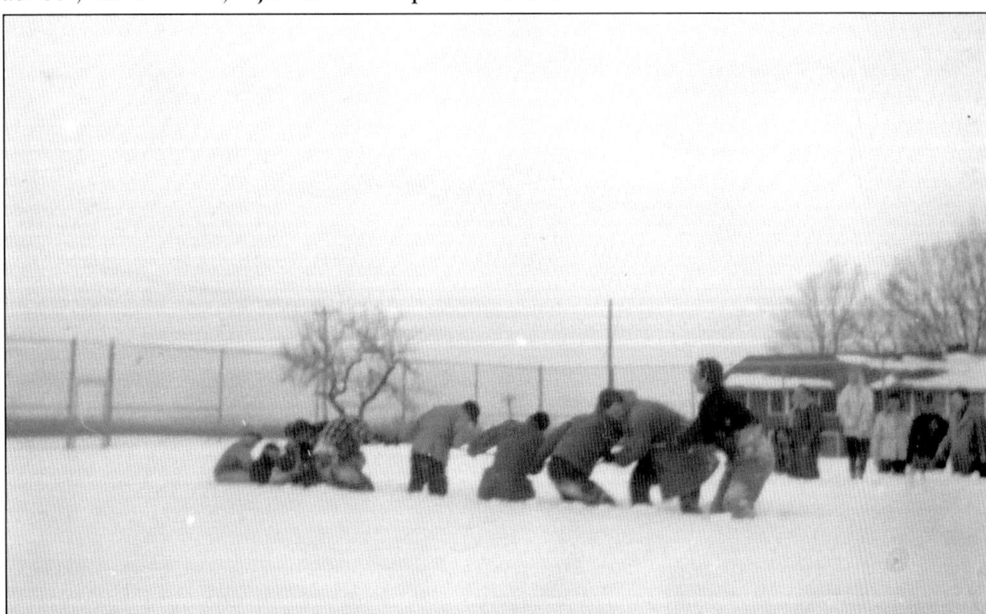

There had been Snow Carnivals in the late 1930s, but the full-blown Winter Carnival or Winter Weekend came in the postwar years. This tug-of-war occurred during the 1949 weekend. A temporary industrial arts building is in the background.

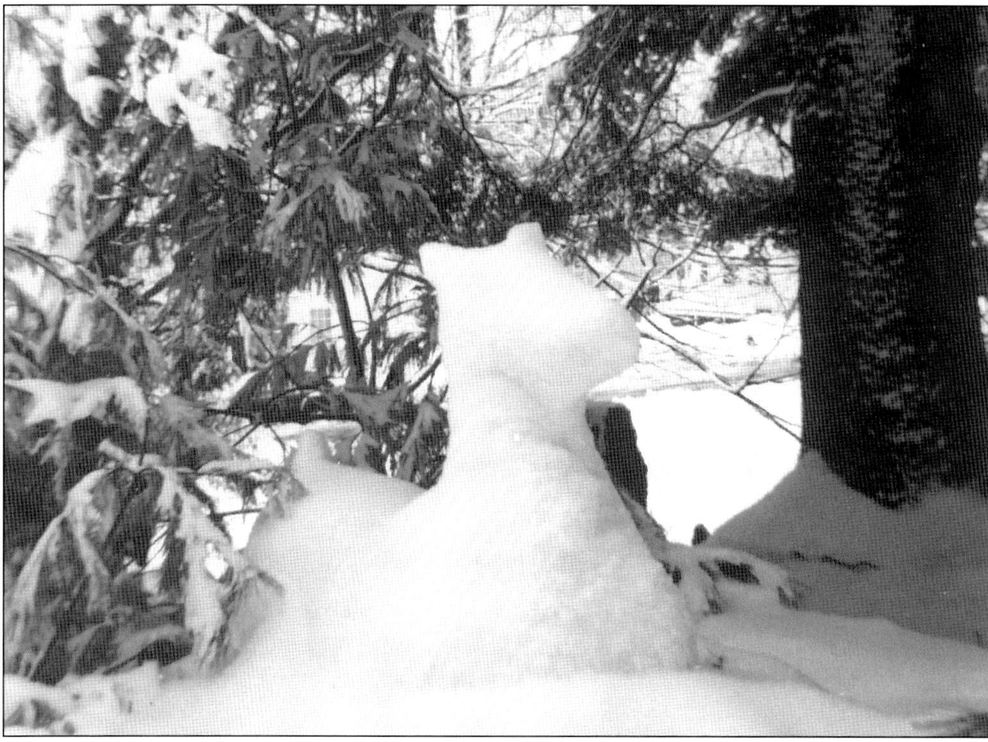

Campus organizations competed with snow sculptures. In 1956, the Art Club's contribution was a deer nestled among the trees and stones of the rock garden.

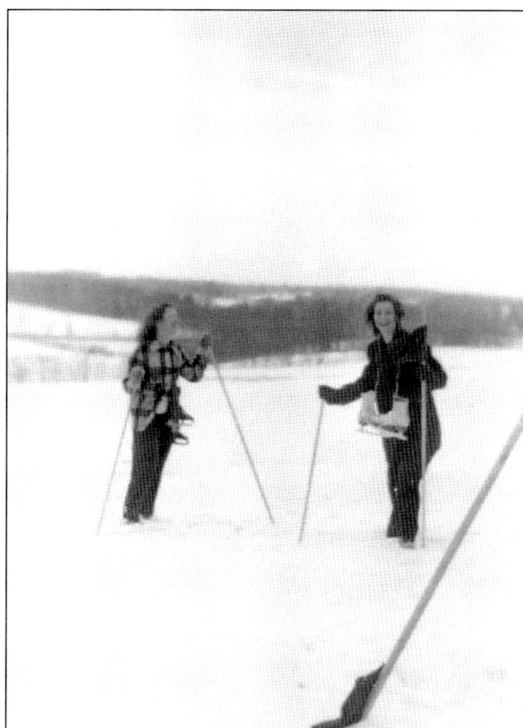

Winter sports did not need organization. When Alden's Pond, located behind the campus, was cleared of snow, students could skate there. Marilyn Baker '51 and Peggy Dayton '51 are shown heading in that direction in the winter of 1948.

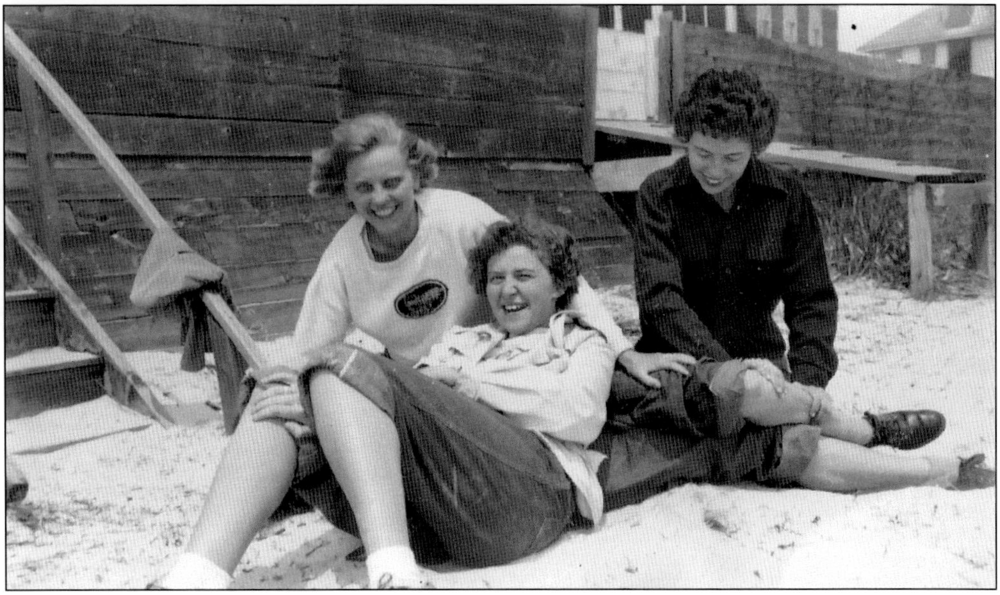

Religion-based clubs flourished. The YMCA and YWCA (combined in 1956 as SCA), Canterbury, and Newman Clubs, all had adherents and sponsored events, including a 1948 YWCA outing at Pine Point. Estelle Pedersen, Pat Stevens, and Norma Naylor, all from the Class of 1949, pose by an oceanside cottage.

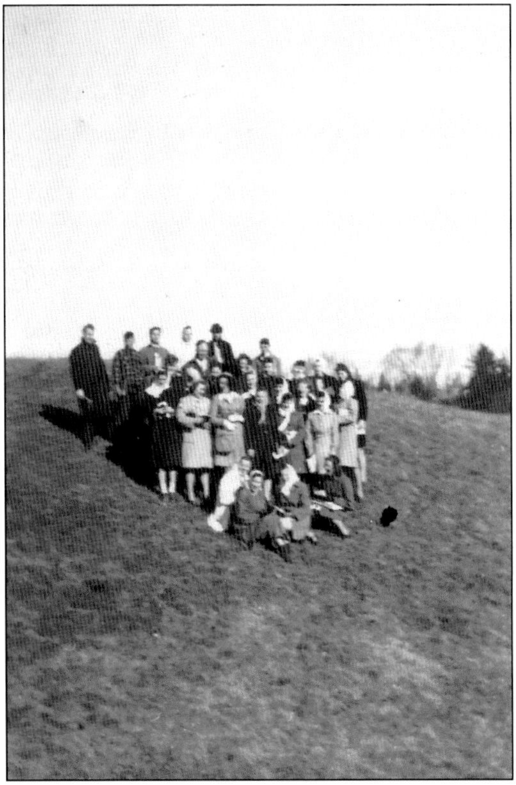

In 1948, the YMCA and the YWCA combined efforts to hold an Easter Sunrise Service on the hill behind campus, probably near where Bailey or Woodward Halls now stand, property then just off campus.

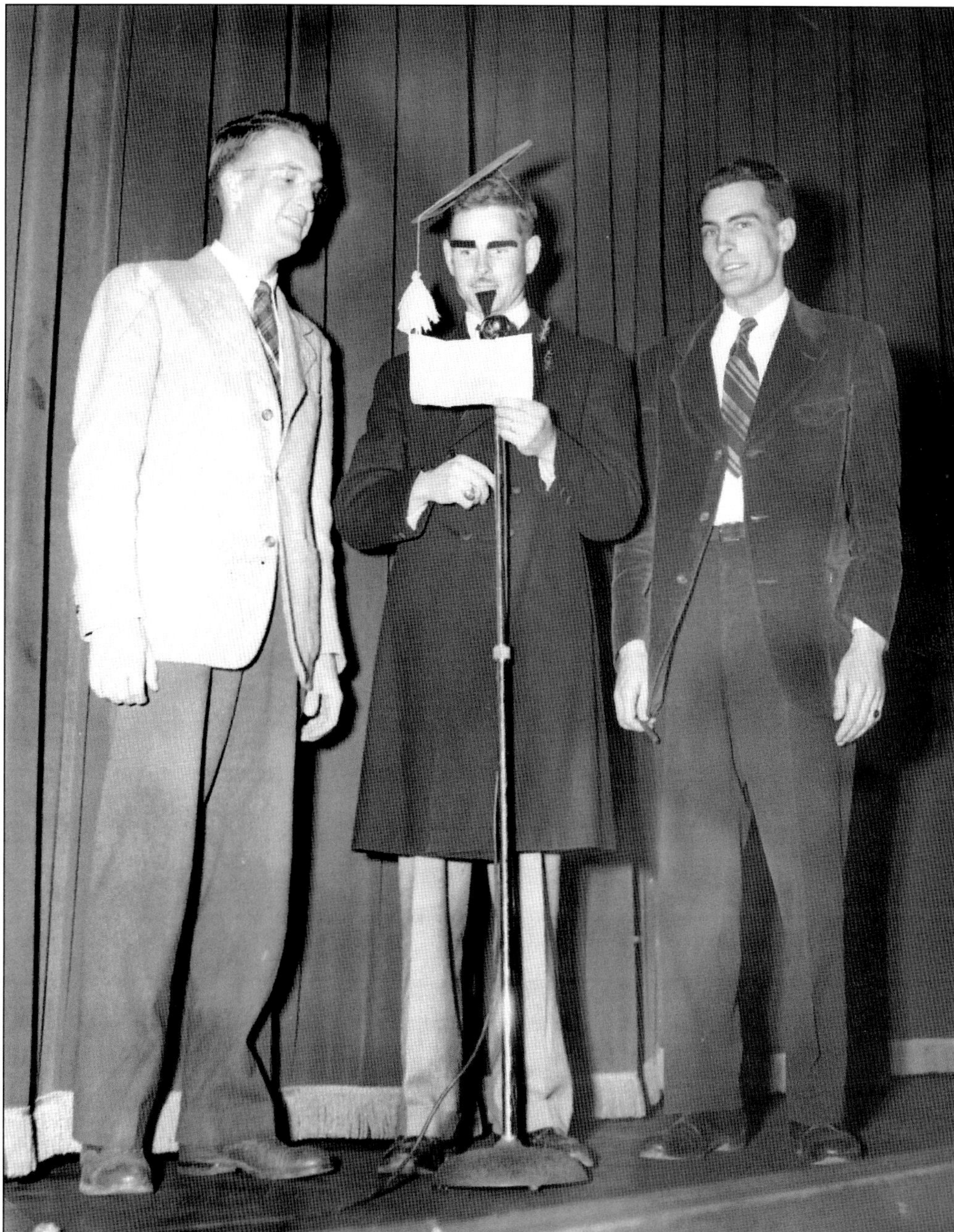

Religious life was fostered by administrative policy, which required attendance at regular chapels or prayer meetings as late as 1960. Held daily in the early years, these meetings were reduced to three times a week in the 1940s. This picture suggests that all were not entirely solemn. The subject matter of the questions asked by this unidentified quizmaster is unknown. The contestants are Don Pierce '48 (left) and Herman Foster '50.

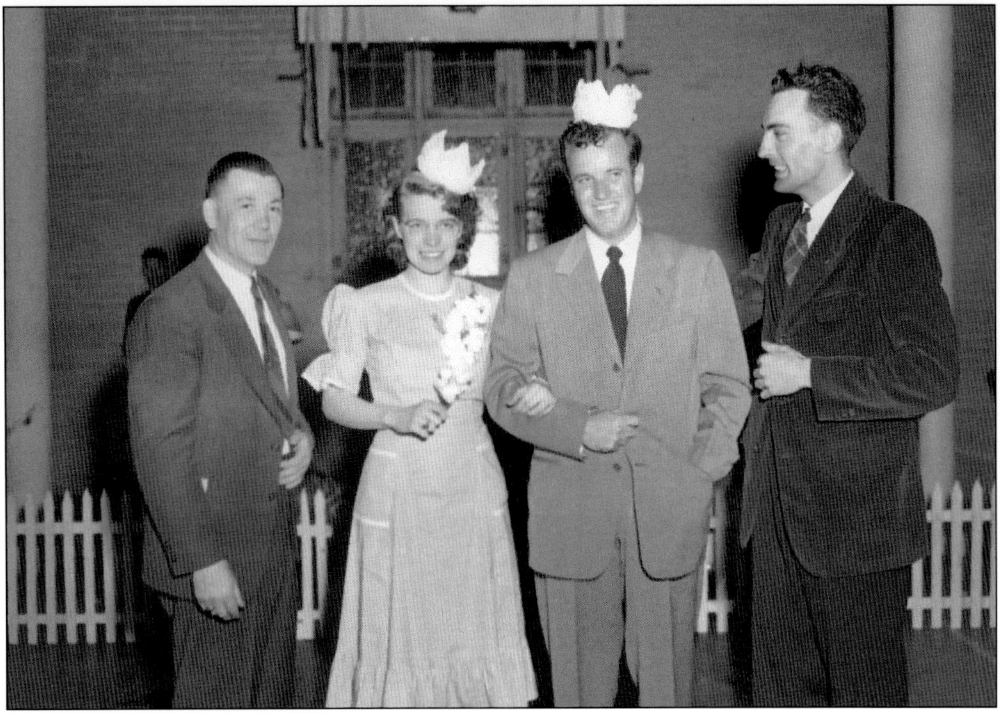

Francis Lucey '49 and Virginia Martin '48 reigned as king and queen at this senior dance in Russell Hall Gym. Robert Miller (left) was the class advisor that year, and Herman Foster (right) was Ginny's date, later her husband.

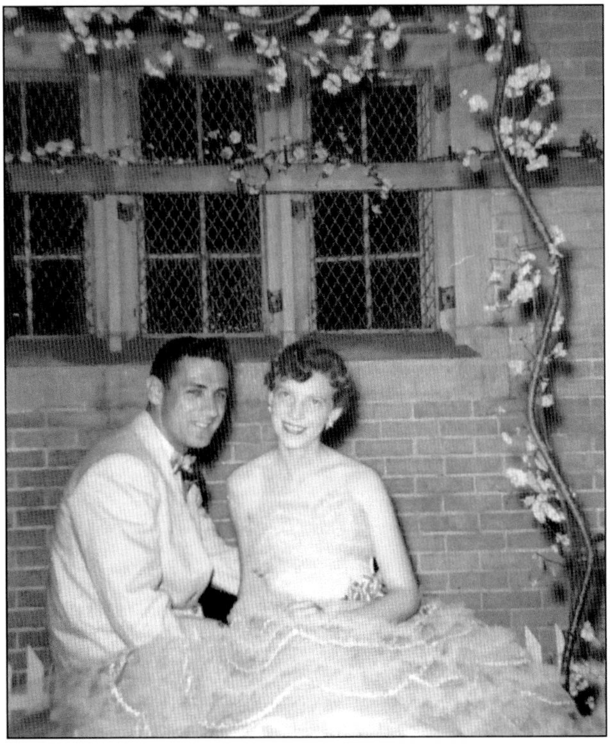

Ten years later, Dick Milligan '58 and Mary Bridges '58 pose in the same gym, with a similar fence and more extravagant flowers. This picture is a reminder of how very difficult it is to disguise a gymnasium.

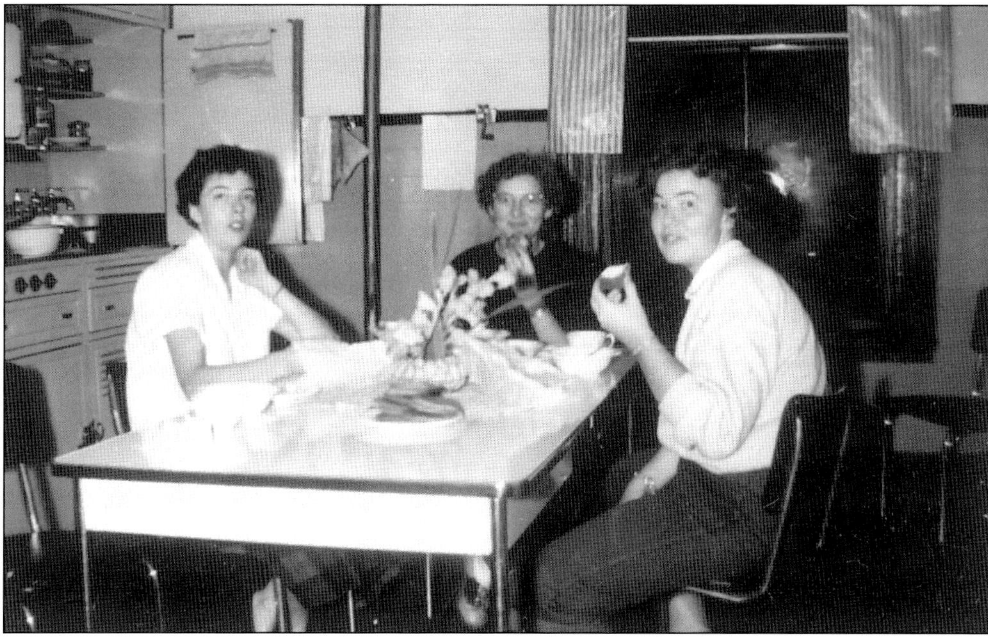

After 1945, life in the dorms went back to normal (no more men in the back part of Robie). Norma Naylor '49, Patricia Stevens '49, and Jean Goodwin '50 are shown having an evening snack in the kitchenette between Robie and East Halls.

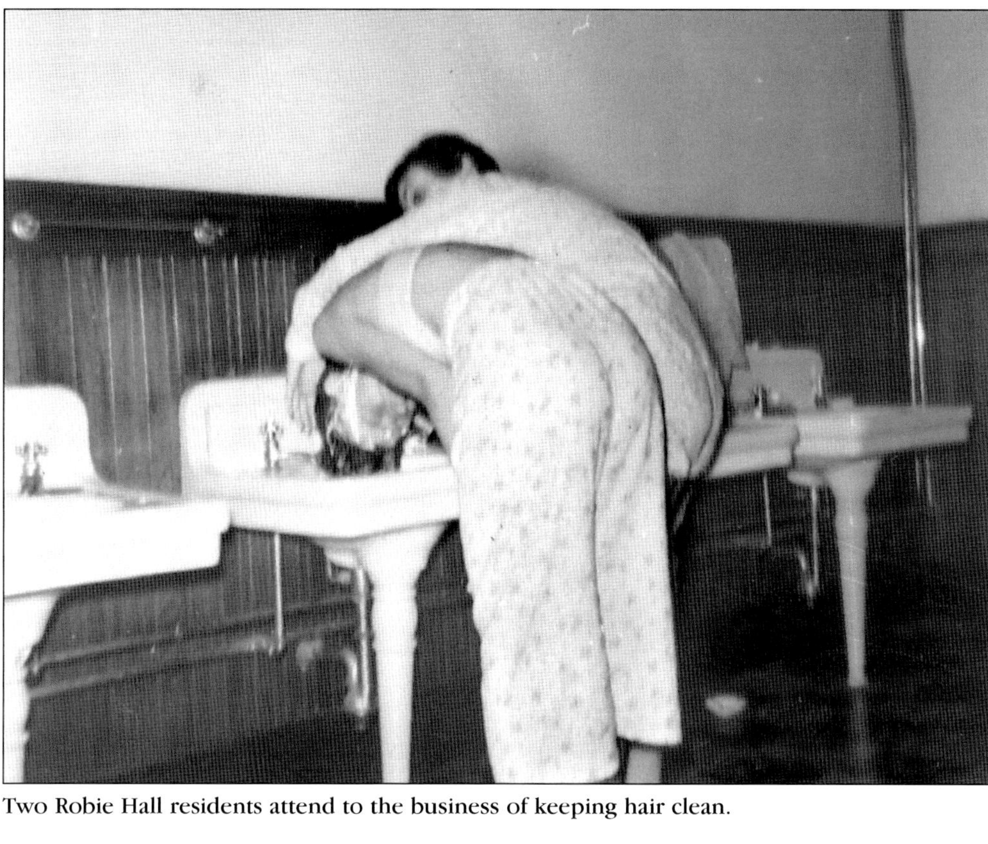

Two Robie Hall residents attend to the business of keeping hair clean.

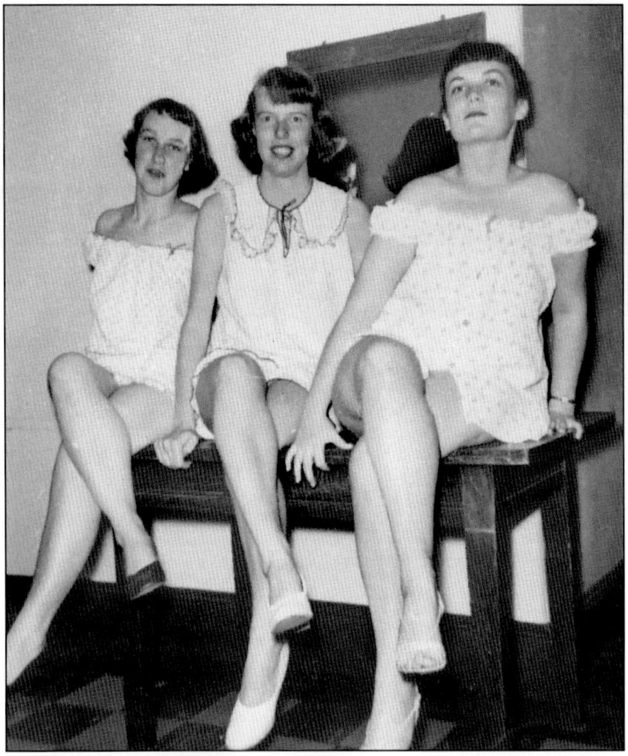

"Shortie" pajamas and shapely legs were in fashion during the 1950s. Janis Rand, Carol Lilly, and Joan Plumpton pose for the camera.

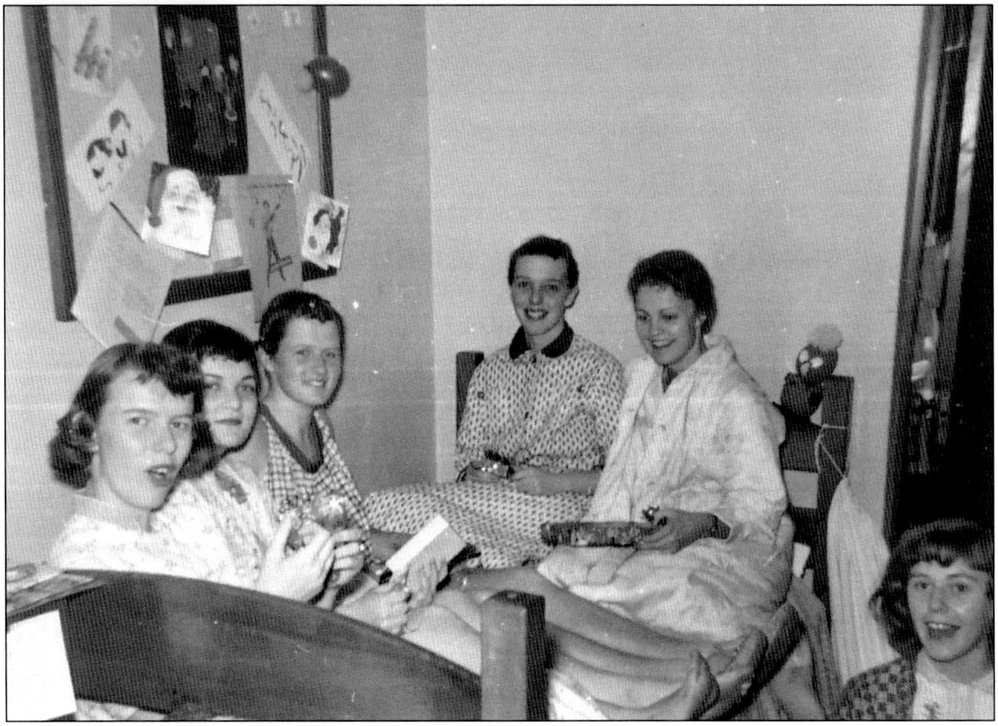

These sophomores are holding a pre-Christmas party in a Robie Hall room in 1956. From left to right are Carol Lilly, Joan Plumpton, Jean Crogan, Marje Johnson, and Madalyn Lucas.

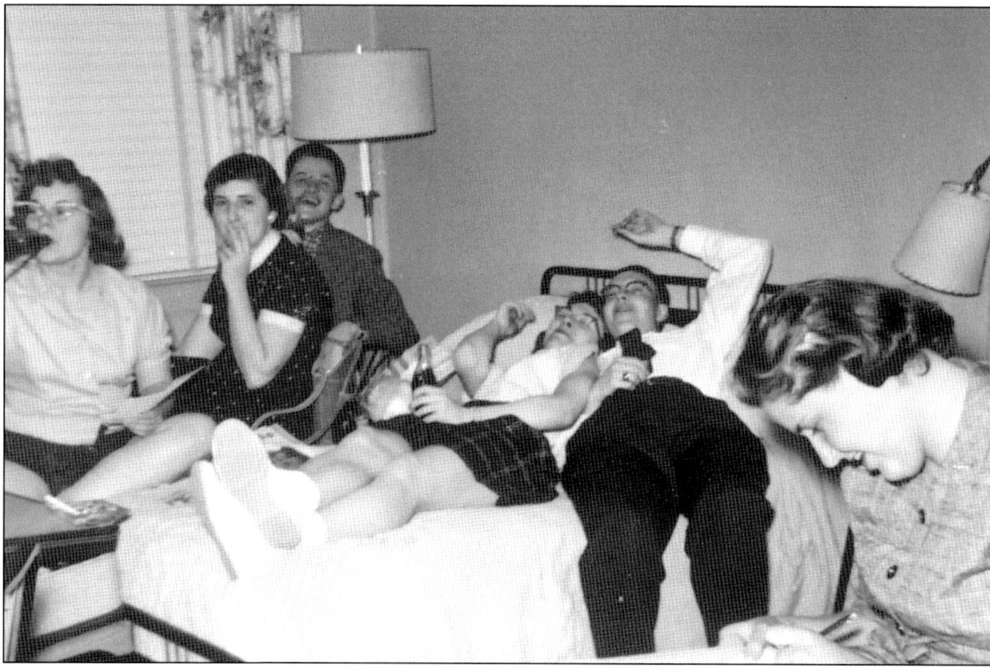

Dormitory rooms were off limits to the opposite sex, but coed room parties were enjoyed on trips, such as the annual educational tours arranged by the North American Travel Association. This 1958 spring trip stopped in Rutland, Vermont, on the way to Niagara Falls.

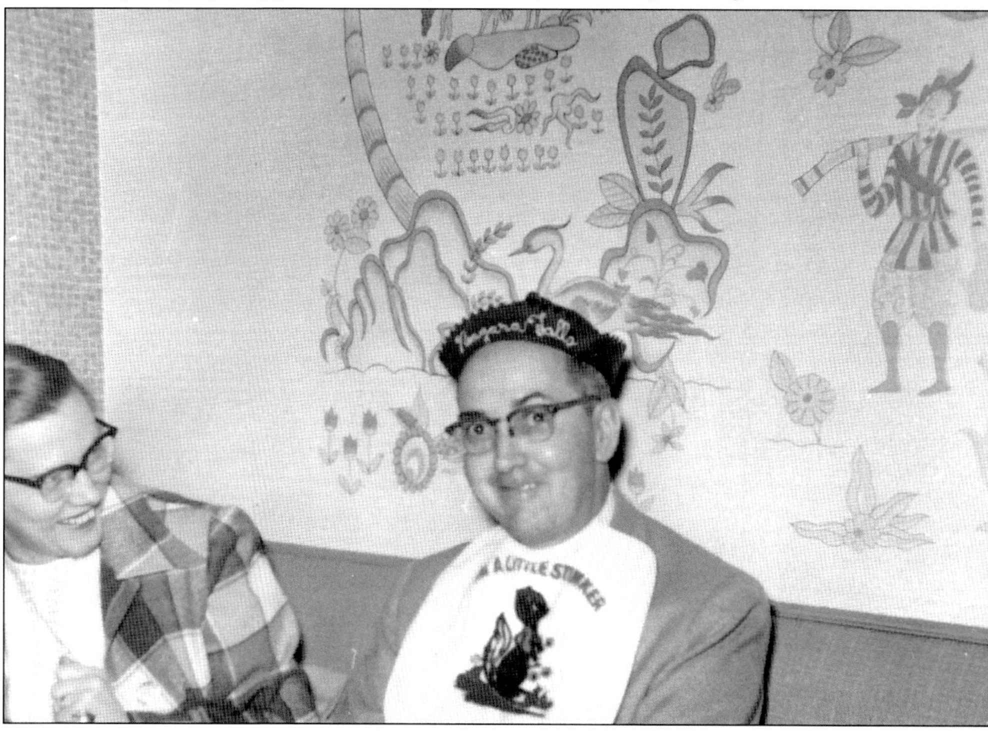

Wenzel Moberg, geography teacher and chaperon, shows off his souvenirs. Elizabeth Moberg (left) at times worked as nurse in the college infirmary.

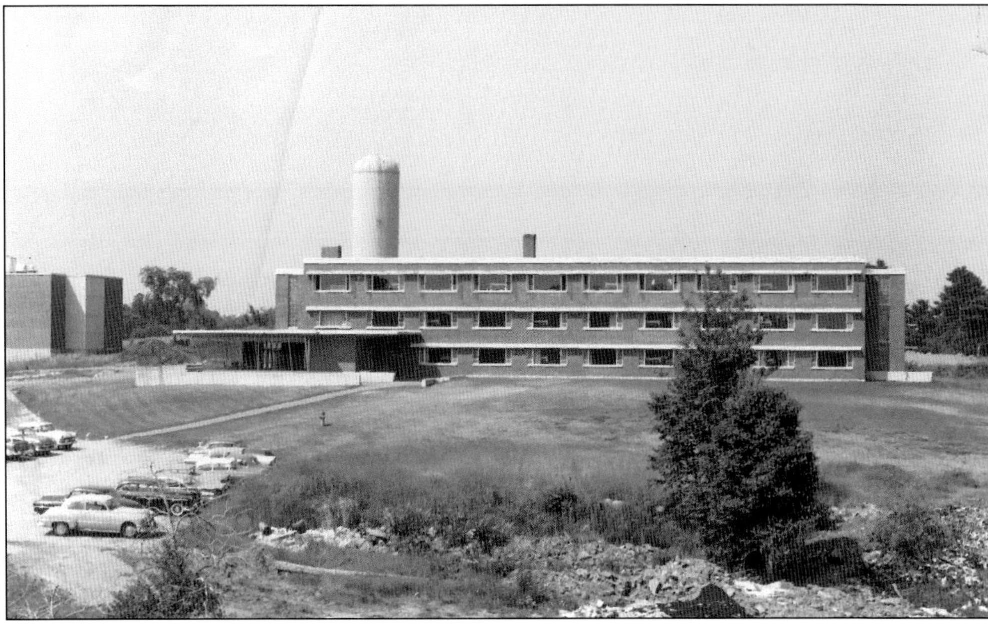

Except for an old barracks moved onto the campus in 1947 to expand the industrial arts program (pages 52, 62, and 89), postwar construction began with the first men's dormitory, opened in 1956 (photographed later). Men by then made up more than a third of the graduating classes. Woodward Hall was named to honor Louis Woodward, a former teacher and administrator (page 20). It was the first building with a design that was not historically derivative.

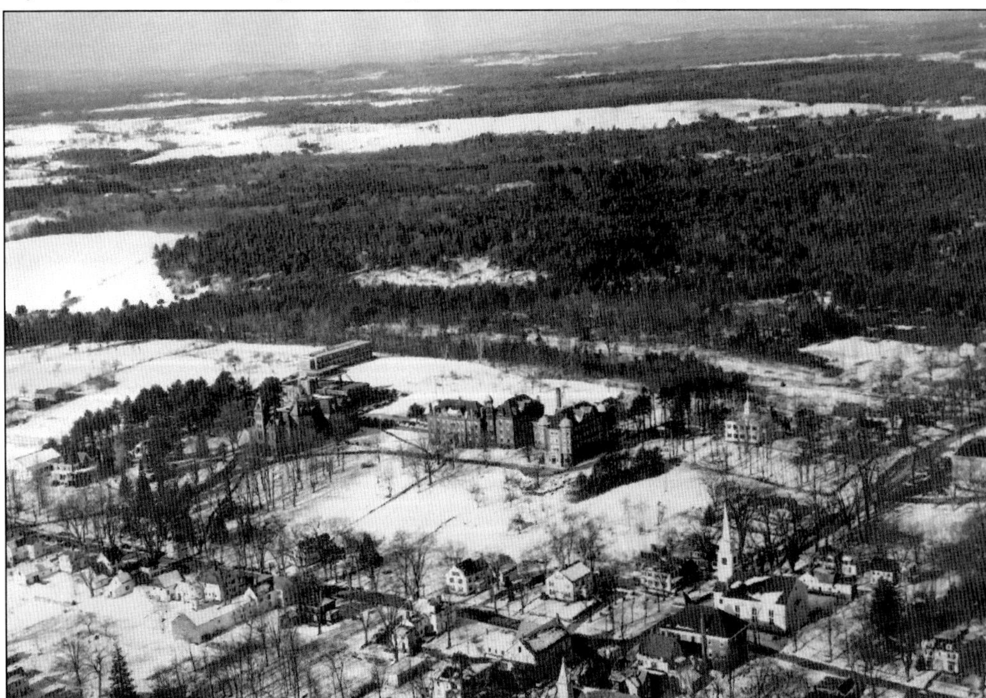

This aerial view of the Gorham State Teachers College campus in the late 1950s includes the new Woodward Hall, left of center.

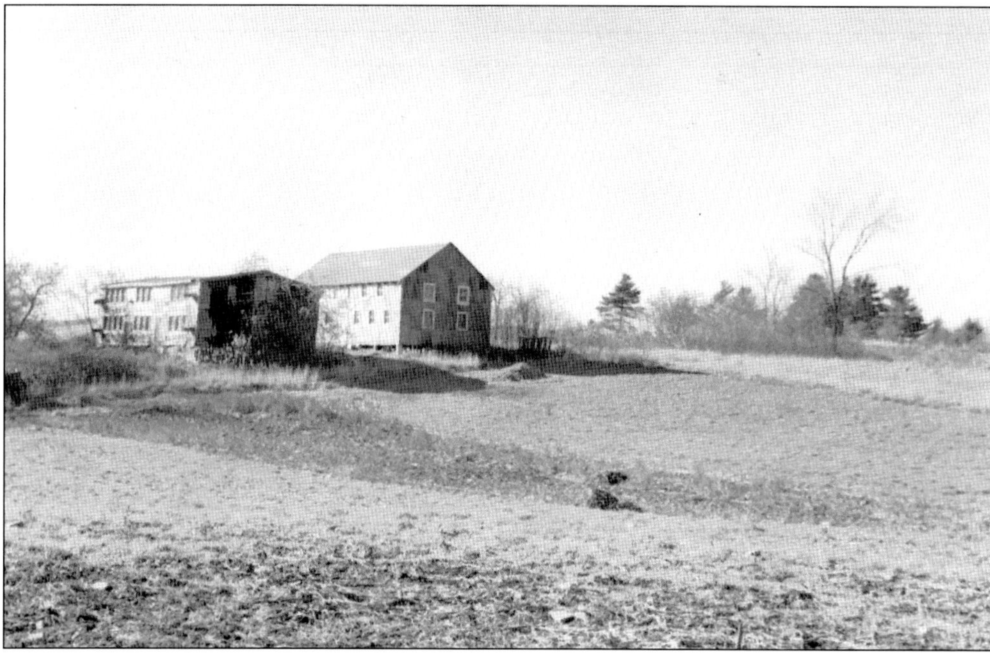

The college's property holdings had to expand before much could be added. In this mid-1950s photograph, farm outbuildings stand on the site that would soon hold Bailey Hall. Compare this picture with the previous one.

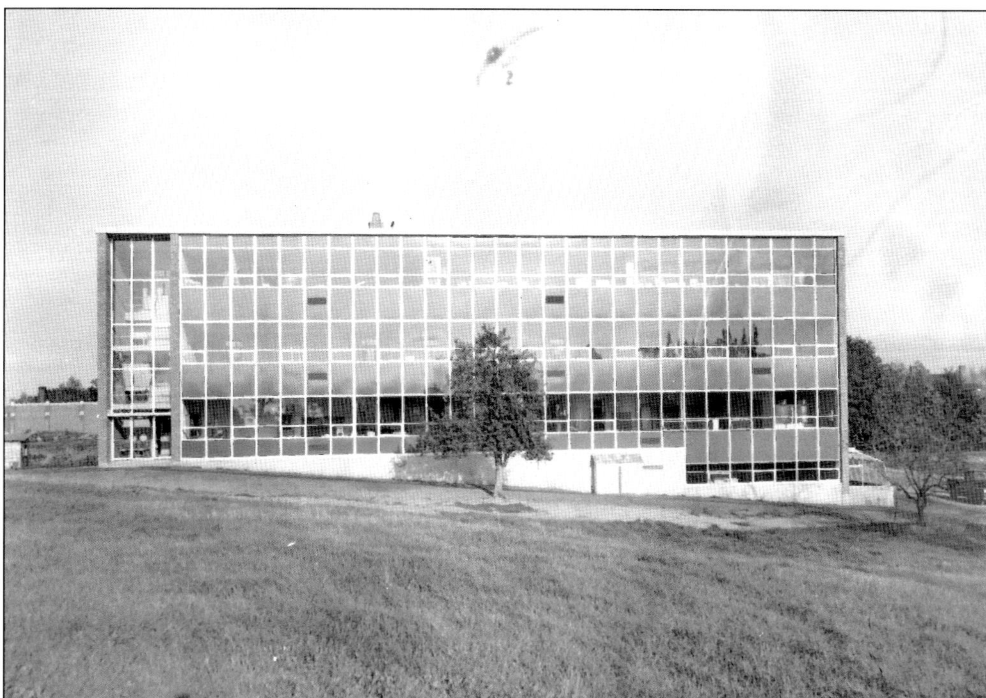

The new classroom complex was planned to be built in three parts. Its first section—the science wing, seen here from the west—opened in the fall of 1958. The structure was later named for Francis L. Bailey, the college president between 1940 and 1960.

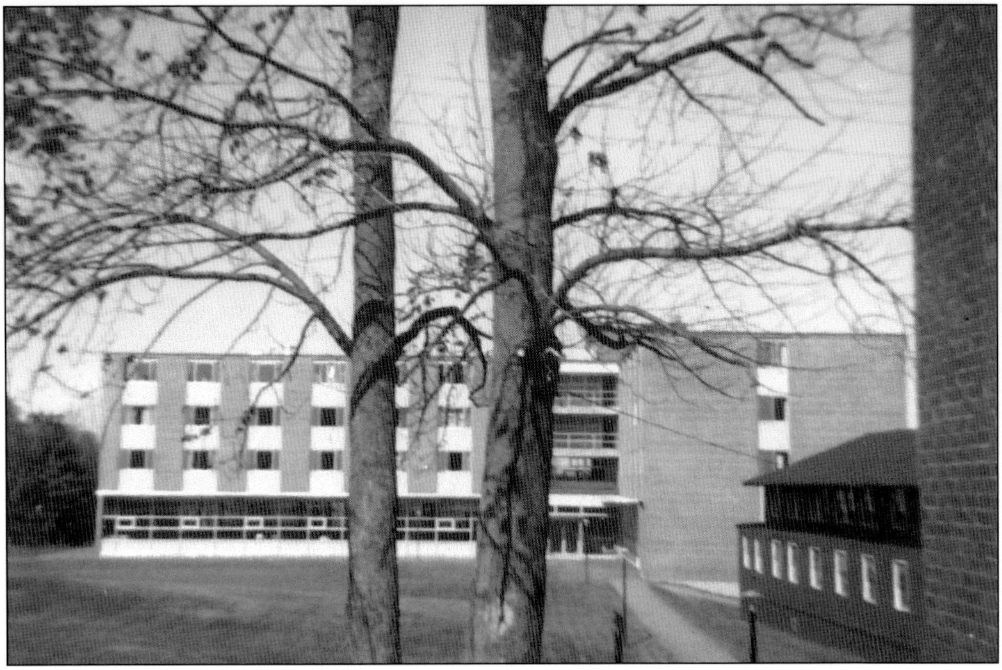

The next building to be completed on campus was another dormitory for women. The L-shaped Upton Hall, opened in 1960, honored Ethelyn Upton, math teacher and administrator since 1945. The recycled barracks building used for industrial arts classes stood nearby (right).

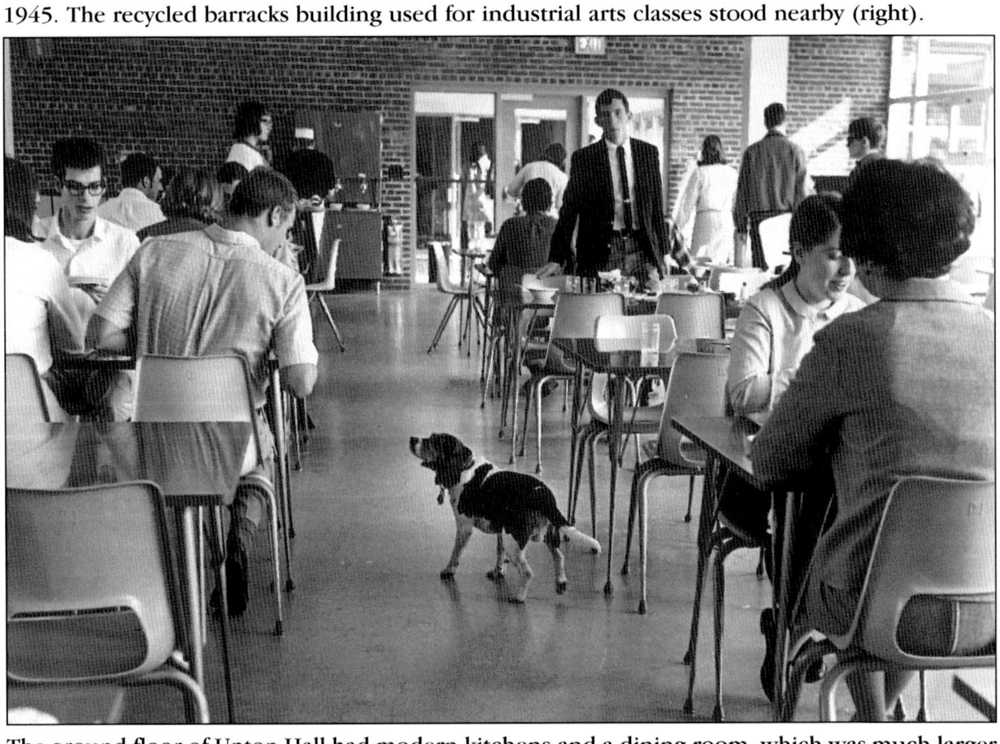

The ground floor of Upton Hall had modern kitchens and a dining room, which was much larger than the previous one in the lower level of Andrews Hall. It served all women residents, male residents, and off-campus men with meal cards.

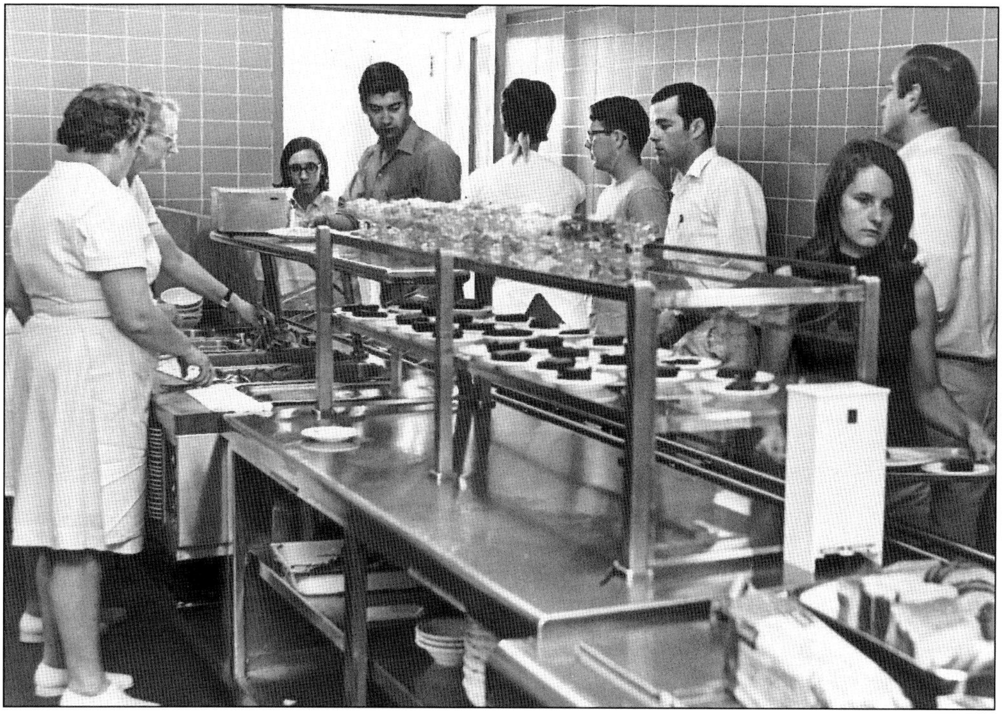

Cafeteria service was more efficient in handling the increased numbers of residents, but it ended a long tradition of family-style dining and marked the end of waiting on college tables as a means of students' helping finance their education.

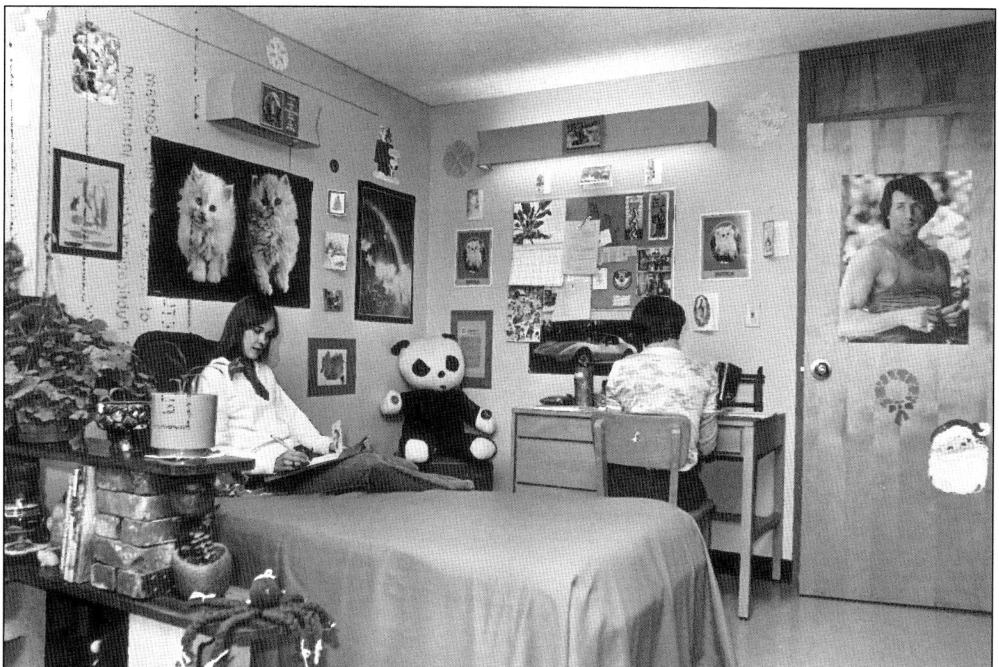

Rooms in the newer dormitories were rather stark, but later residents made them personal with varied decorations.

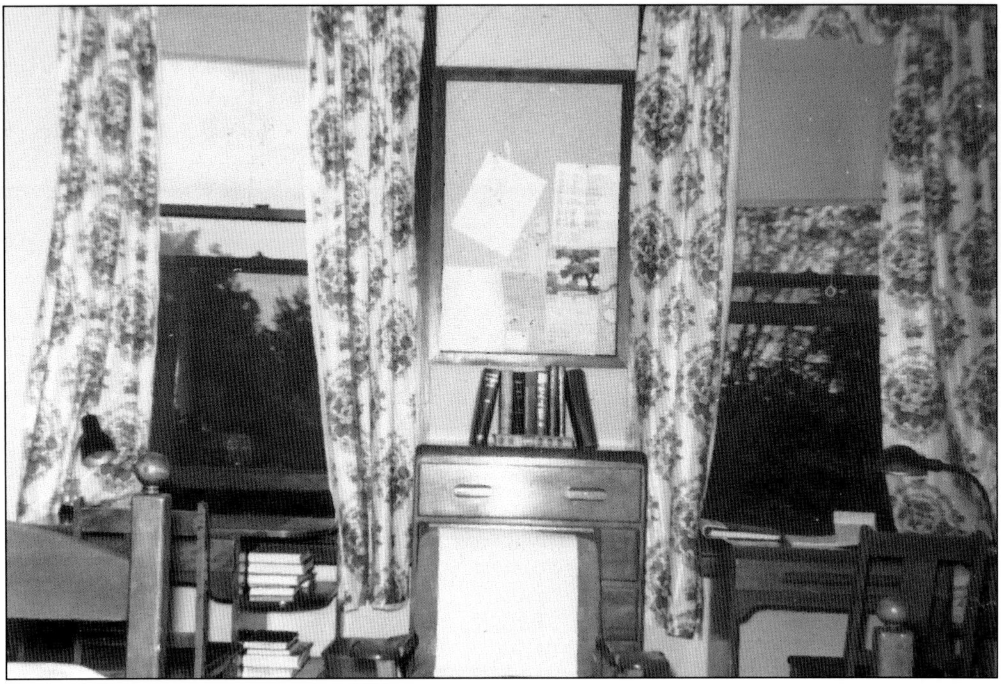

For contrast, note this 1963 photograph, taken by a freshman living in Andrews Hall. Some women preferred the older buildings, finding them cozier.

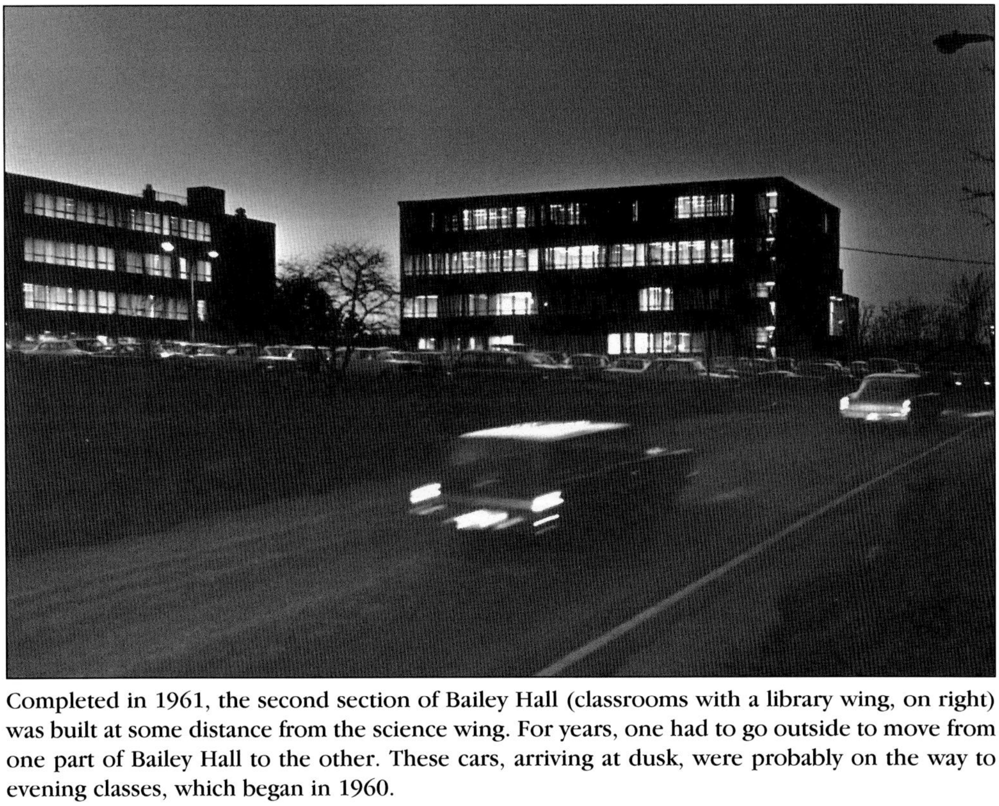

Completed in 1961, the second section of Bailey Hall (classrooms with a library wing, on right) was built at some distance from the science wing. For years, one had to go outside to move from one part of Bailey Hall to the other. These cars, arriving at dusk, were probably on the way to evening classes, which began in 1960.

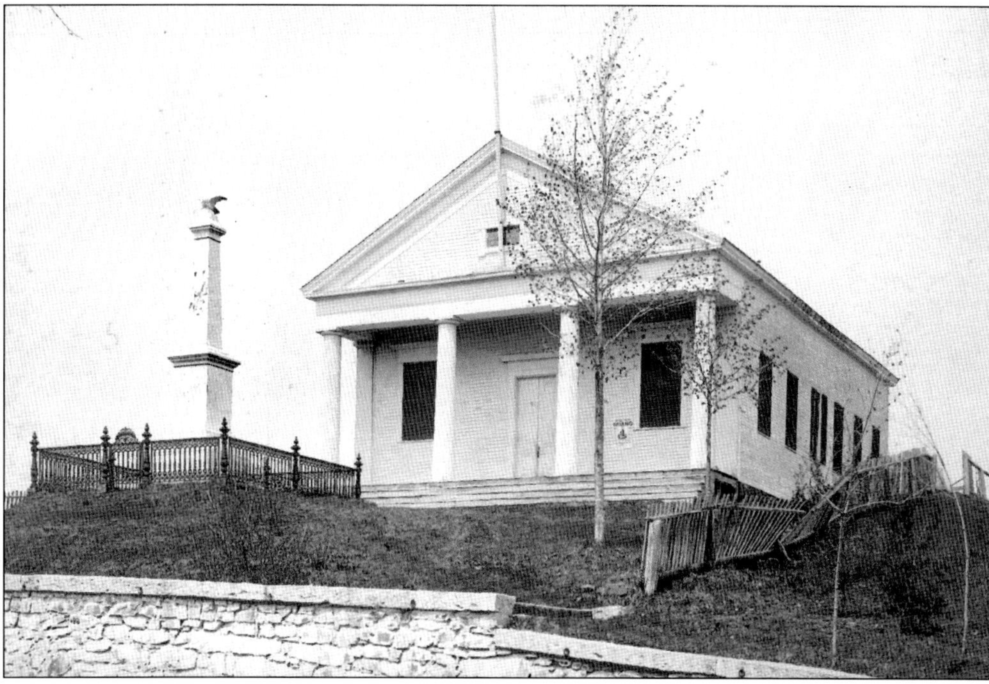

In the meantime, the town of Gorham found its town hall (page 13) too small and turned it over to the college in 1961. Students worked to convert the building into a chapel. Underused, it eventually became an art gallery.

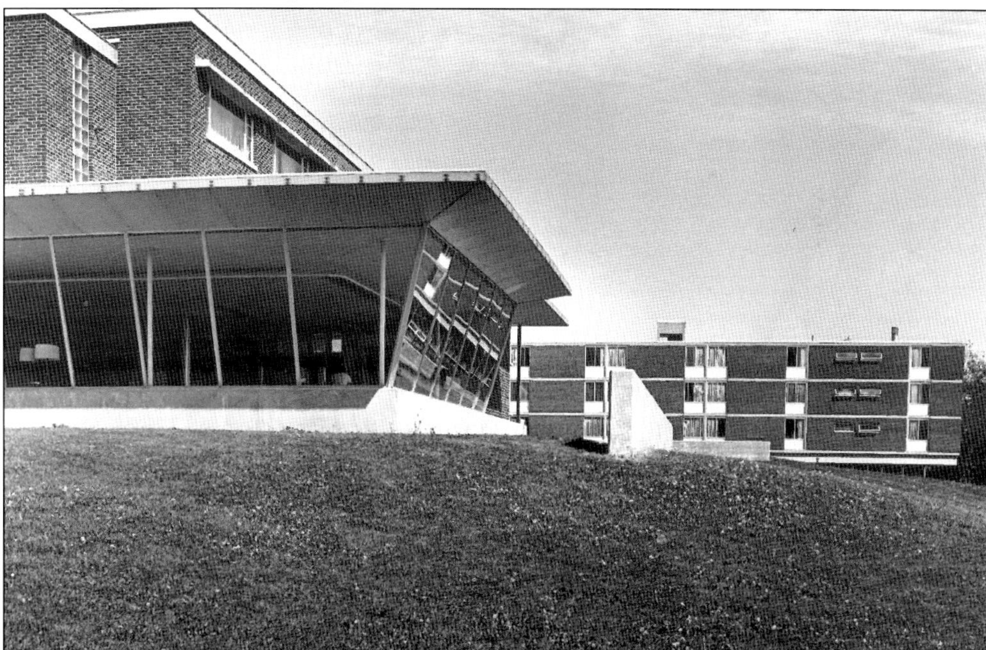

In 1963, increased enrollments necessitated a second men's dormitory, built at right angles to Woodward (left) and called Anderson Hall. Hayden Anderson, for whom it was named, was an alumnus (Class of 1925) who held posts with the Maine Department of Education.

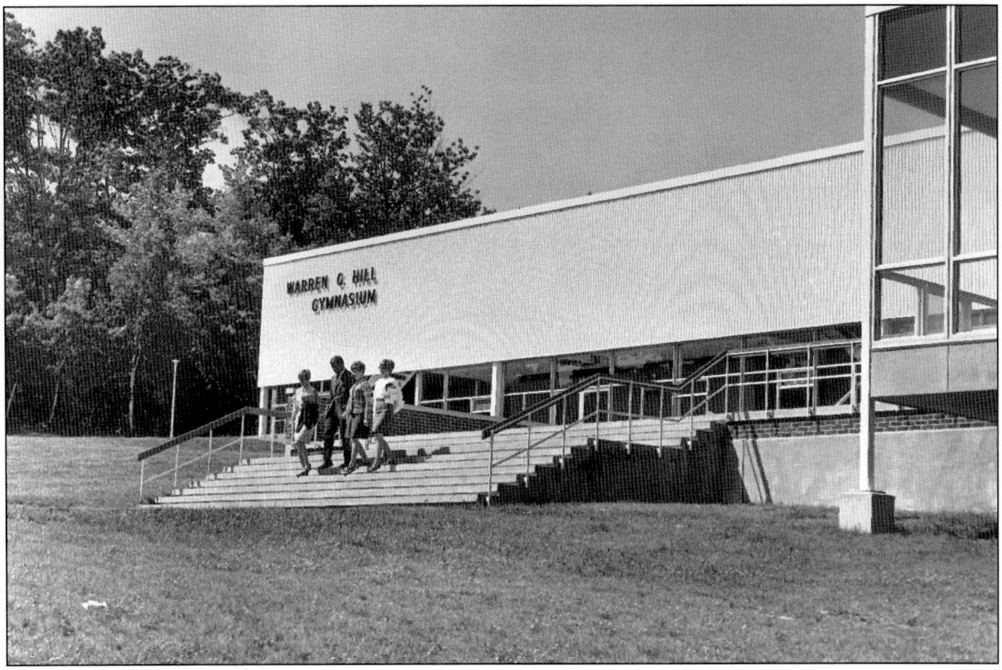

This gymnasium, built in 1963, was named for alumnus Warren G. Hill '39, who served as the state commissioner of education. The building provided interior space for ceremonies and offered a regulation-size basketball court for college teams.

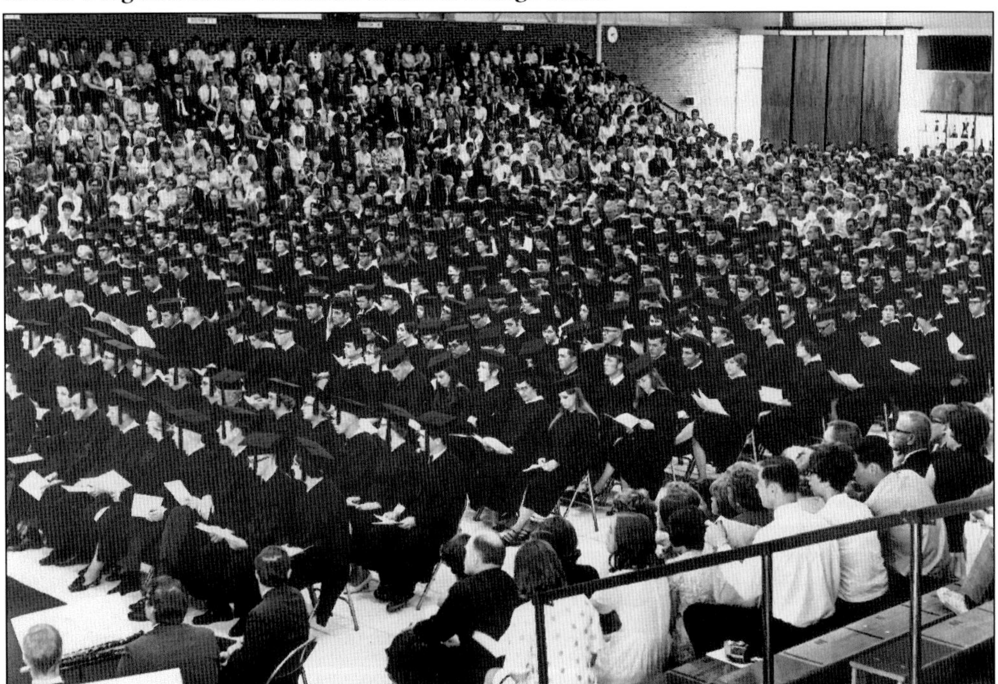

After the new gymnasium was completed, commencement exercises were held there. (Portland City Hall had been used previously.) As this 1965 picture indicates, however, the area was later too small for growing student enrollments.

Five

University of Maine at Portland, 1957–1970

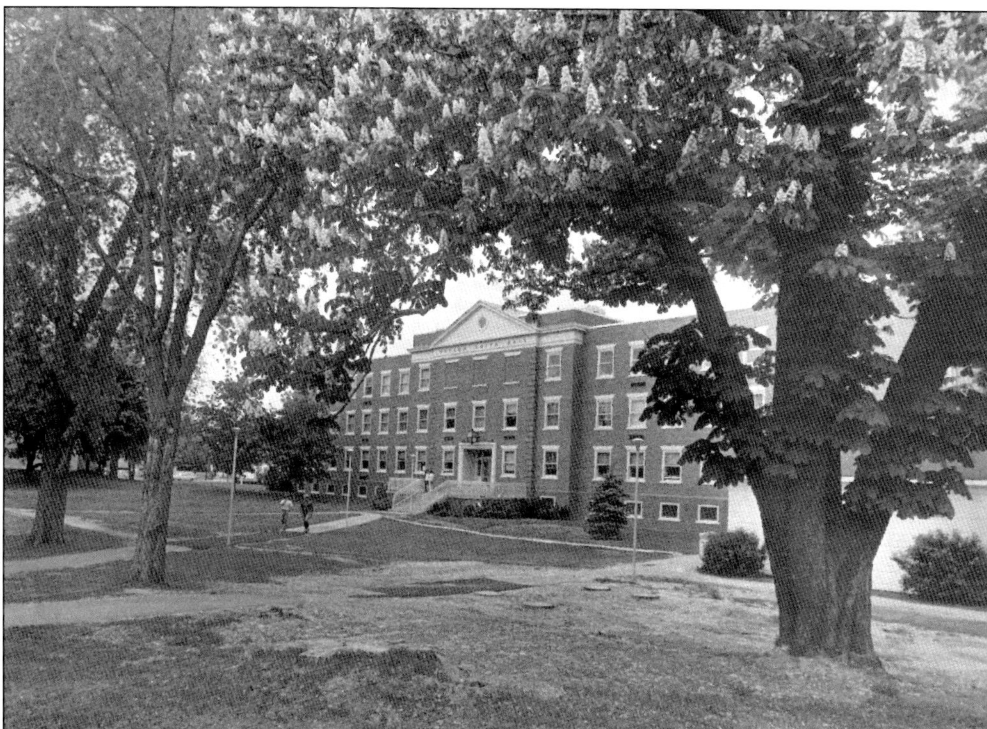

Early in 1957, a merger between Portland Junior College and the University of Maine was announced. University officials planned to take over the small private institution and operate its own two-year college, the University of Maine at Portland (UMP) on the premises, now enlarged by another four acres. Instead of being called "seniors," second-year men were called "sophomores" and were expected to transfer to the Orono campus to complete their education. Changes came slowly during the first three years but included new school colors (the light blue and white of the University of Maine) and new names for publications and on sports uniforms (although the basketball team remained the Stags for years). More classrooms were planned in 1958, but Payson Smith Hall was completed only for the fall of 1960.

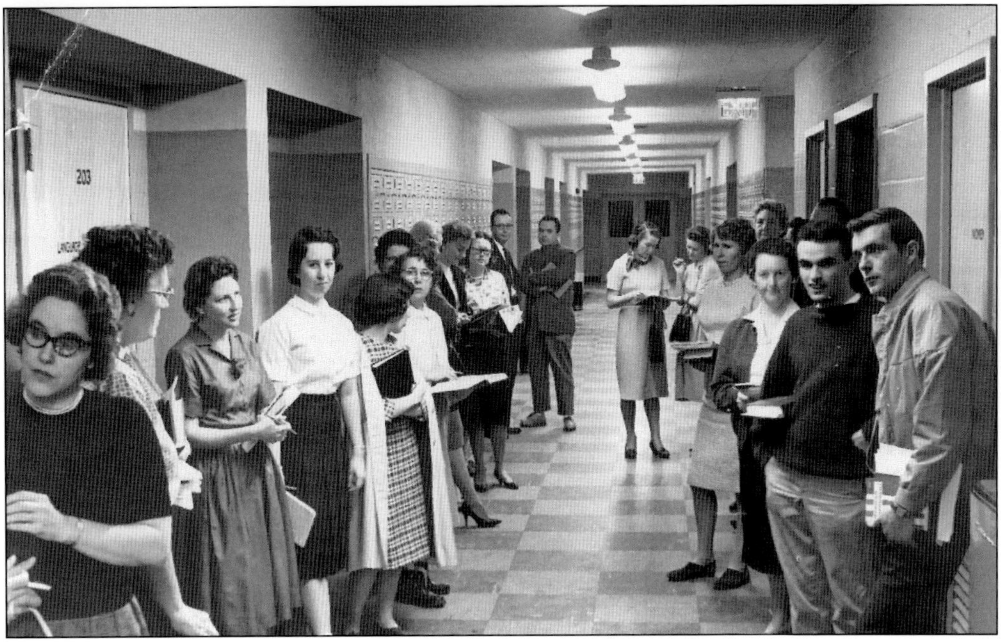

The opening of Payson Smith Hall (named for a commissioner of education and Portland native) touched off a period of real growth. Additional classrooms made it possible to admit more students—including, for the first time on that campus, women. In this photograph, both men and women line up in a hallway of the new building at registration time.

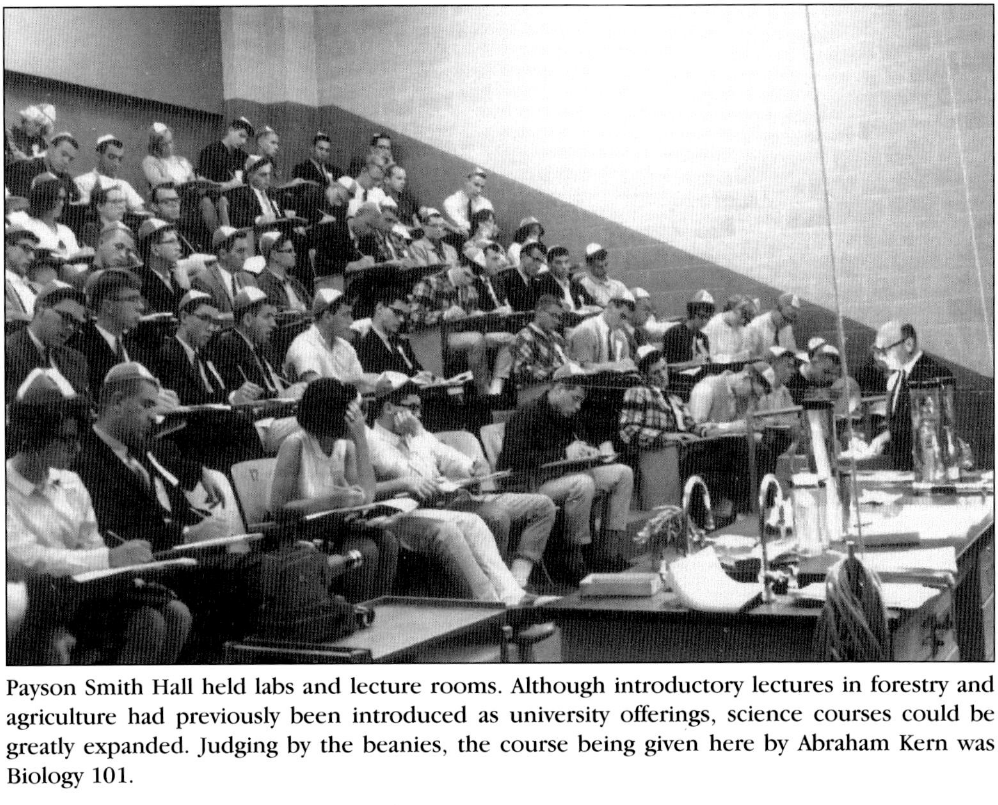

Payson Smith Hall held labs and lecture rooms. Although introductory lectures in forestry and agriculture had previously been introduced as university offerings, science courses could be greatly expanded. Judging by the beanies, the course being given here by Abraham Kern was Biology 101.

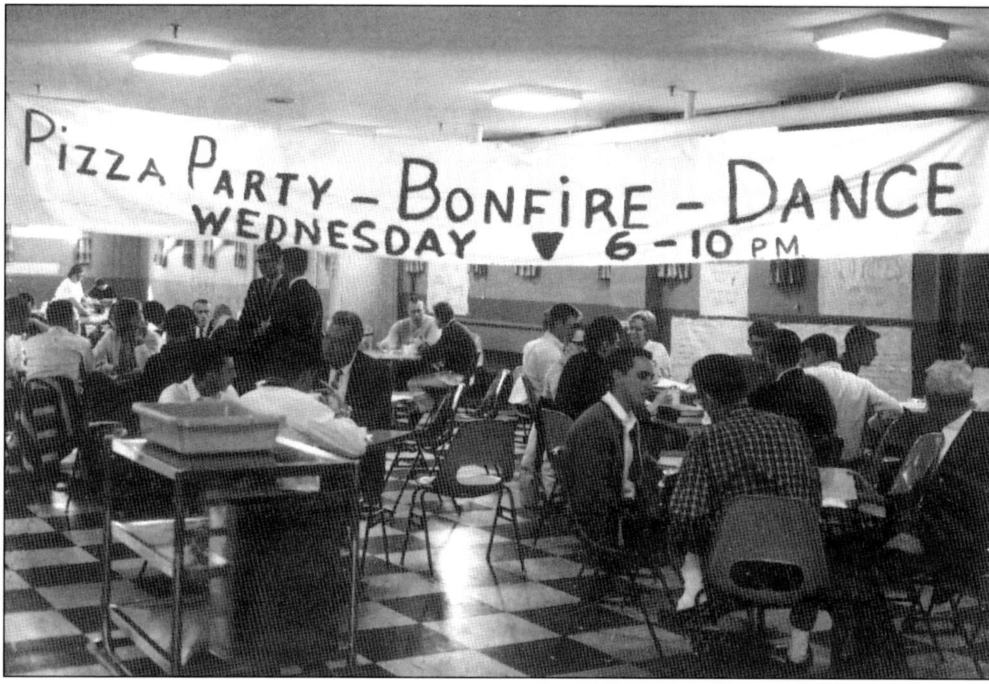

Also located in the new building were an expanded library and a better cafeteria. The latter served as a rendezvous spot as well as a place to advertise campus events.

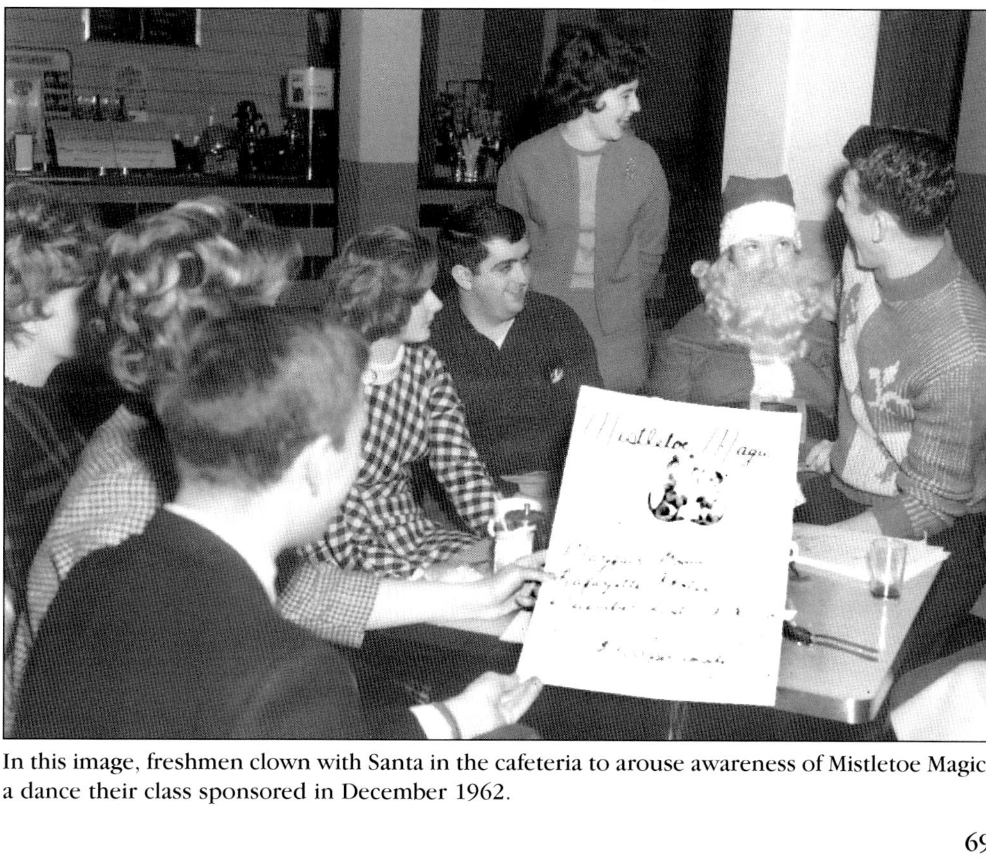

In this image, freshmen clown with Santa in the cafeteria to arouse awareness of Mistletoe Magic, a dance their class sponsored in December 1962.

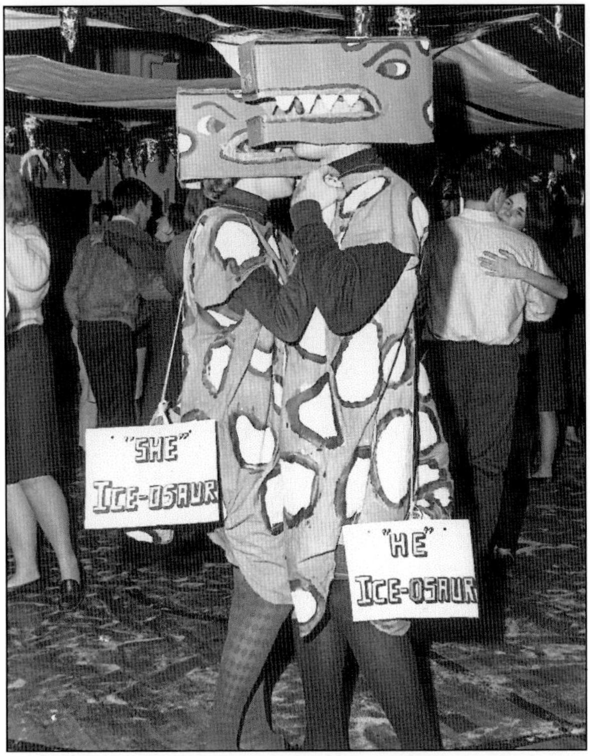

Some earlier social activities continued, such as Winter Carnival theme dances. The 1966 theme was "Pleistocene," with cavemen and dinosaurs enlivening the dance floor.

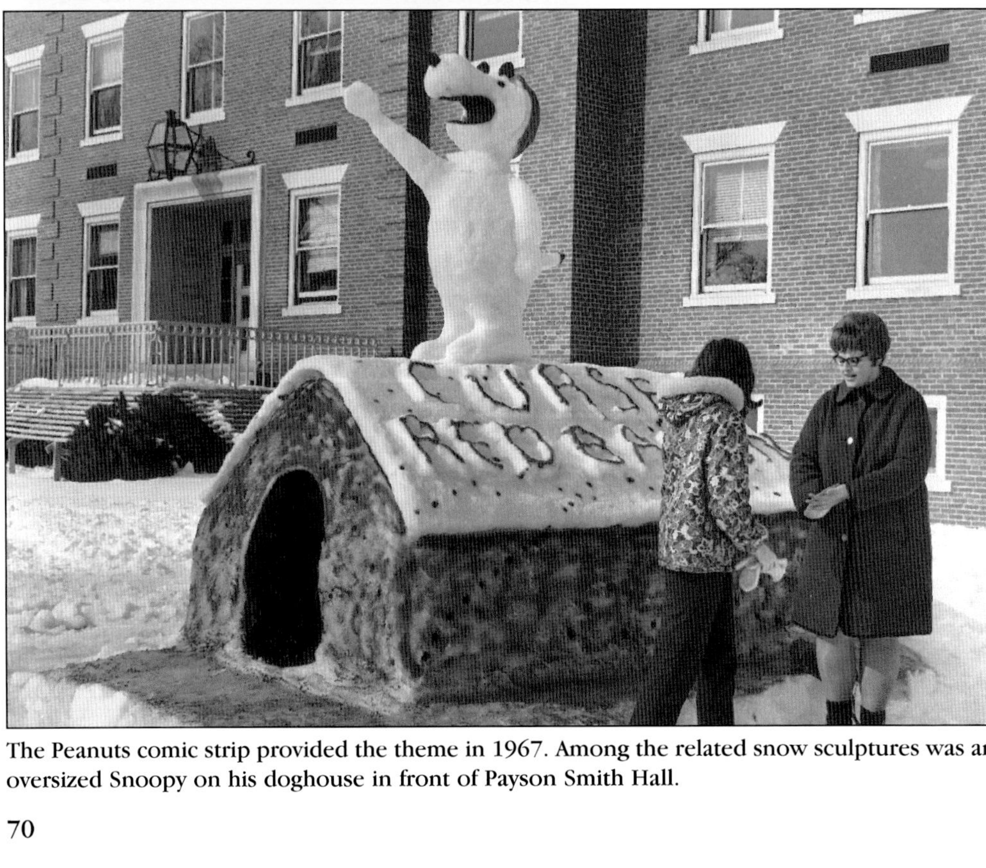

The Peanuts comic strip provided the theme in 1967. Among the related snow sculptures was an oversized Snoopy on his doghouse in front of Payson Smith Hall.

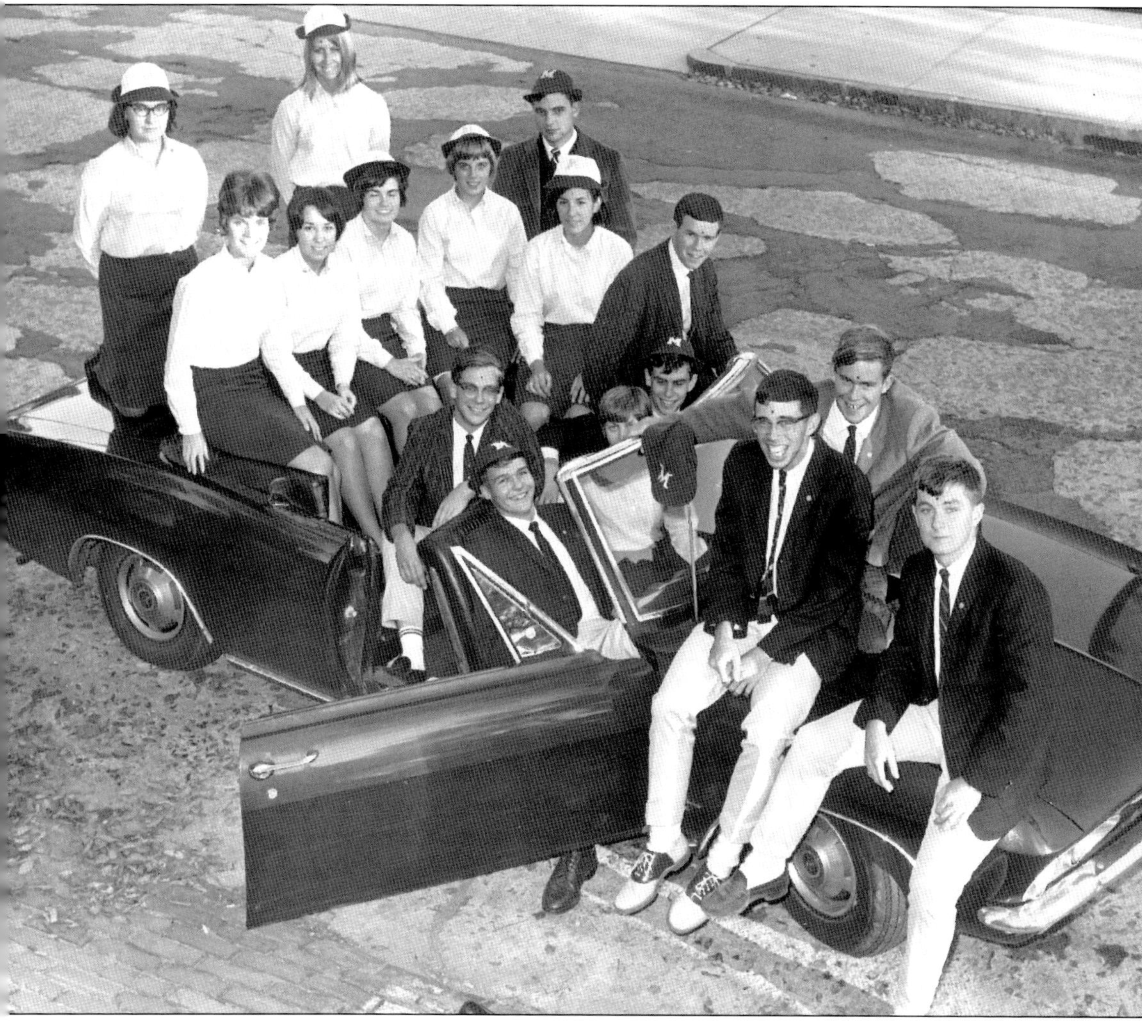

By 1962, the Orono practice of selecting a few men (Owls) and women (Eagles) in May of their first year to help acclimate the next season's freshmen was adopted in Portland. As sophomores, the Owls and Eagles were essentially in charge of freshman orientation. While "on duty" they wore face patches: a small star for the Eagles, a dot for the Owls. The 1966–1967 Owls and Eagles in this convertible were, on the hood, from left to right, Fred Bonaventure, Paul Strout, and Dean Atwood. In the front seat were John Trewergy, Ellen Thompson, and Michael Tewhey, while Ken Jones and Martin Gouzie were just behind them. Beth Coombs, Nancy Hunter, Barbara Knight, Wanda Stover, and Sheila Libby squeezed into the rear seat, and Carol Kealhier, Ellen Conant, and Bob Williamson were on or near the trunk.

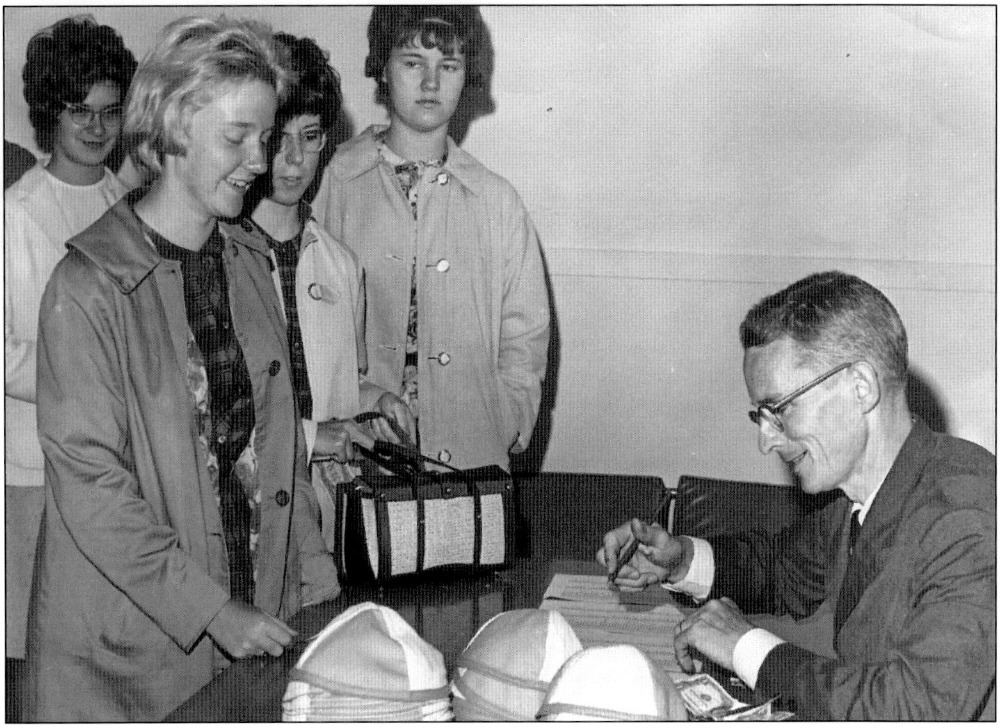

Whether because of Orono customs or simply because it was the 1960s, a new stress on being "collegiate" appeared, along with freshman beanies. John Jaques (assistant dean) is shown distributing beanies to new students. Freshmen who failed to wear them properly were taken to "Kangaroo Court" by the Owls.

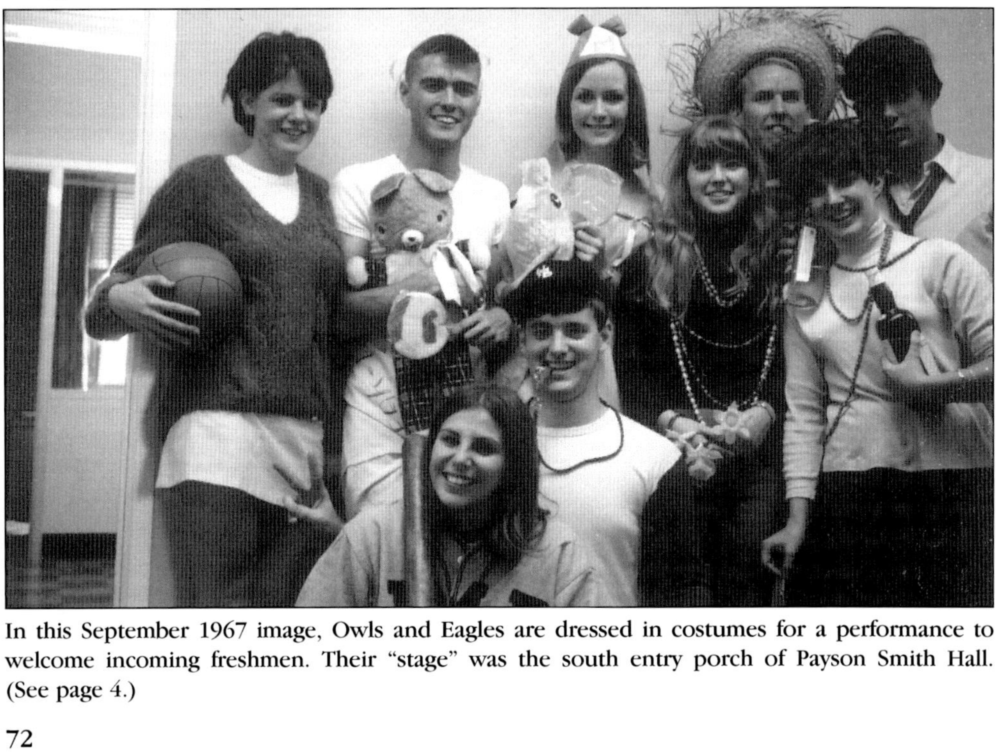

In this September 1967 image, Owls and Eagles are dressed in costumes for a performance to welcome incoming freshmen. Their "stage" was the south entry porch of Payson Smith Hall. (See page 4.)

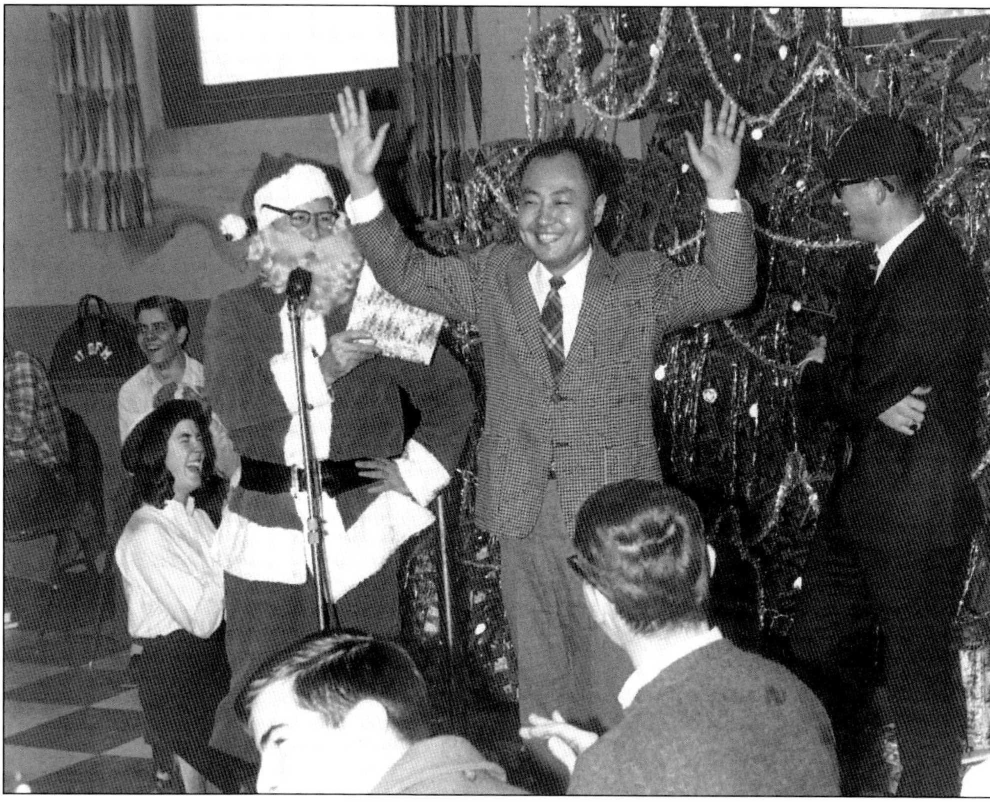

The two organizations also sponsored Christmas parties. In 1965, Hirofumi Matsusaki (business education) is shown receiving a gift of a "playboy" award from Santa (Alfred Clarke, admissions) to the amusement of an unidentified Eagle (left) and Head Owl Charlie Cragin.

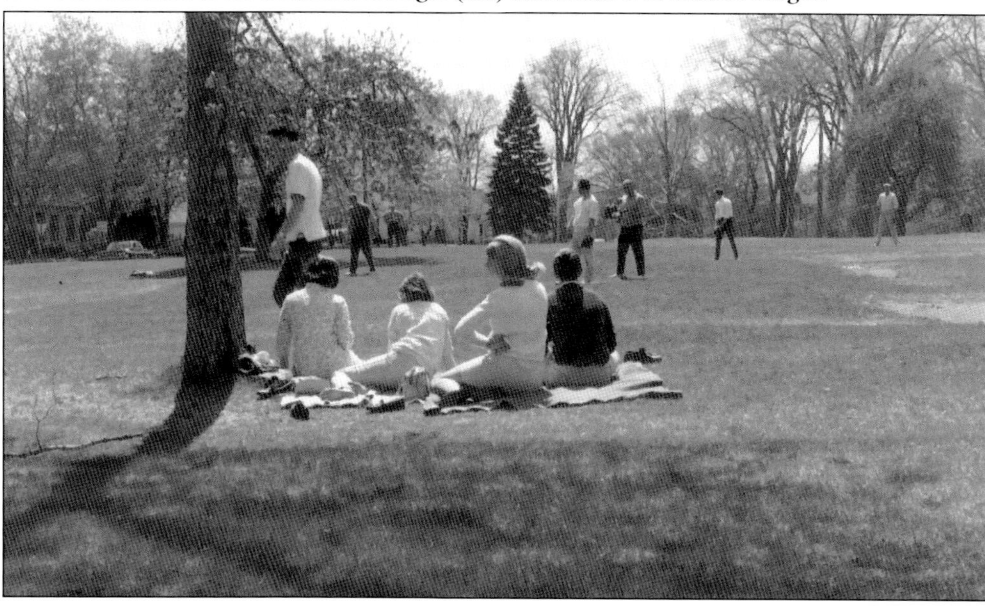

The front lawn of the campus was an inviting spot to relax between classes or even to engage in an informal ball game.

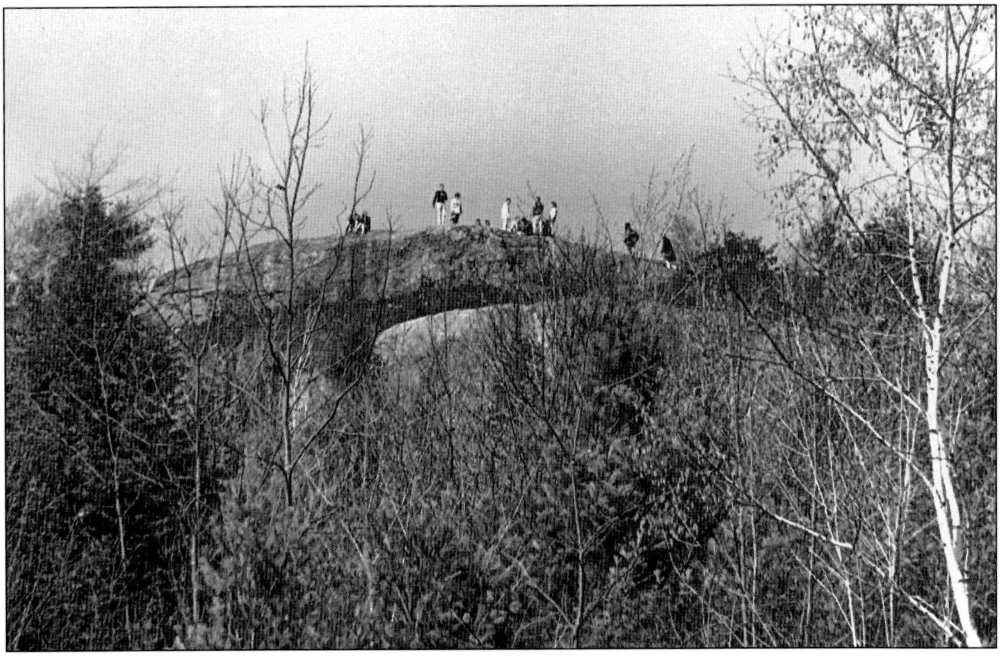

One Portland Junior College tradition that was preserved was Mountain Day, in its later years scheduled for an autumn Sunday. In this 1964 photograph, students of the University of Maine at Portland are shown on top of Bradbury Mountain.

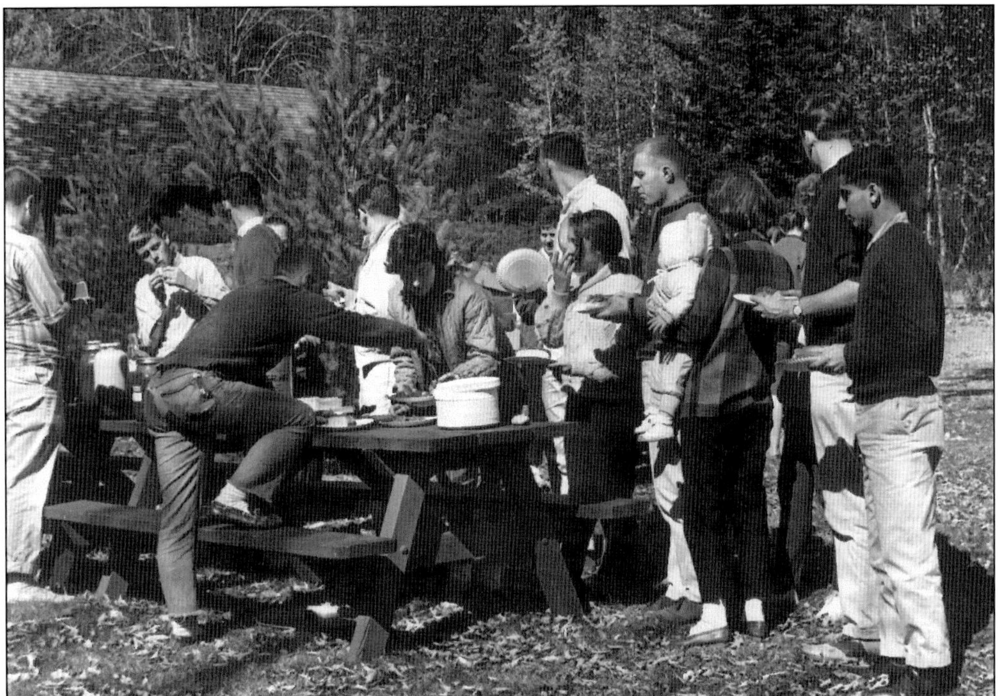

Luncheon was an important part of the day. Judging from this 1964 picture, the original practice of each participant bringing his own lunch was no longer in effect. The one student identified is Ramzi Karam (right).

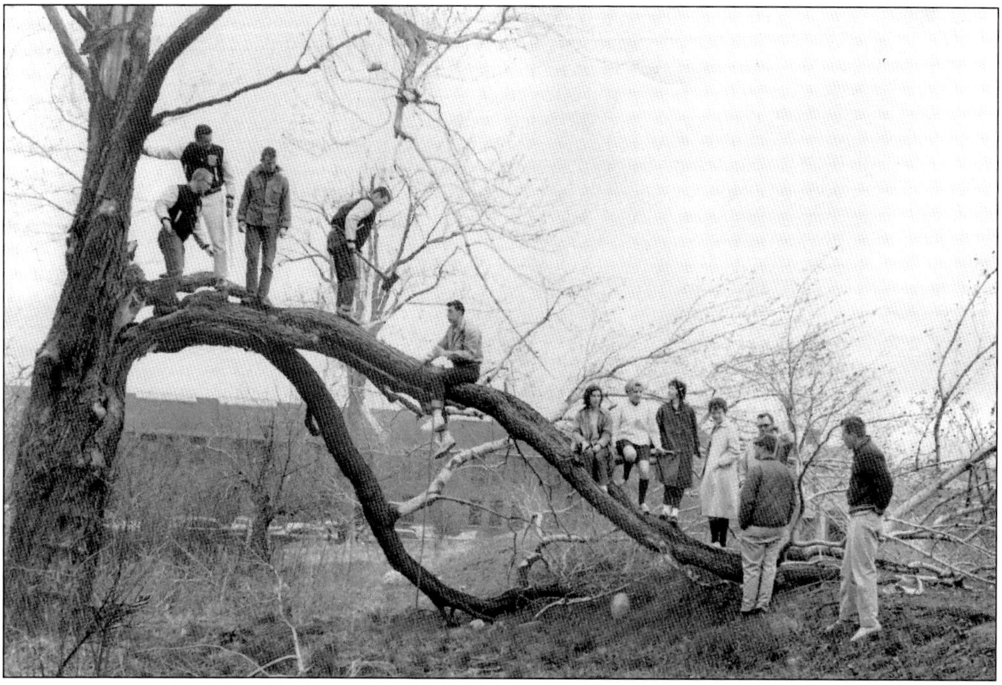

Maine Day, an Orono springtime custom, involved some campus cleanup. In 1960, the gymnasium got a new coat of paint. In 1962, students took down and cleared away this dying elm tree by the parking lot.

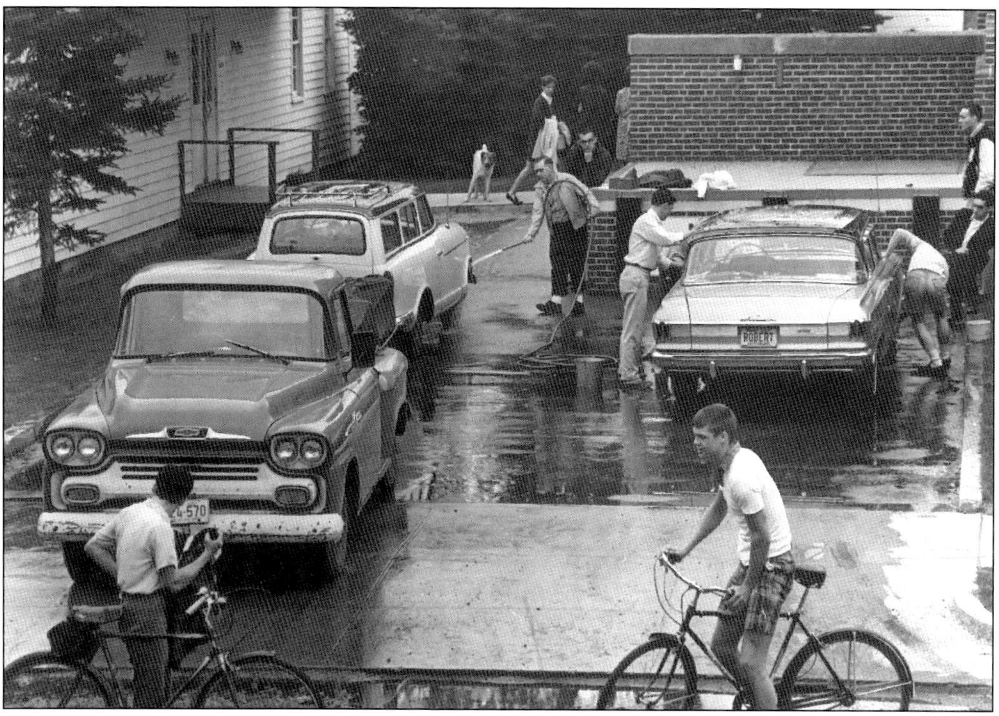

In 1964, students and some faculty (Owen Hall, accounting, is in the center) washed cars in the area between buildings, off Falmouth Street.

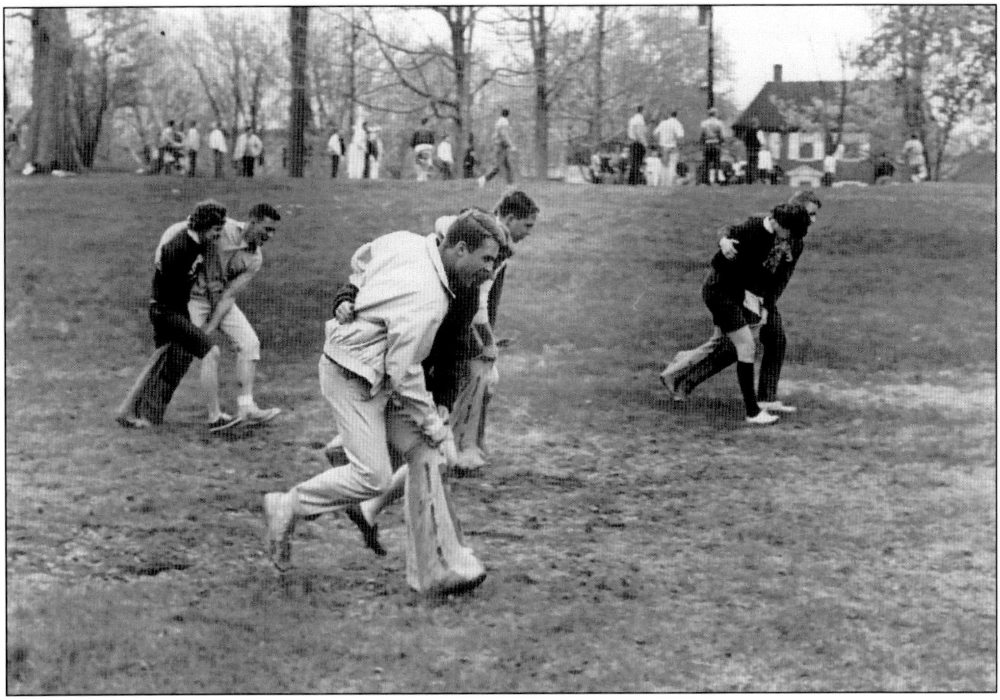

Maine Day also regularly included various out-of-doors activities, such as a tug-of-war, a softball game, or a three-legged race such as the one shown here in 1963. An off-campus clambake might follow.

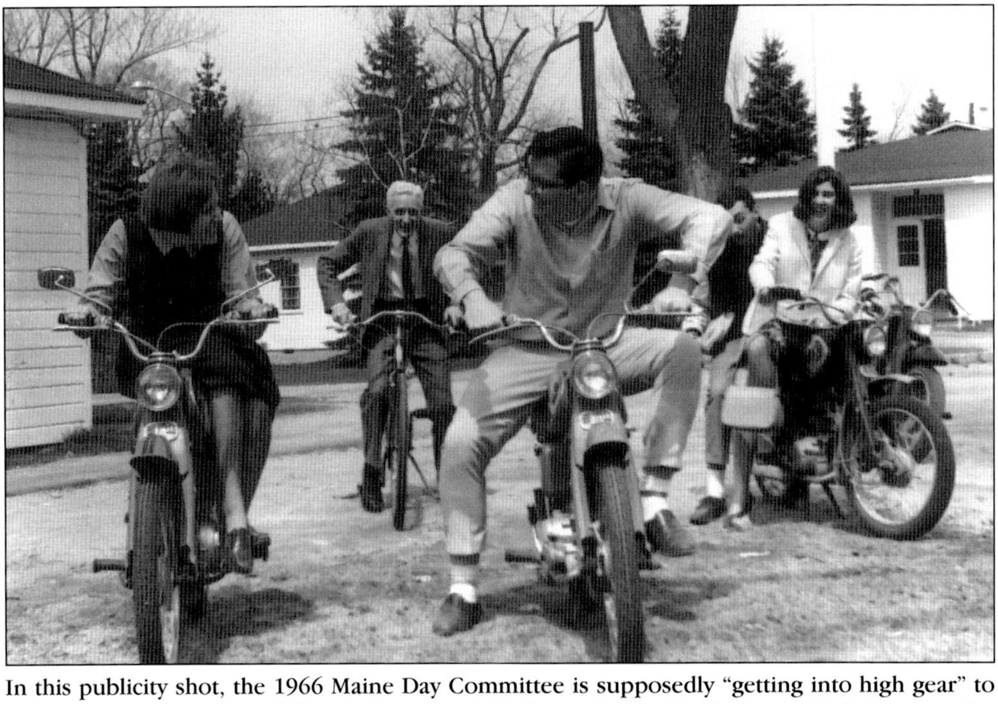

In this publicity shot, the 1966 Maine Day Committee is supposedly "getting into high gear" to plan the day. Shown from left to right are Jean Dickson, George VanAmburg, Mark Eastman, Pat Feury, and Jane Jacobs. The early classroom buildings are visible in the background.

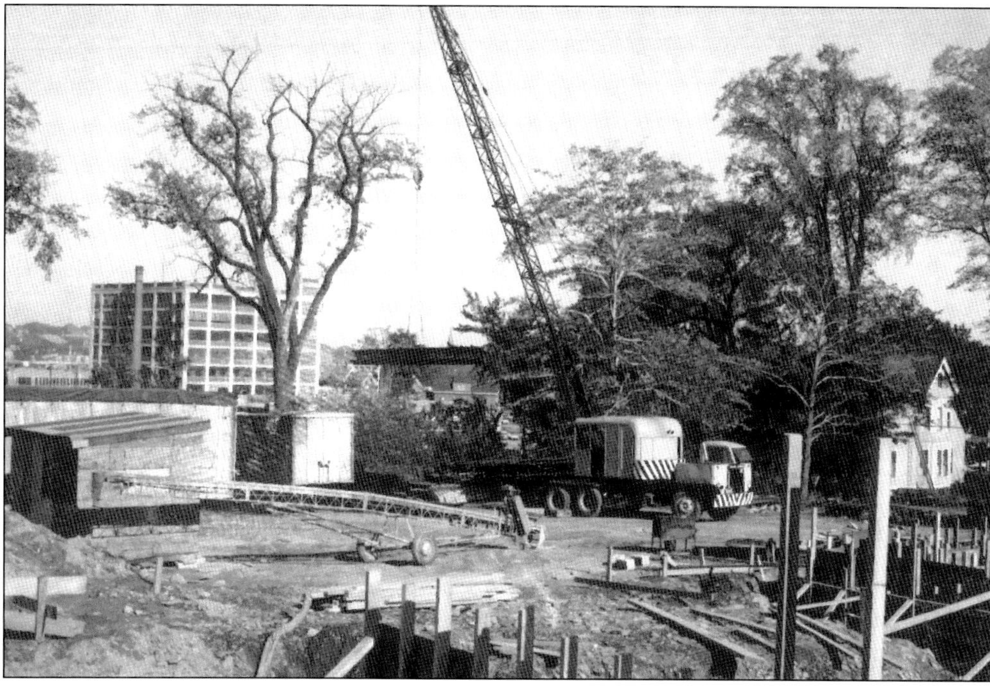

The construction of a second large classroom edifice on campus was begun in 1964 on the site of the old Deering mansion. The National Biscuit Company bakery (later made into a library) can be seen in the background.

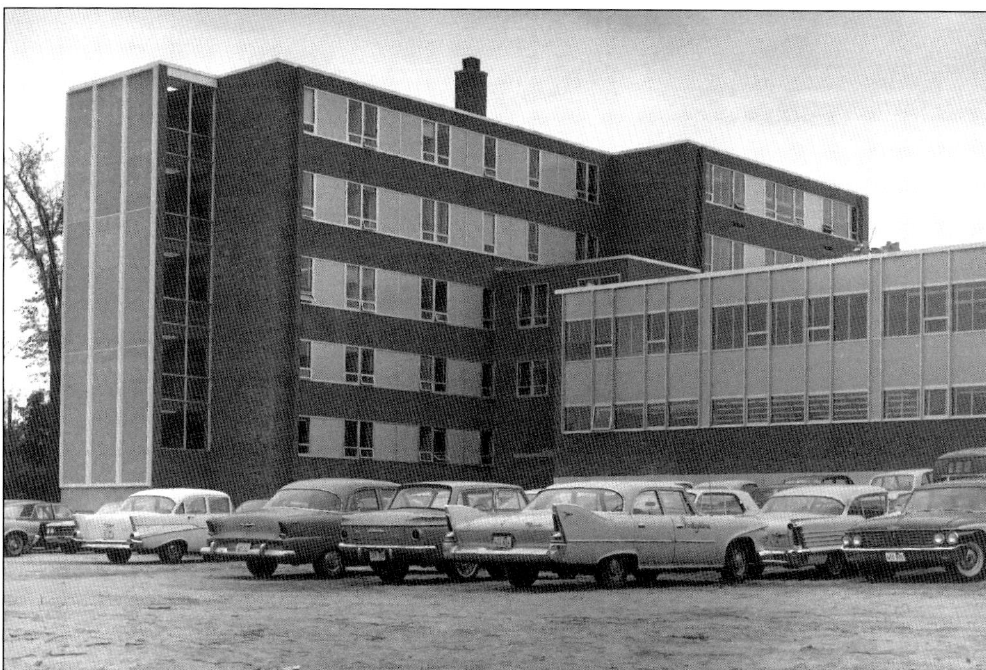

Luther Bonney Hall, named to honor the last dean of Portland Junior College, was dedicated in 1965. It held classrooms and offices, plus a library wing (right). More classrooms meant more students and more cars that required parking spaces.

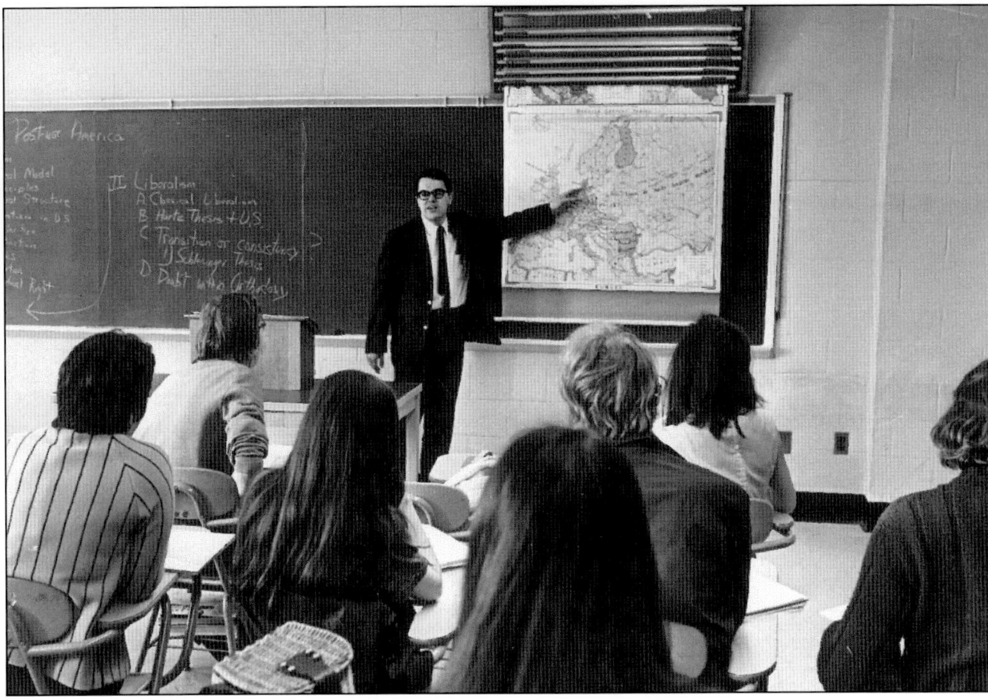

The social sciences made good use of the new rooms. Allan Whitmore's specialty was American history, with emphasis on its social and intellectual aspects.

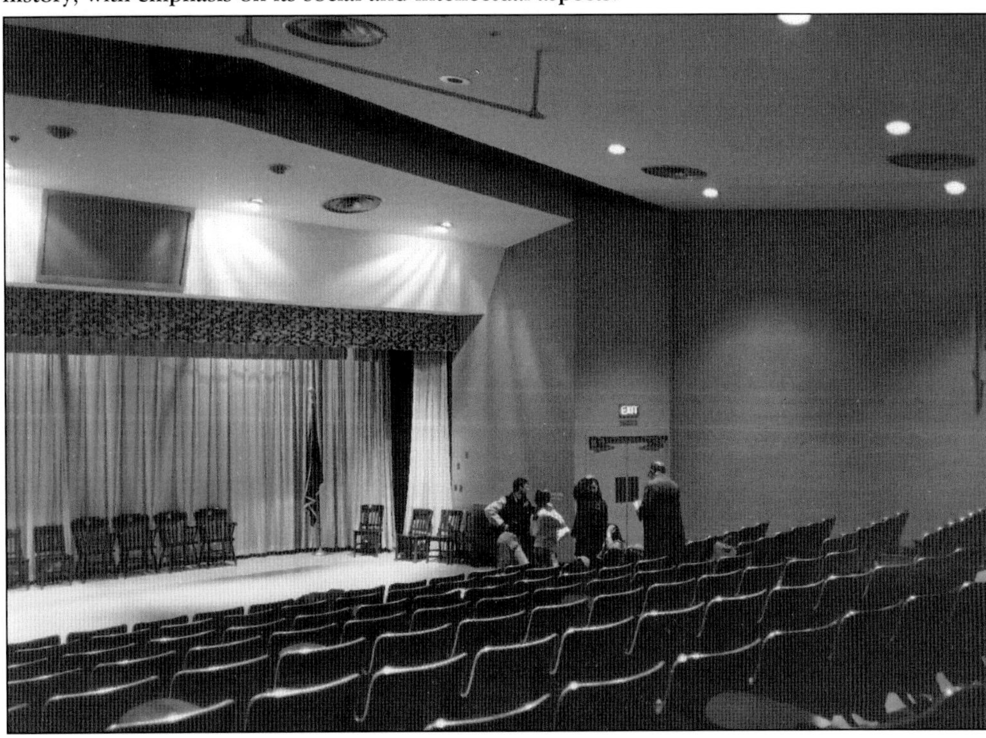

An auditorium on the first floor of Luther Bonney served as a theater for dramatic performances and also as a location for lectures. This group seems to be planning an event there.

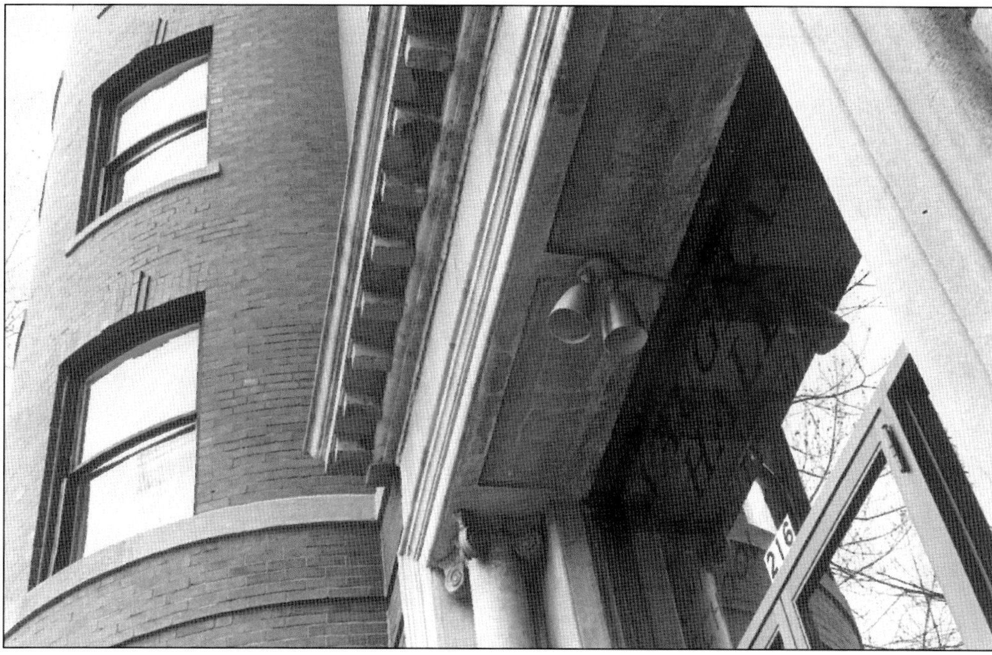

At the beginning of the 1966–1967 year, the University of Maine at Portland acquired a temporary dormitory. The University of Maine leased Vaughan Hall on Vaughan Street to house nursing students from Orono who were getting practical training at Maine Medical Center and taking a few courses on the Portland campus. In 1969, the entire nursing program would be transferred to Portland.

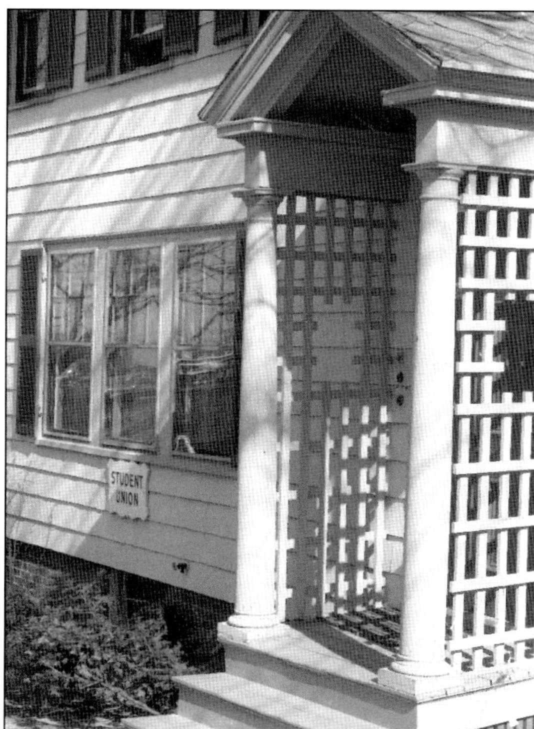

A building across Bedford Street from Luther Bonney Hall was purchased and renovated for the Student Union to occupy in September 1967. During the following years, more private homes in the area would become university property, some to be used as offices, others to be razed for parking—not always in accord with owner or neighborhood wishes.

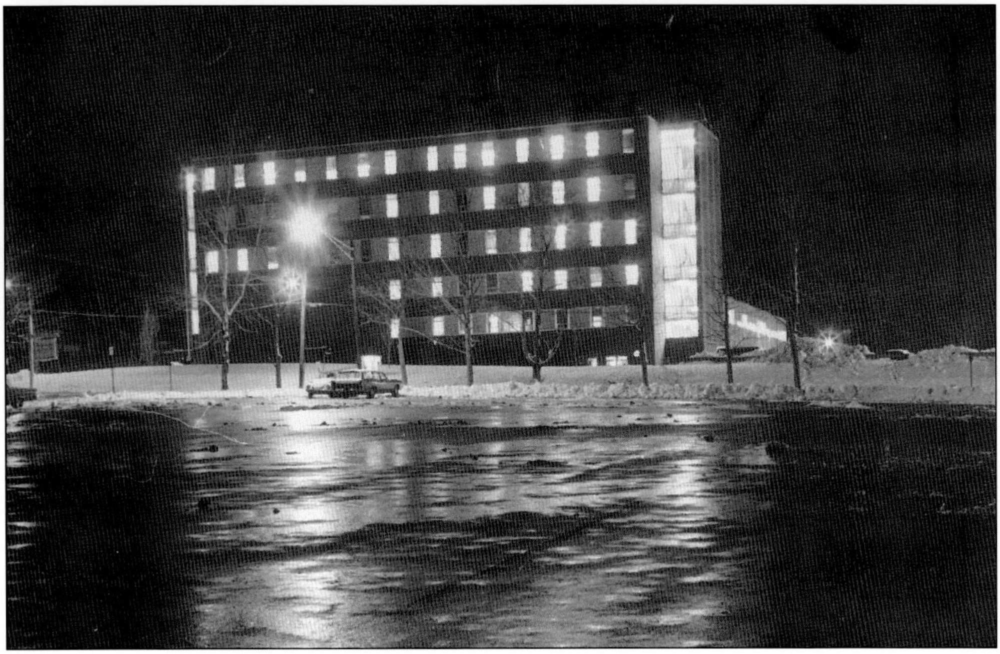

This view of Luther Bonney Hall at night should be familiar to the many students who enrolled in the UMP Continuing Education Division (CED), begun in the spring of 1963 and offered in the evenings, replacing earlier University of Maine extension courses.

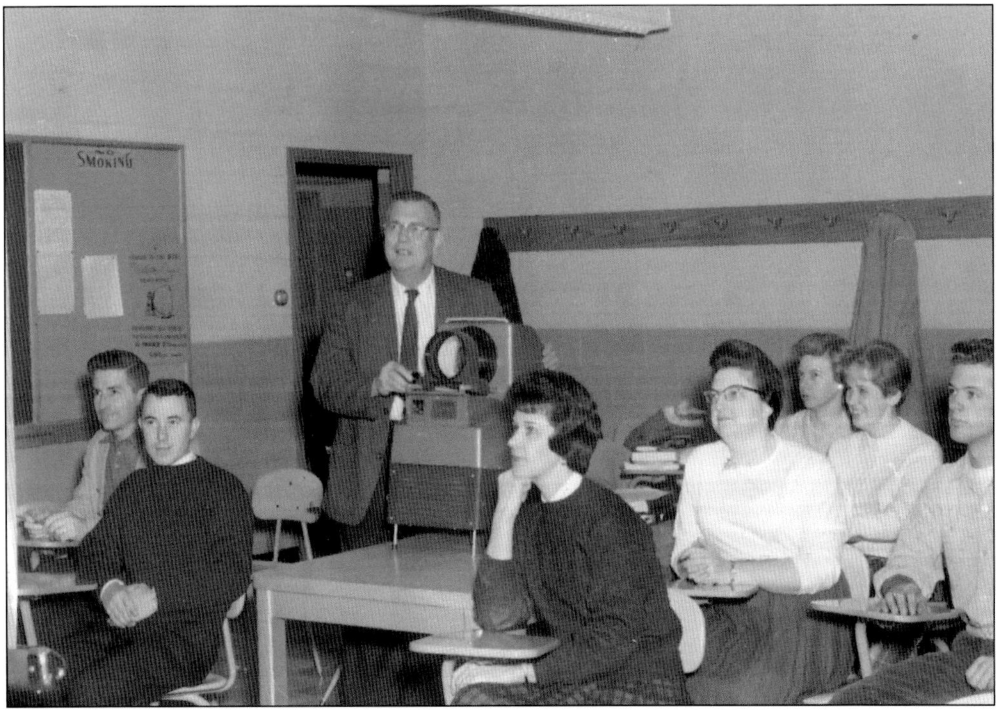

Alvin Rogers taught business courses. To help his 1963 CED students in Functional English to improve their writing, he projected samples of their essays on a screen and invited comments from the class.

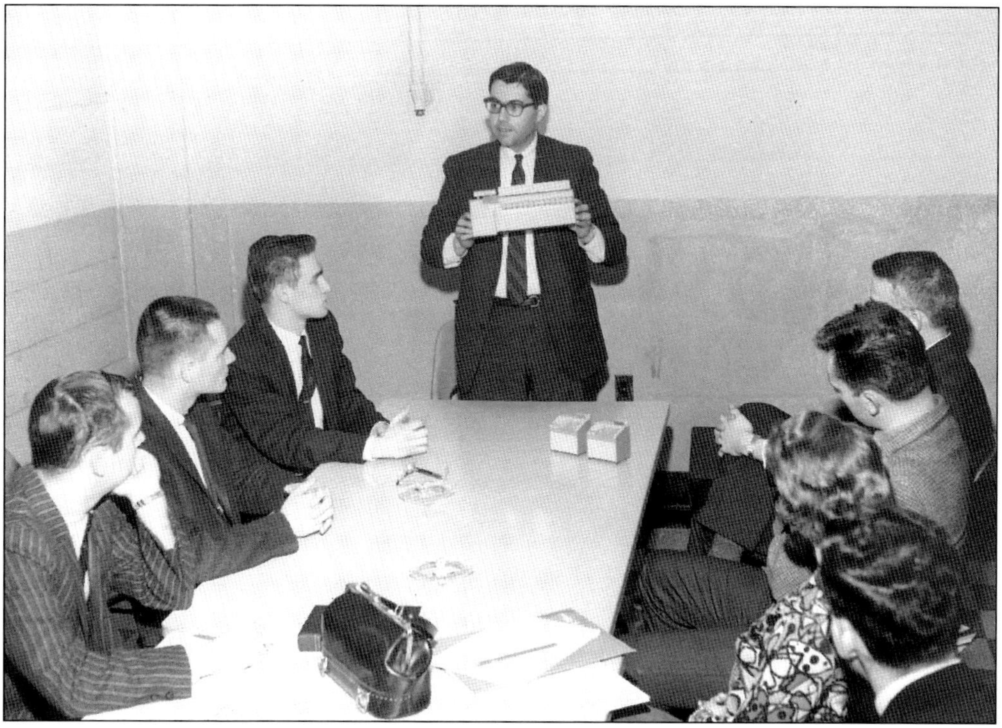

Business students formed the "Businessman's Fraternity" and invited men in the field to speak. Here, a representative from the Burroughs corporation explains the wonders of card-punch processing to this 1964 gathering.

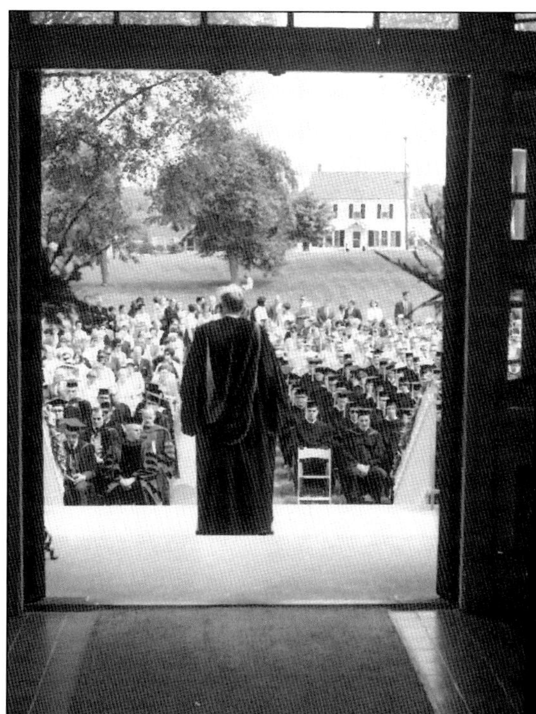

Administrators from Orono maintained a presence in Portland. Here, University of Maine Pres. Lloyd Elliot delivers the 1964 commencement address from the steps of Payson Smith Hall. Note the varied regalia. Faculty (with hoods) are in the very front. The black caps and gowns behind them represent bachelor's degrees, and the lighter ones farther back are for two-year graduates.

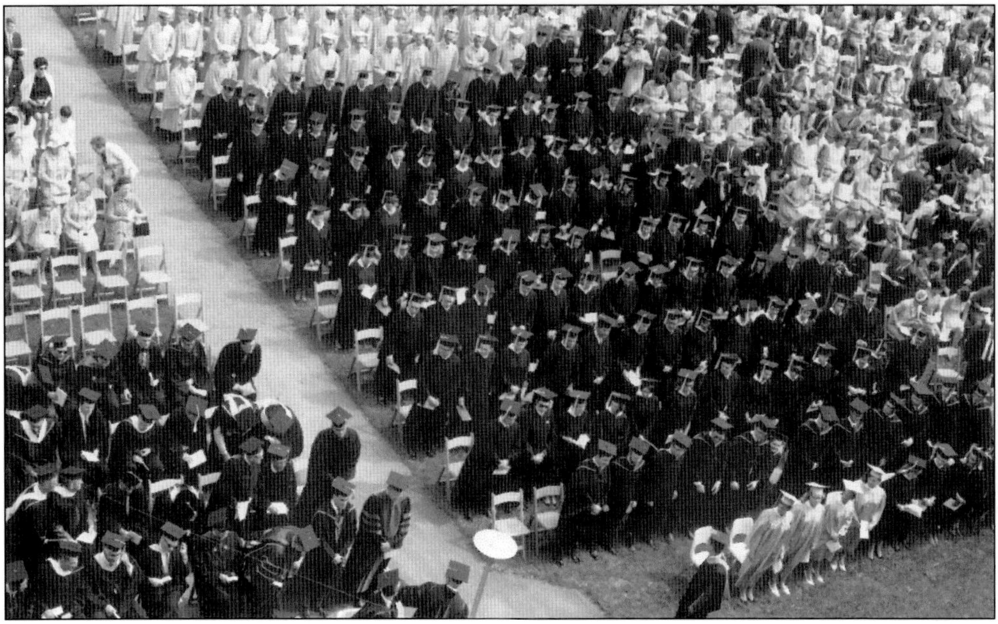

Despite plans to maintain the University of Maine at Portland as a two-year "feeder" campus, the business program, with its bachelor of science course, opened a door. Students who did not wish to spend two years in Orono and faculty who felt fully qualified to teach advanced courses demanded other bachelor's degrees for Portland. The commencement program for the 1965 graduation listed 15 four-year degrees given in education and one in English, in addition to business and law degrees.

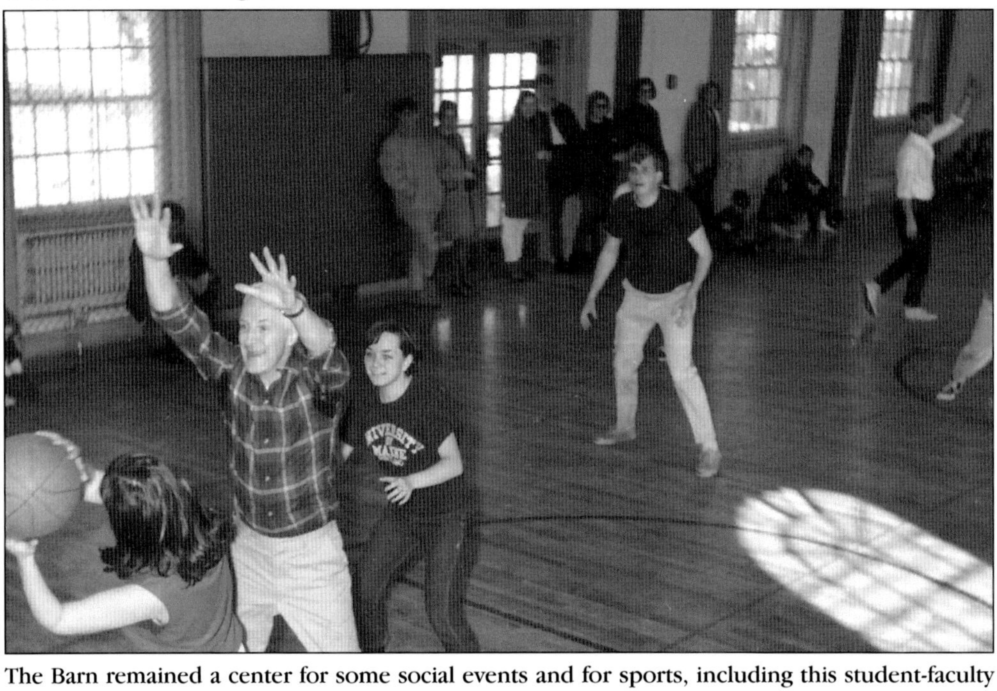

The Barn remained a center for some social events and for sports, including this student-faculty game in 1965. Staff members facing the camera are George VanAmburg (left), of Student Services, and Phillip Cole (right of center), who taught history.

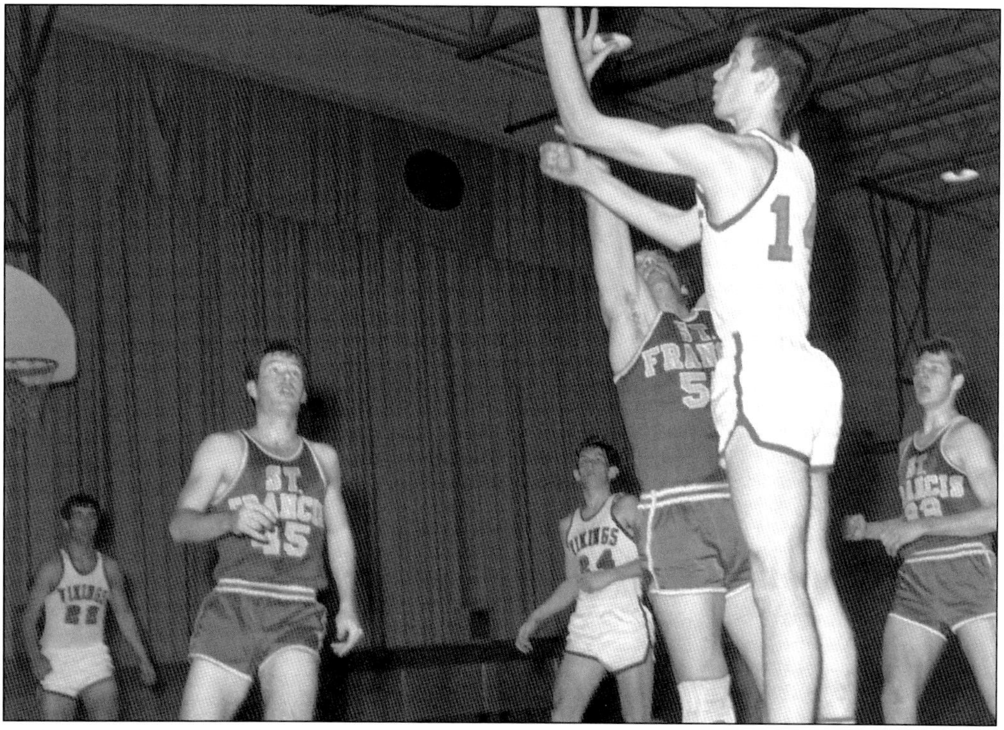

Both intercollegiate and intramural basketball games were scheduled. St. Francis (later New England) College, in Biddeford, is shown playing against the University of Maine at Portland, sometime after the 1962 change of team uniforms to reflect the new name "Vikings."

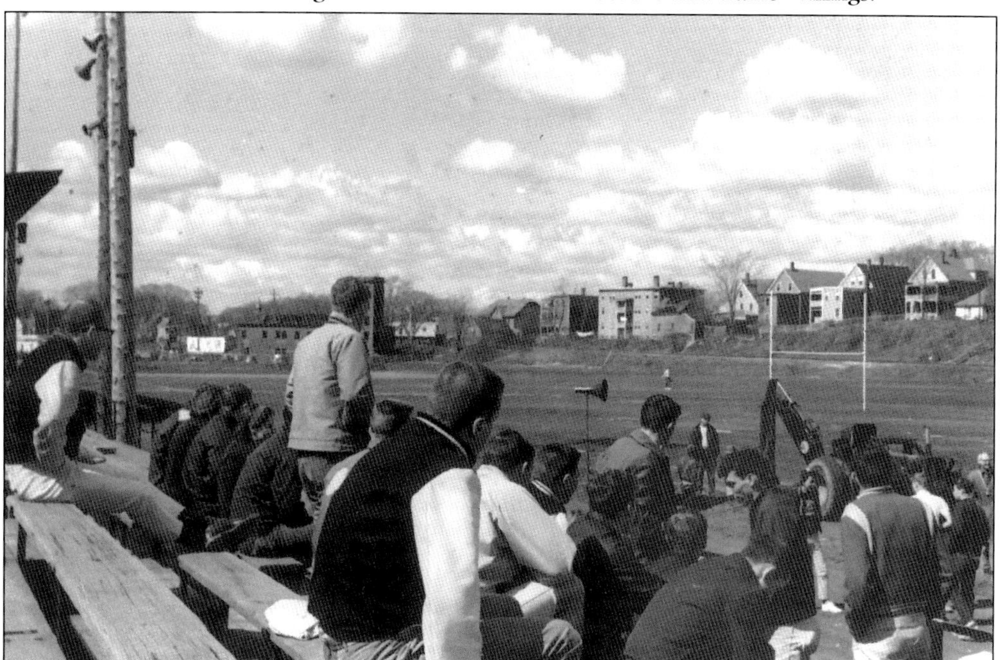

After many open areas on campus became parking lots, city property nearby could serve for other athletic events. Here, a group gathers on the bleachers at Portland Stadium.

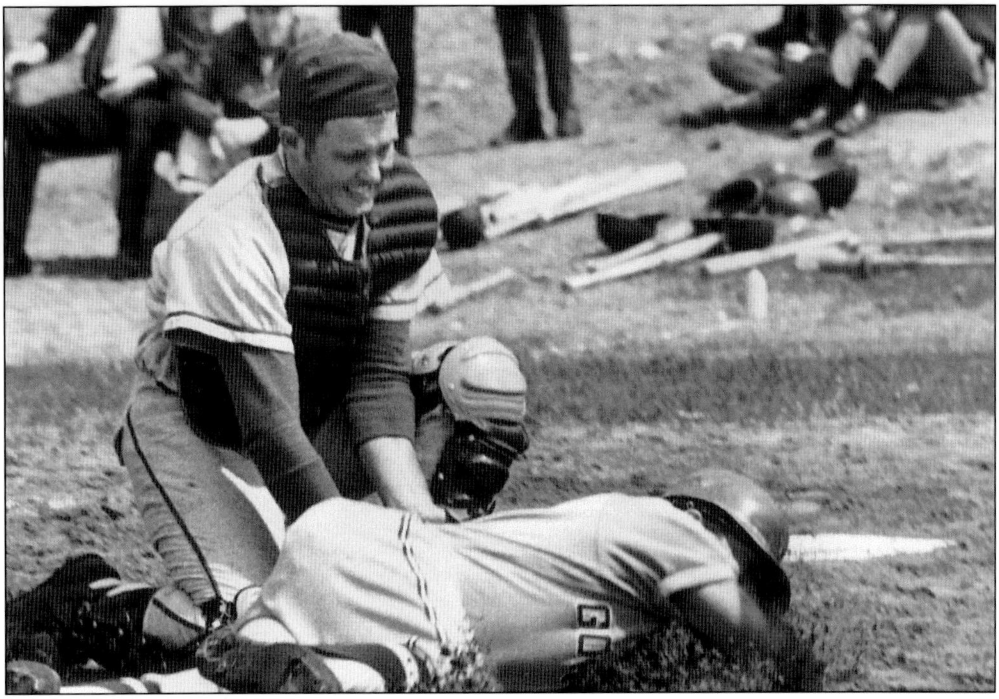

In this 1969 baseball match, the opposing team was Gorham State College.

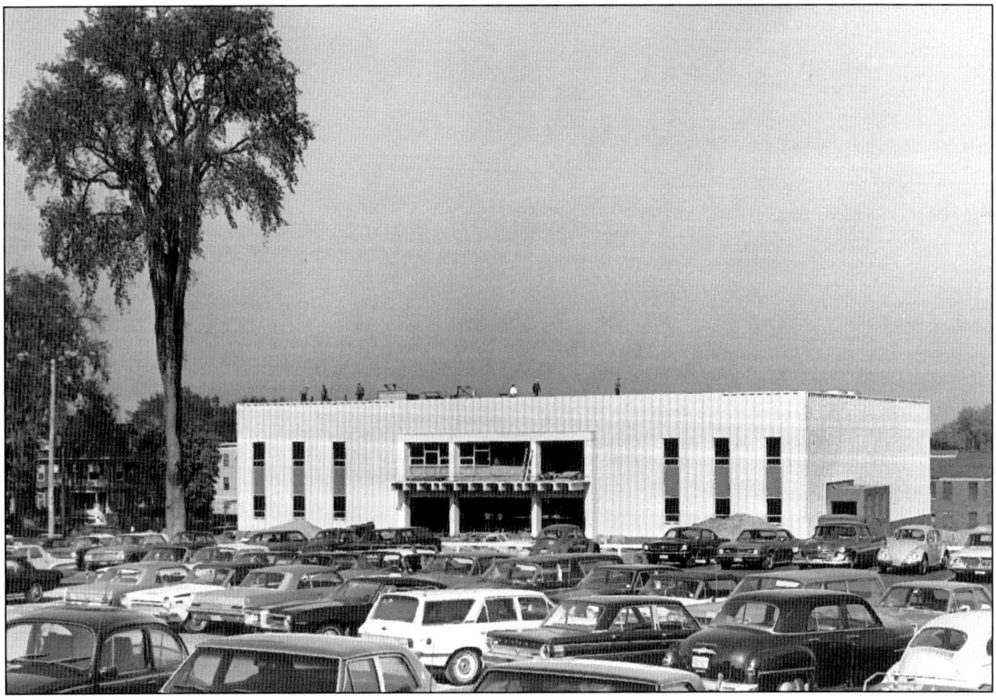

By the mid-1960s, more interior space was needed for sports. The legislature therefore allowed money for a new physical education building, shown here under construction. Opened in 1969, it contained a gymnasium, classrooms, and a health center. Twenty-four years later, it was named for James Sullivan (page 125), longtime director of athletics on that campus.

At the same time, the Science Building, shown going up behind the Barn, was erected on space previously occupied by North and East Halls, which had been torn down in the fall of 1967. It held a variety of science facilities, including a planetarium donated in memory of publisher Constant Southworth. West Hall, on the left, then housed the University Store.

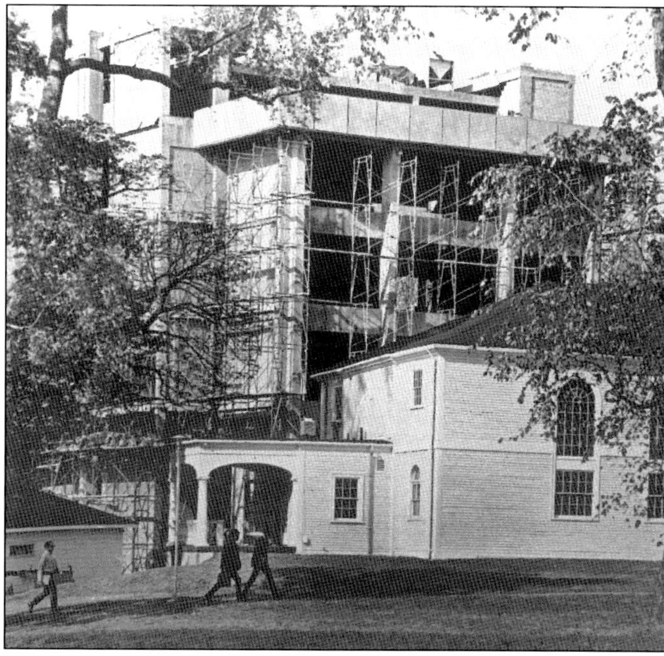

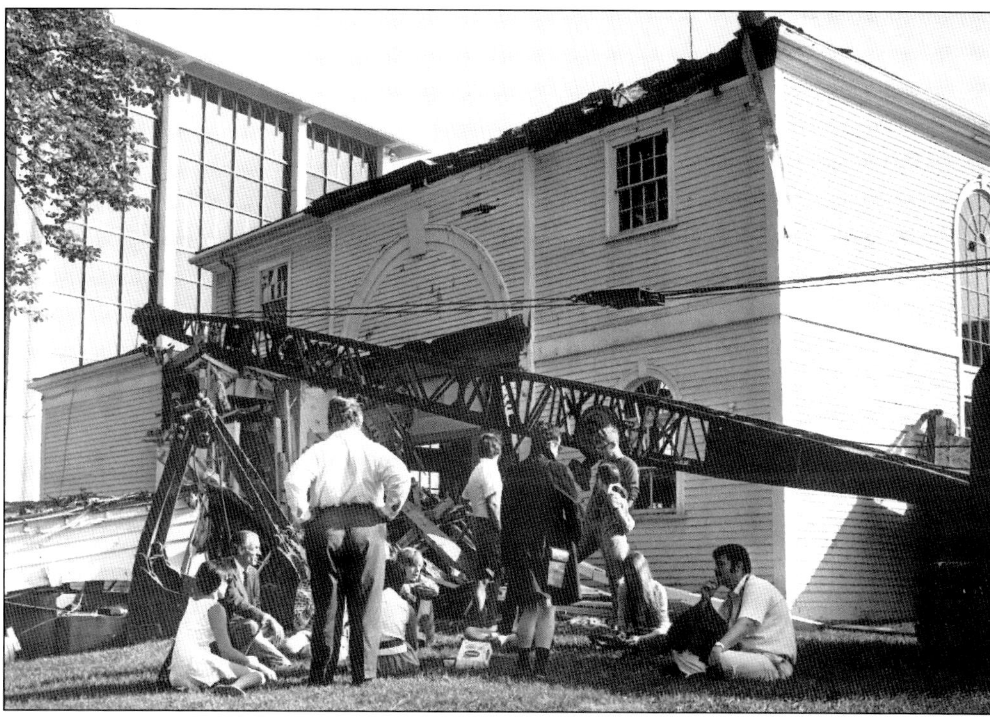

Despite its longtime position as campus centerpiece and of earlier university publicity, which had touted its unique wooden-pegged frame, the old Barn was proclaimed an inauthentic eyesore by administrators and trustees who ordered its destruction. Protests from students, faculty, and preservationists at local, state, and national levels (who were investigating alternatives) were unheeded. The 1805 building was demolished in August of 1969—but only after an injunction removed demonstrators blocking the crane.

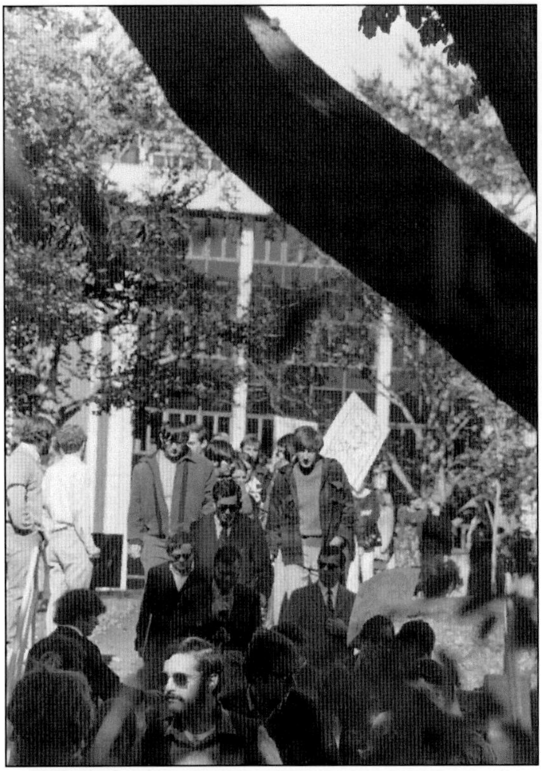

The 1960s brought campus unrest all over the country, as students launched antiwar protests. This October 15, 1969 peace rally began on campus, where participants gathered south of the Science Building.

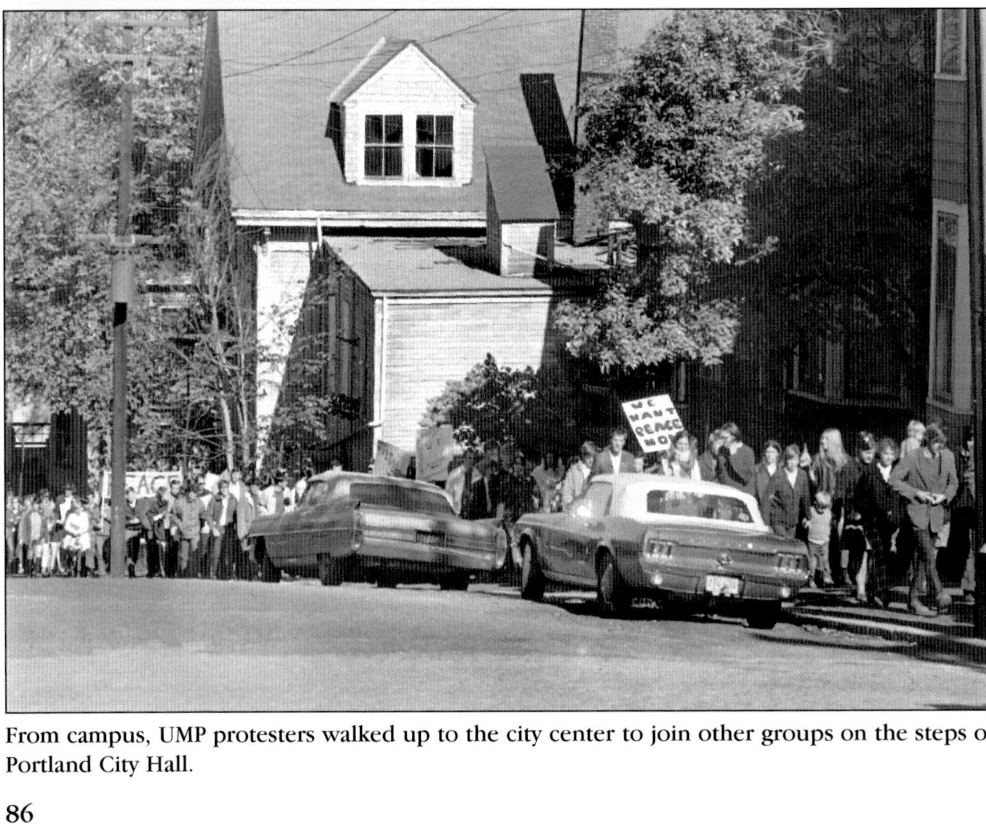

From campus, UMP protesters walked up to the city center to join other groups on the steps of Portland City Hall.

Six

Gorham State College and Gorham State College of the University of Maine, 1965–1970

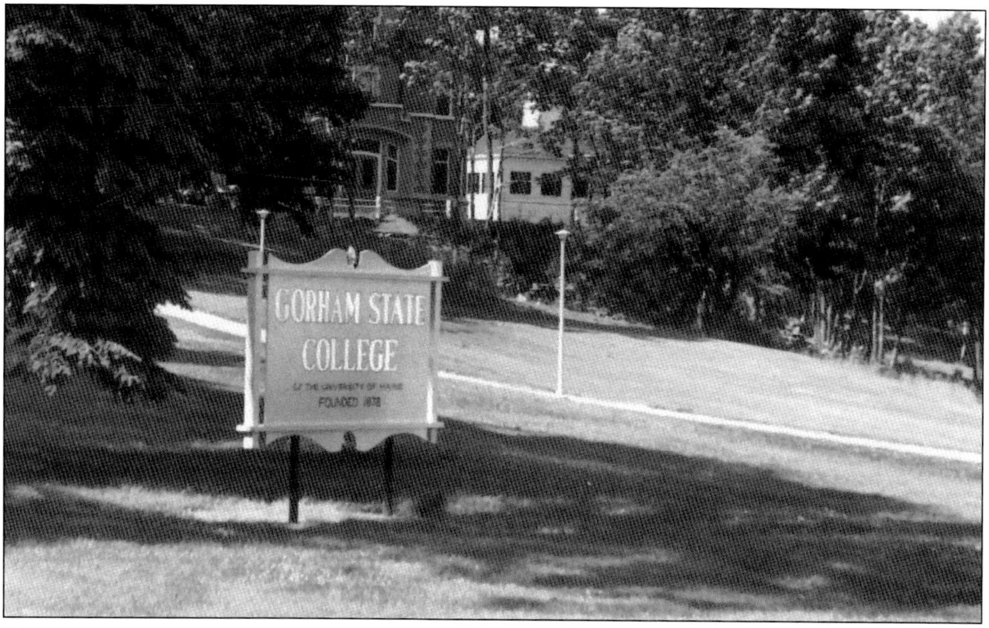

After two decades as a teaching college, the Gorham institution experienced another name change, which again reflected increased offerings, as additional academic courses in the arts and sciences became available. The new Gorham State College continued to offer undergraduate and graduate studies in education, but could also could give baccalaureate degrees in other fields. To this end, the state legislature made funds available for an unprecedented increase in faculty. The sign on the lawn had to be changed again. The academy building is visible among the trees on the right. (Detail.)

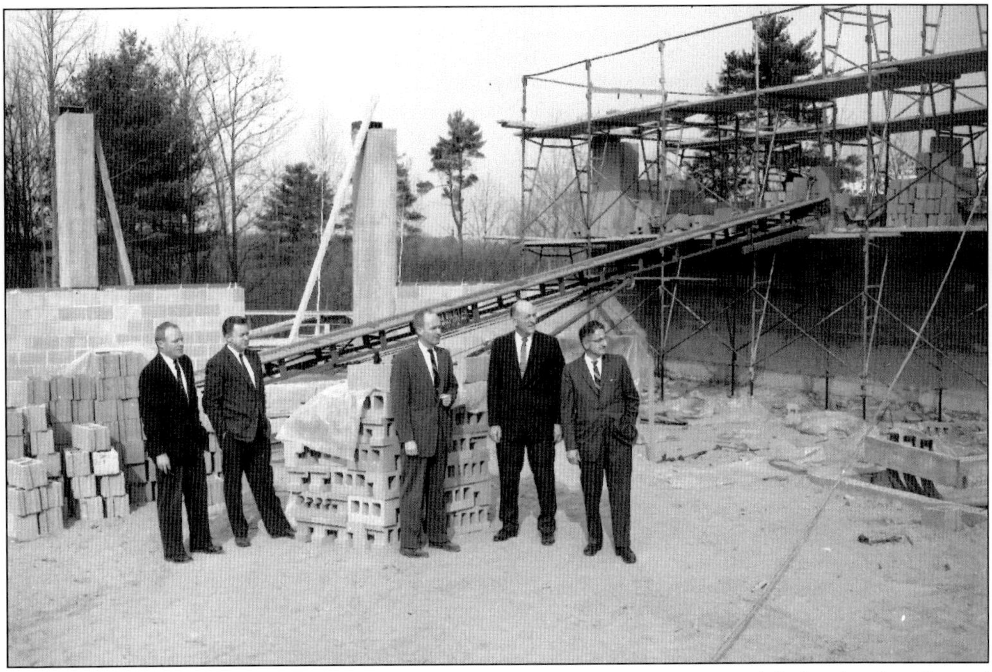

Older programs grew as well. Faculty of the industrial arts program were delighted to be allowed a modern building. Touring the site early in 1965 are, from left to right, Arthur Berry, Richard Carter, John Greer, John Falls, and John Mitchell.

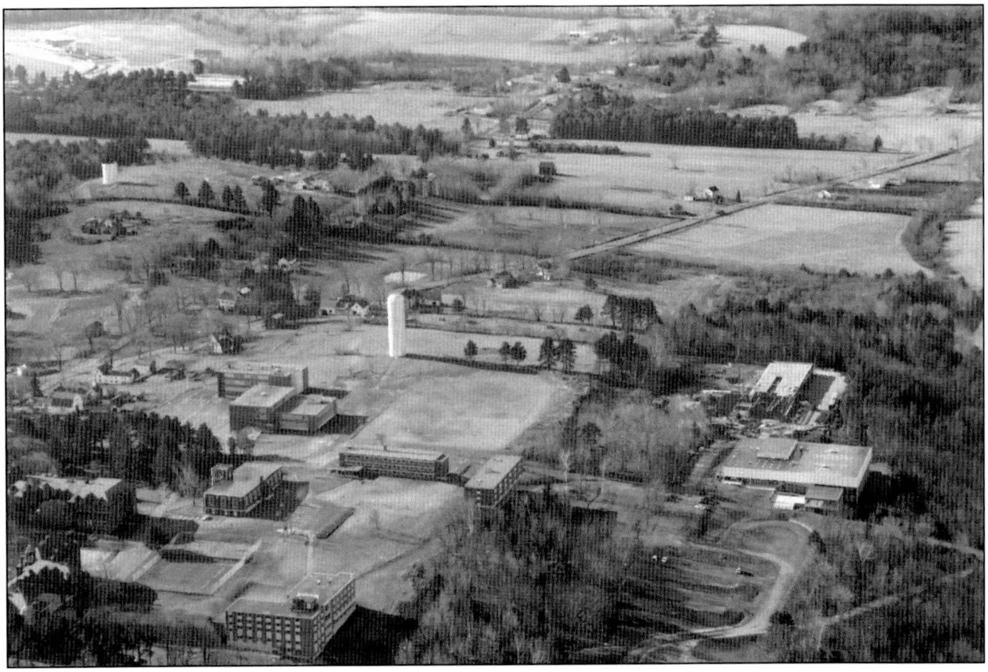

This aerial view shows the new industrial arts building under construction (right), while the temporary structure is the dark area seen through trees to the left of Upton Hall (lower left). Note that Bailey Hall was then still in two parts. The water tower behind had been erected in 1958, at the same time as the science wing.

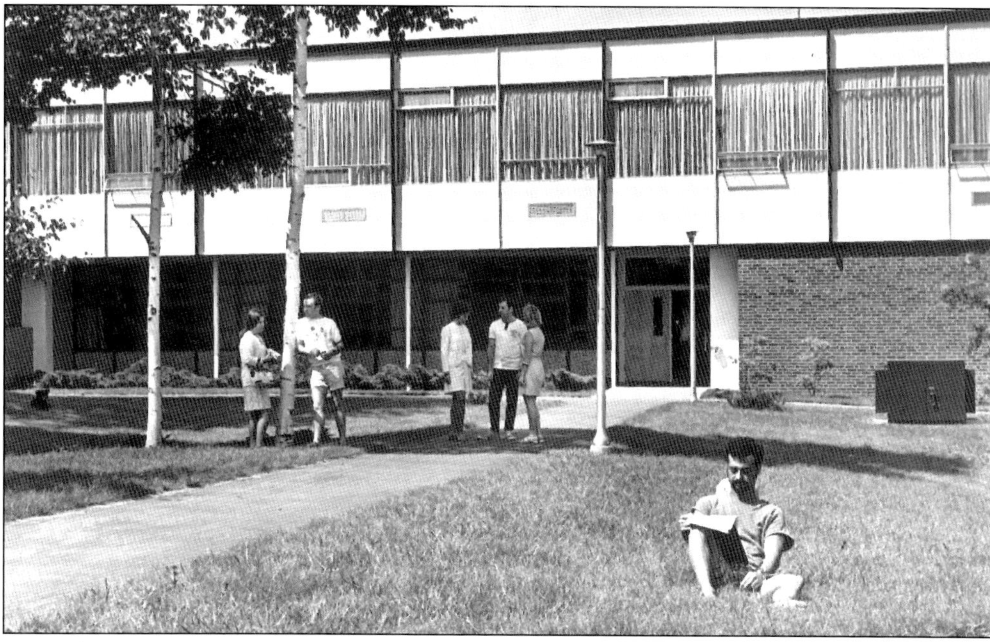

The industrial arts building was completed in time for the 1965–1966 academic year, but it was not named for John Mitchell until the summer of 1994. As soon as the new space was ready for equipment to be moved, the old barracks building, located between Robie and Upton Halls, was destined to be torn down, while Academy Hall would be turned over to the art department.

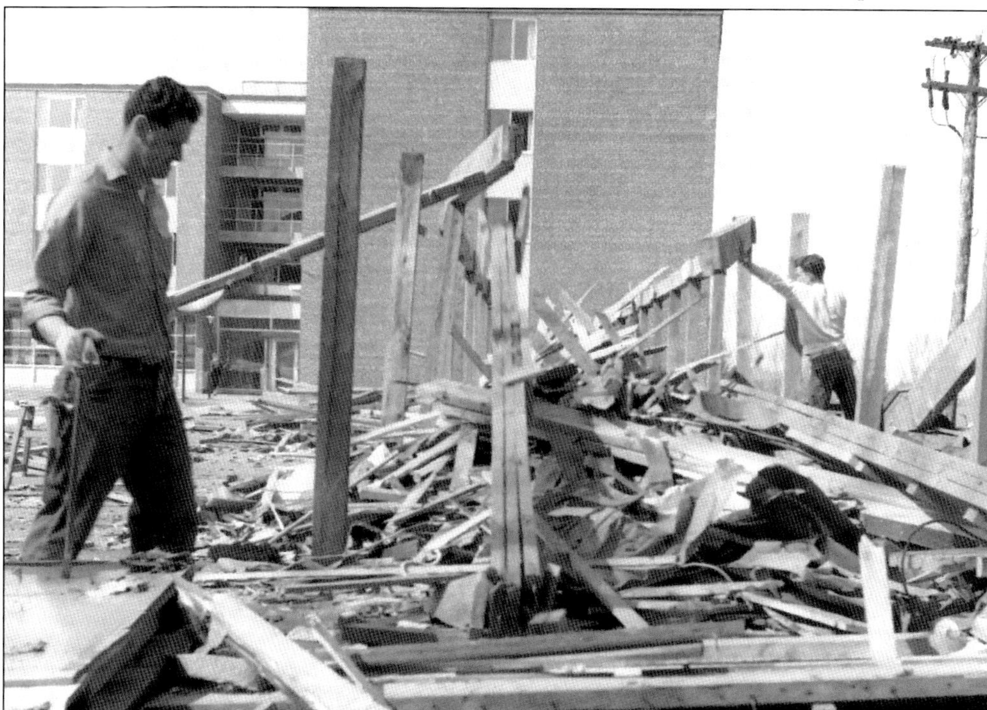

Barracks demolition is nearly complete in this picture. Within a few days unsalvageable debris would go up in flames.

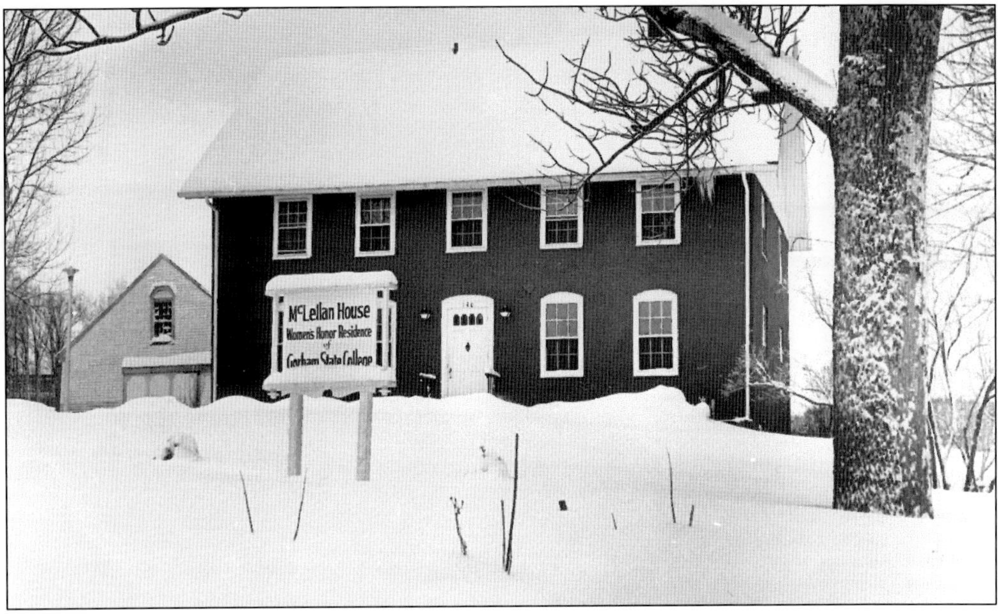

The 1773 Hugh McLellan House, the oldest brick home in the county, was acquired in 1966 and used as an "honor dorm," where a select group of women made their own rules. Student government within dormitories had begun with the women in Academy Hall, 1910–1915, and then expanded to the bigger residences. However, strict rules remained in effect for women (if not for men), even those living on campus.

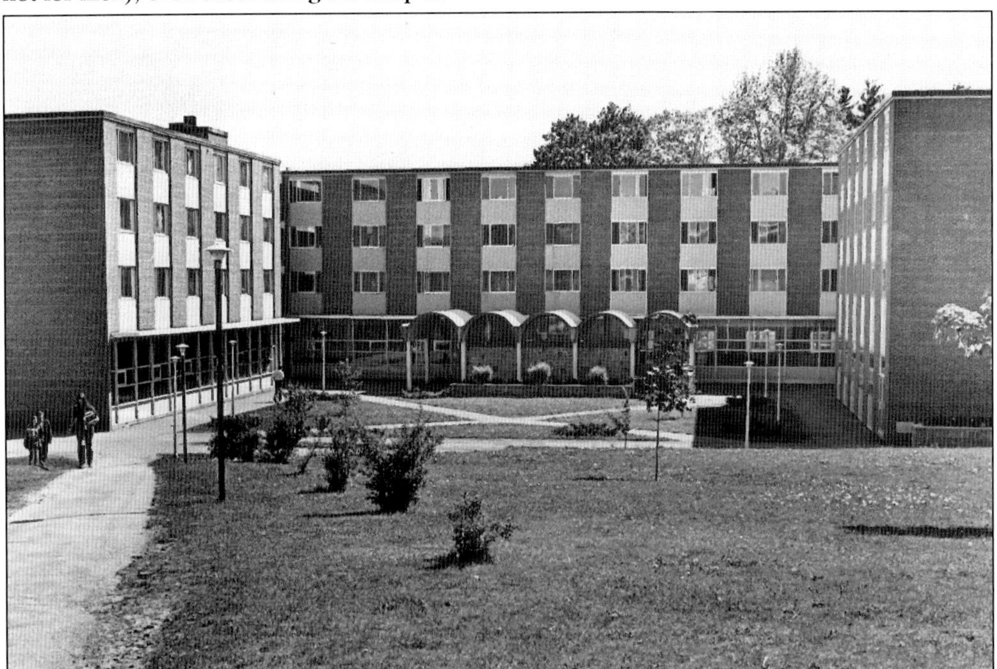

Women's dormitory space was again increased in 1968, when the L-shaped Hastings Hall (right) was attached to Upton Hall, creating a large U-shaped building. Mary Hastings was director of student teaching from 1919 until 1945.

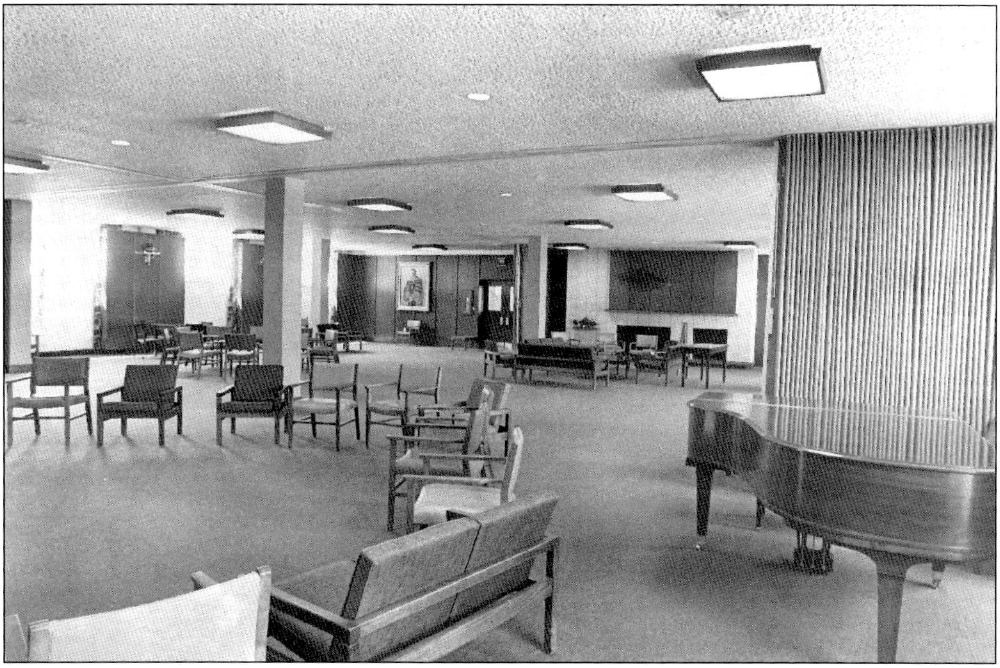

Hastings Formal Lounge, a large first-floor space with a small food serving area attached, could be subdivided by folding walls if desired. It is used for many campus functions. The portrait on the far wall is of Kenneth T.H. Brooks, college president from 1960 to 1970.

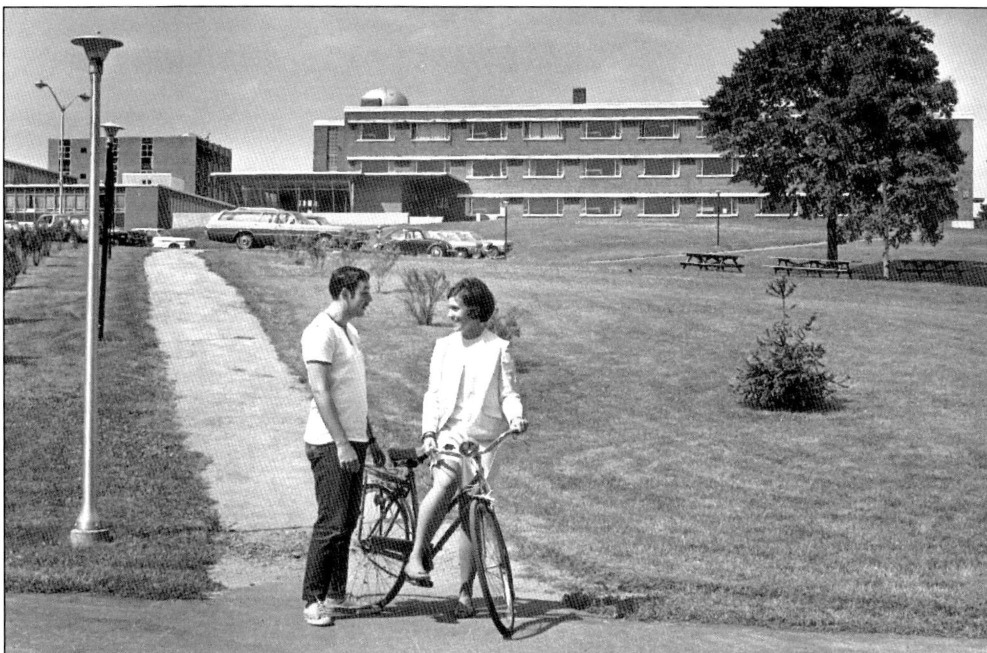

The "missing link" in Bailey Hall, completed in 1969, stood two stories taller than the earlier wings. It held classrooms, including a large auditorium, as well as numerous offices. This photograph was taken from a spot near Upton-Hastings, with Bailey Hall on the left and Woodward Hall on the right.

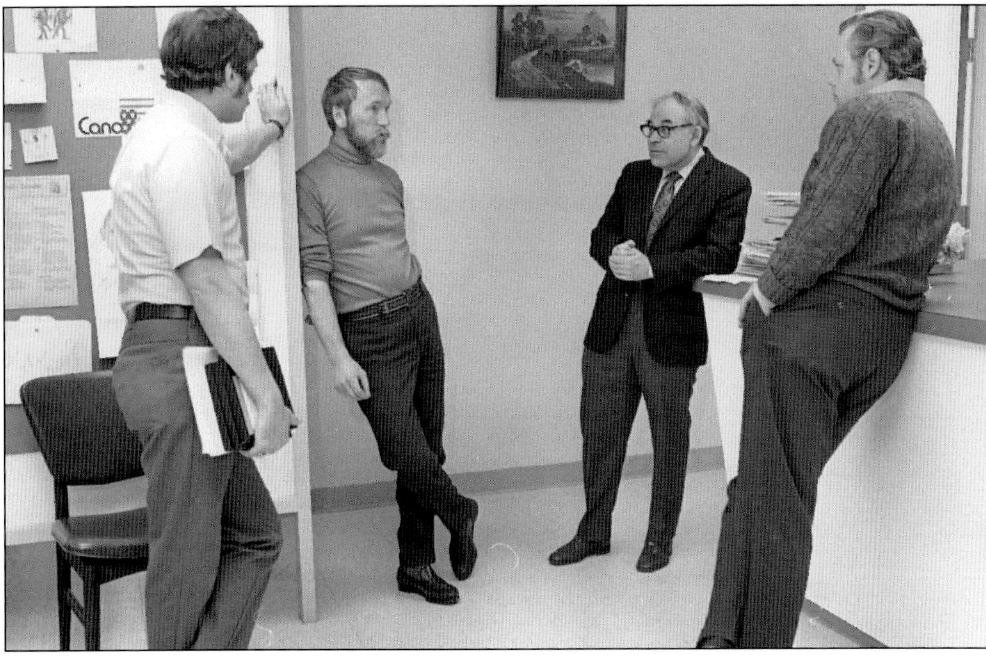

Faculty offices were in suites in the new section, where space on the fourth floor was used by faculty in education and psychology. Here, Robert Southworth (second from left) and James Whitten (third from left) chat with two students outside their offices. Southworth, a Portland Junior College graduate, was in the Class of 1949 (page 46).

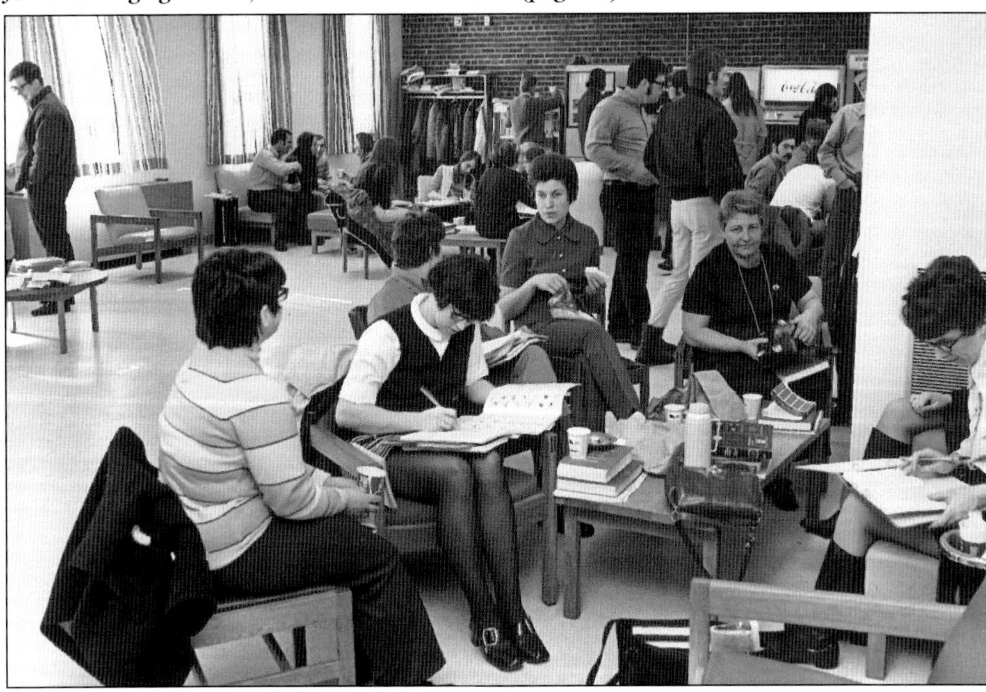

The Bailey Hall addition included a sizable student lounge, planned especially for commuter students. In addition to comfortable chairs in which students could relax or study, the lounge offered vending machines for quick snacks.

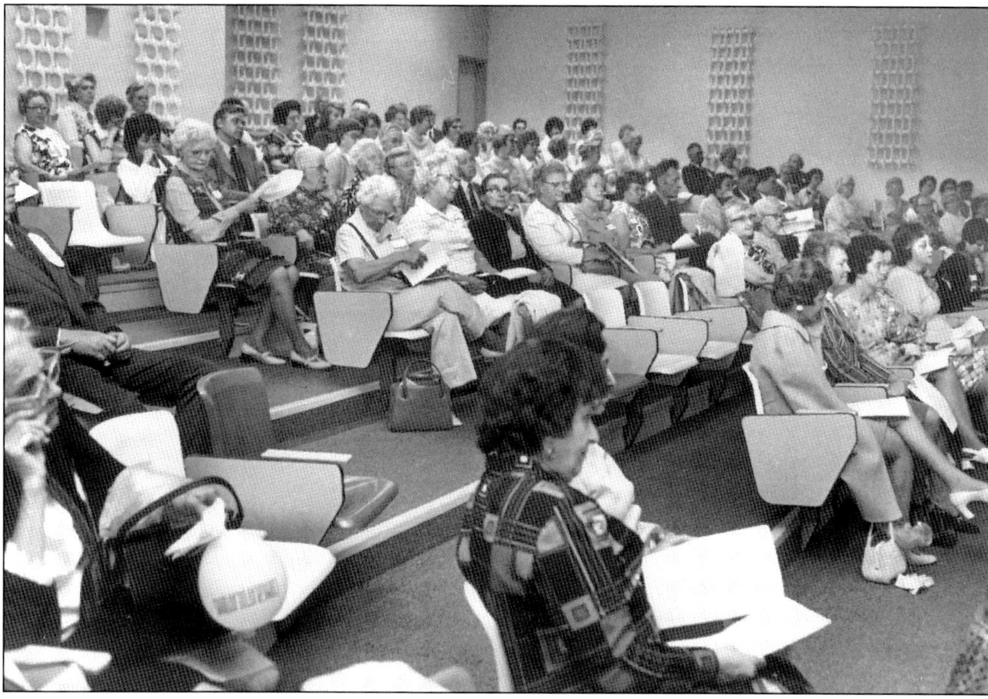

The lecture hall served for "Sunday night flicks" as well as for large classes and meetings, such as this summer gathering of alumni.

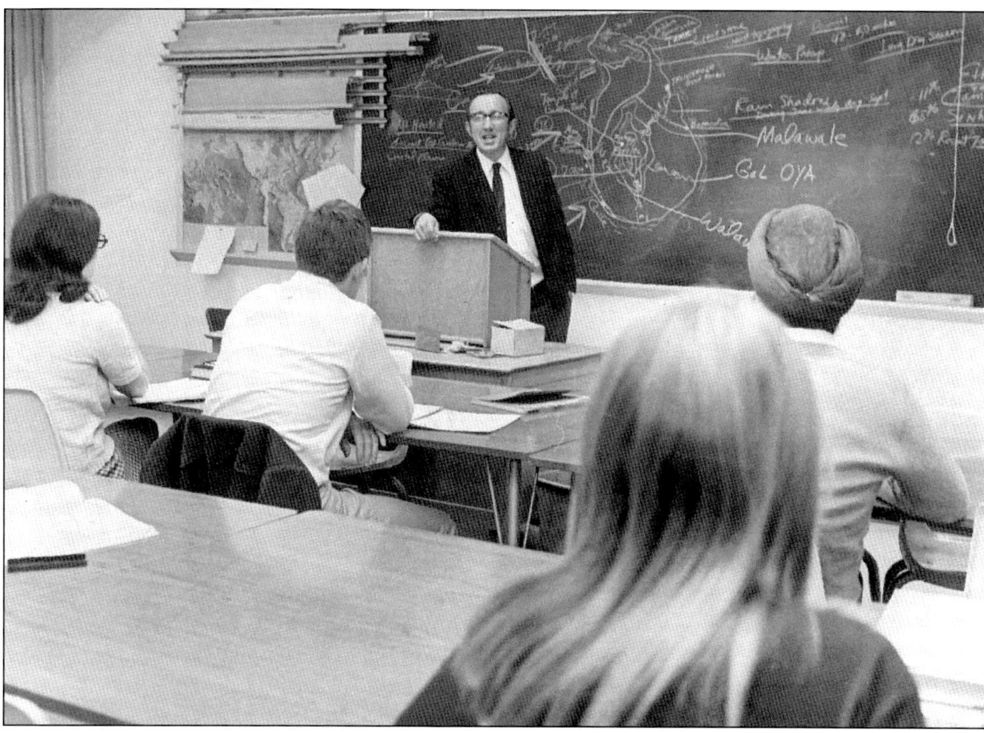

The geography classroom, part of an earlier wing of Bailey Hall, was kept lively by the enthusiastic lectures of Franklin Hodges.

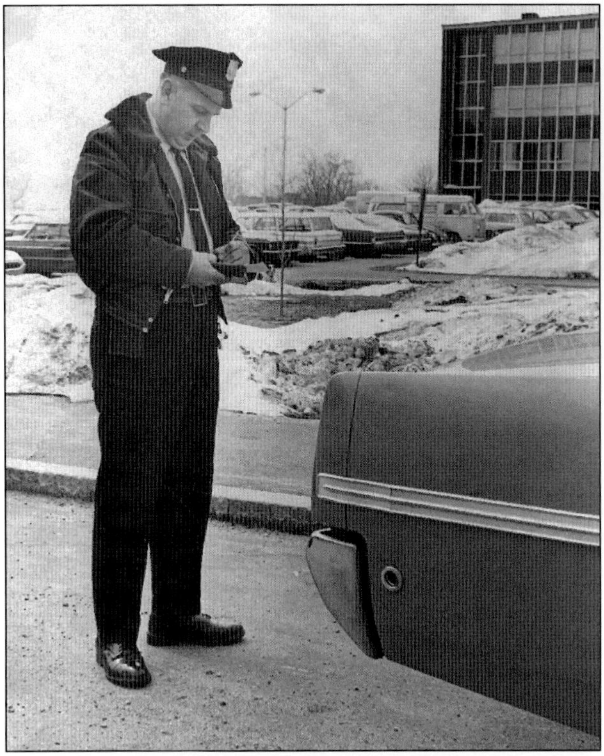

New dorms and new buildings meant more students and more automobiles. The college had to have its own security force, with the power to ticket cars parked improperly. Here, Joe Cross writes a ticket for a car near Bailey Hall.

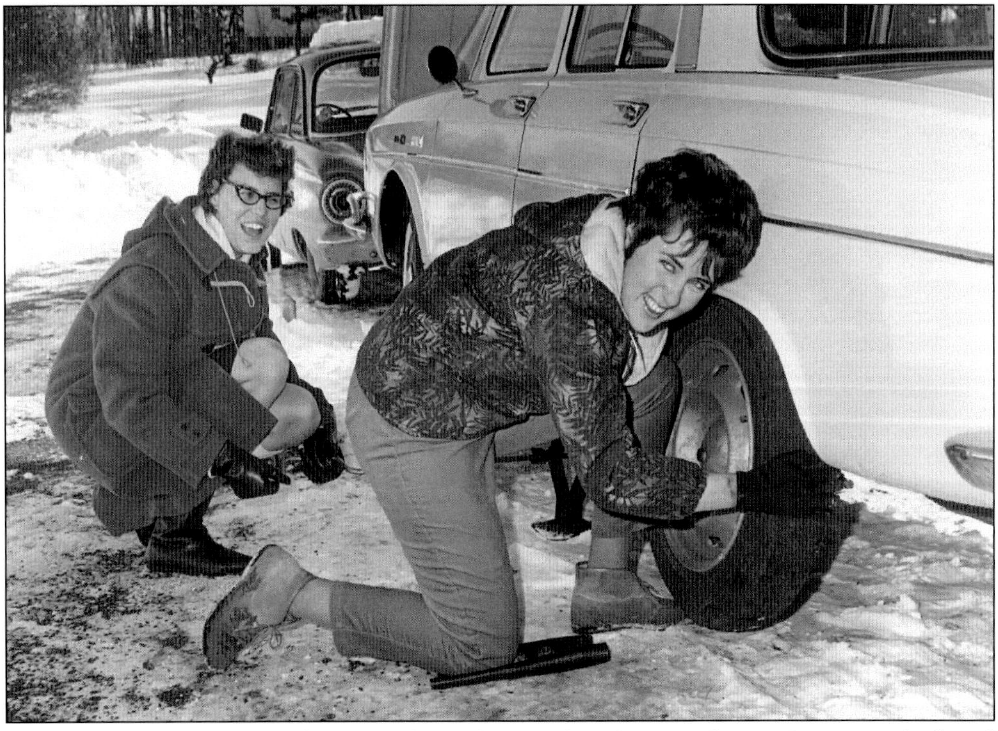

Sometimes the cars were problems in themselves. In this photograph, Kay Gagnon and a friend have to change a tire before they can leave campus.

Recognition Day, a spring event in which individuals were given various awards, began in the 1950s. In the 1960s, faculty attended the ceremony in academic regalia. Shown in 1968 are George Barker (biology), at left, and Wenzel Moberg (geography), the recipient of that year's yearbook dedication. Both men would retire within a few years because of debilitating illnesses.

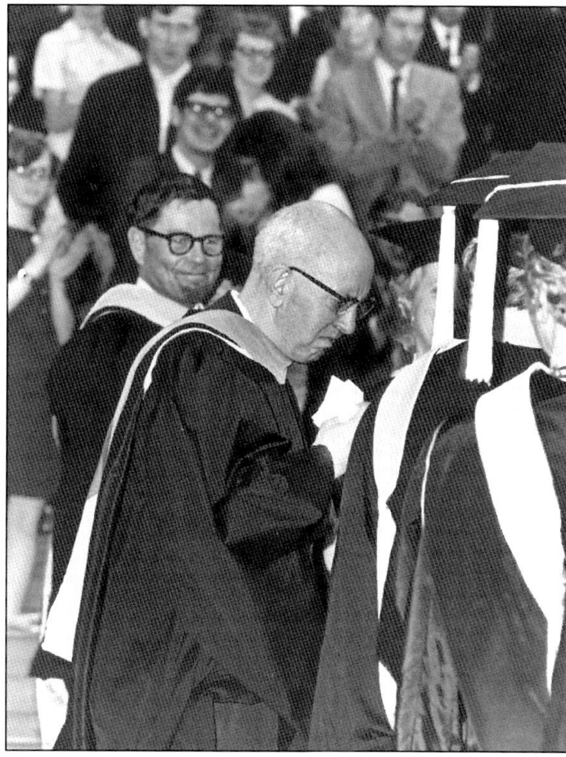

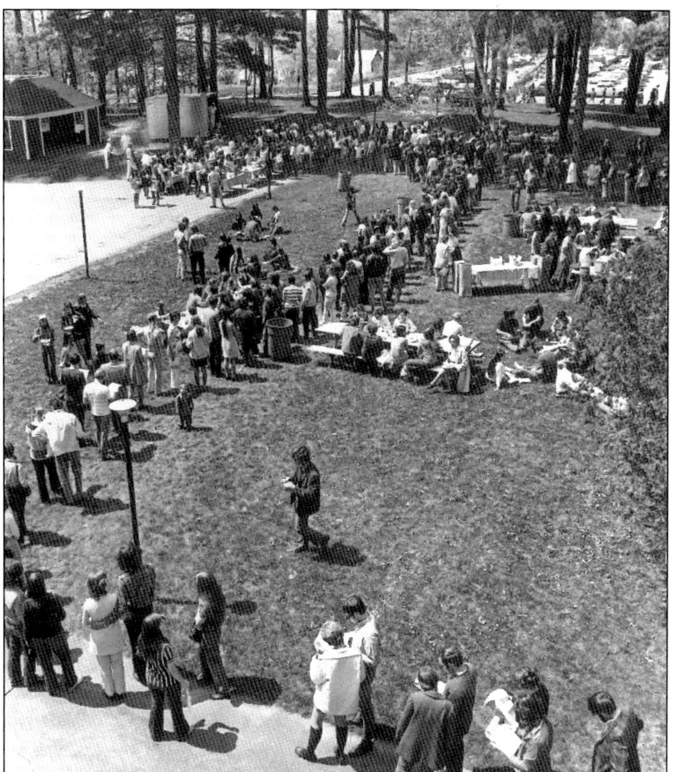

A picnic was often planned to follow the ceremonies and was served in the pine grove near Corthell Hall.

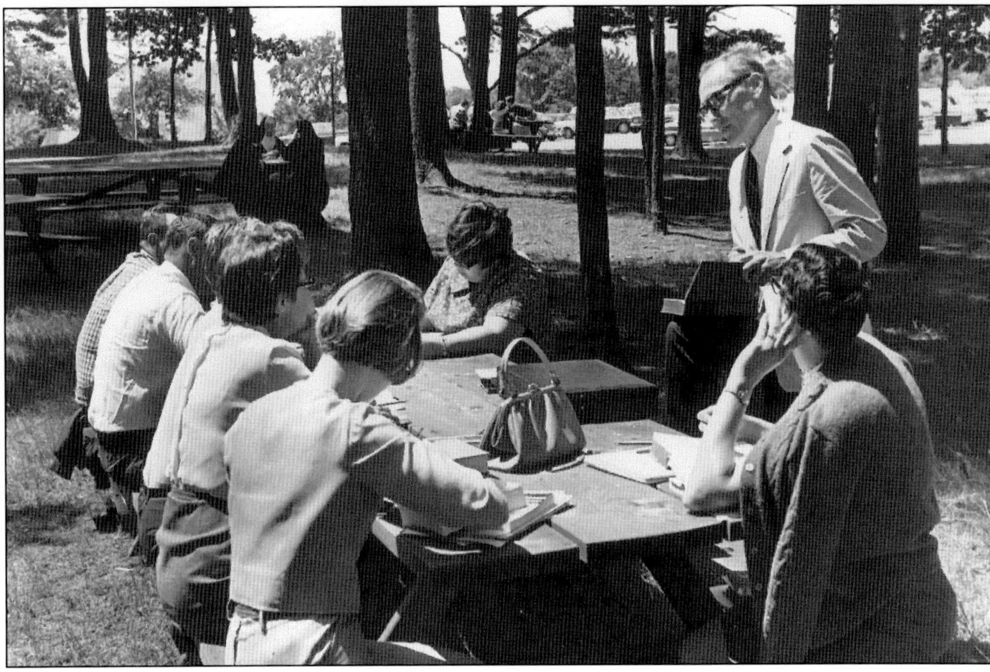

The picnic tables in the grove could be used for classes on fine days, particularly in the summer, when many teachers arrived to take course work, either to keep up certification or to work toward master's degrees, given at Gorham starting in 1964.

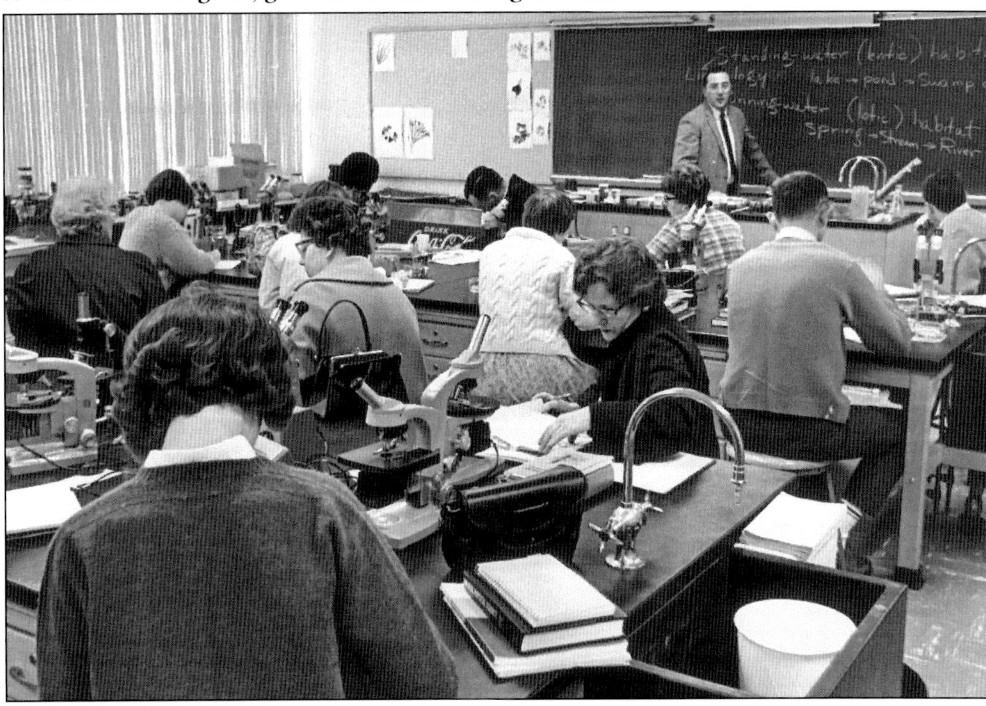

Here, Remo Riciputi teaches biology to another mixed-age group in the summer of 1967. It should be noted that nontraditional college students (those not going straight to college after high school) had come to be expected in all classes at the college.

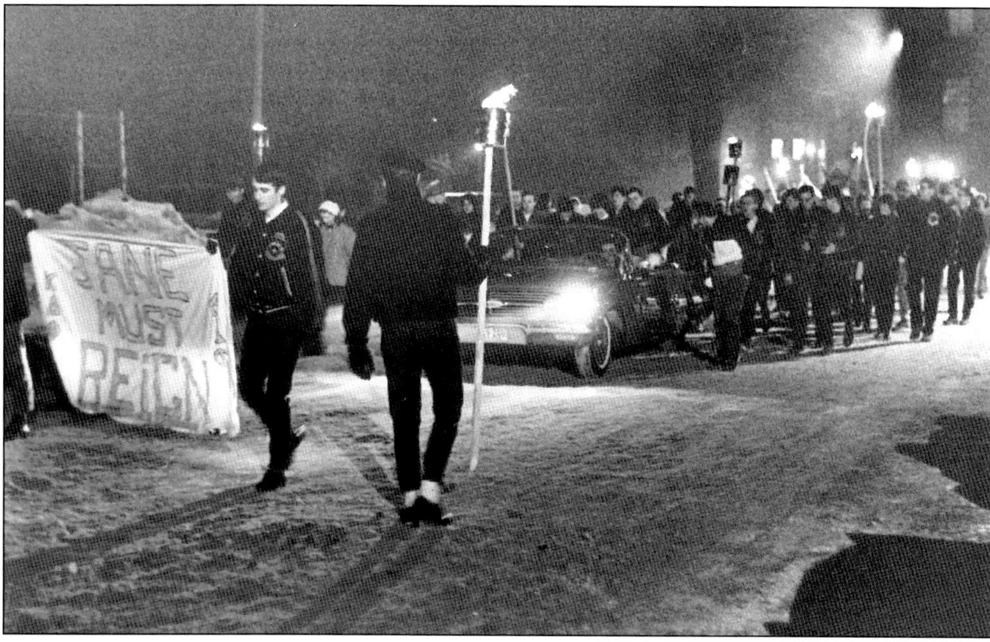

Preparations for Winter Carnivals featured elections for a "mayor" and "queen." Queen candidates were nominated by clubs, of which the fraternities were most active, staging campaigns with torchlight parades. This one took place in 1967, but Jane did not reign that year.

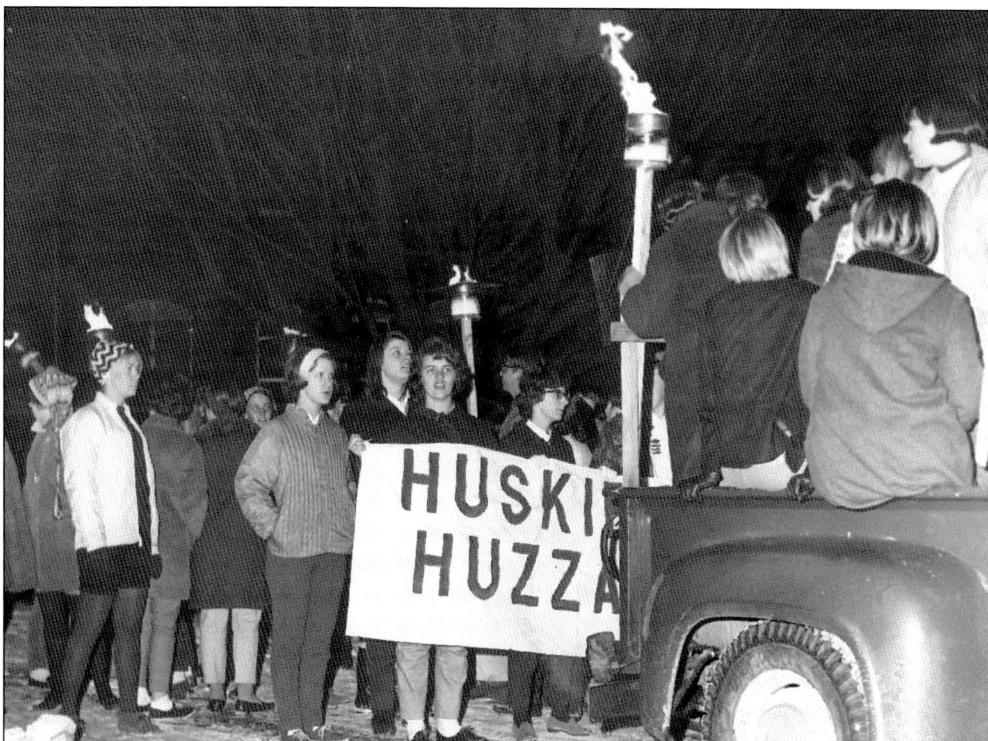

Torchlight processions also lighted mayoral campaigns and other events like the 1968 Huskies Huzzah, sponsored by the Student Council.

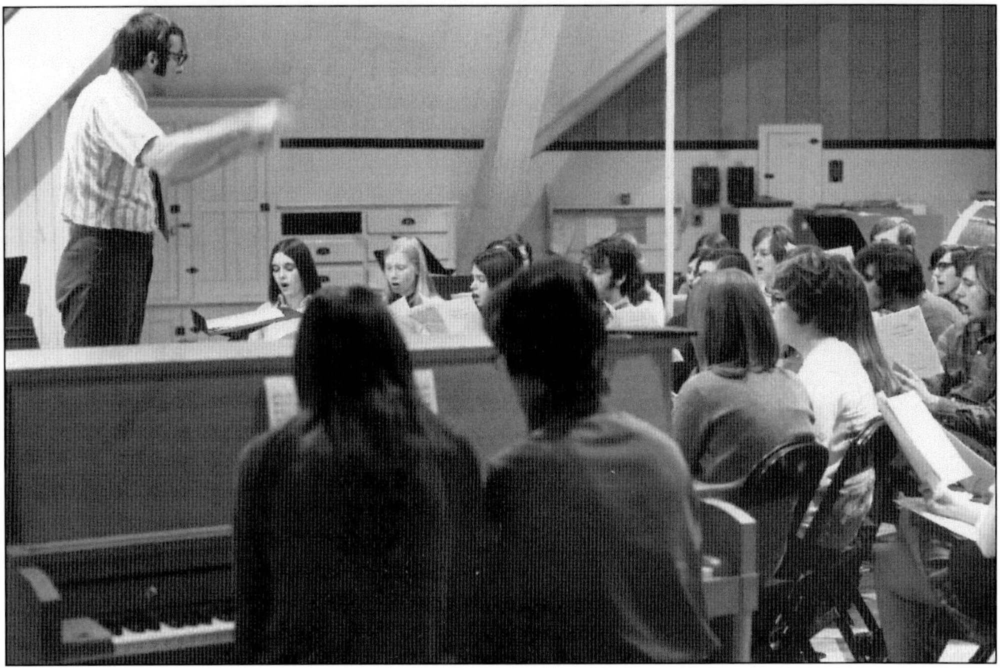

Gorham State College was the only such college offering a major in music. Music education expanded in the 1950s and 1960s, its courses eventually taking over the upper floor of Corthell Hall. Note the sloping ceilings of this classroom, where Ronald Cole is holding a class.

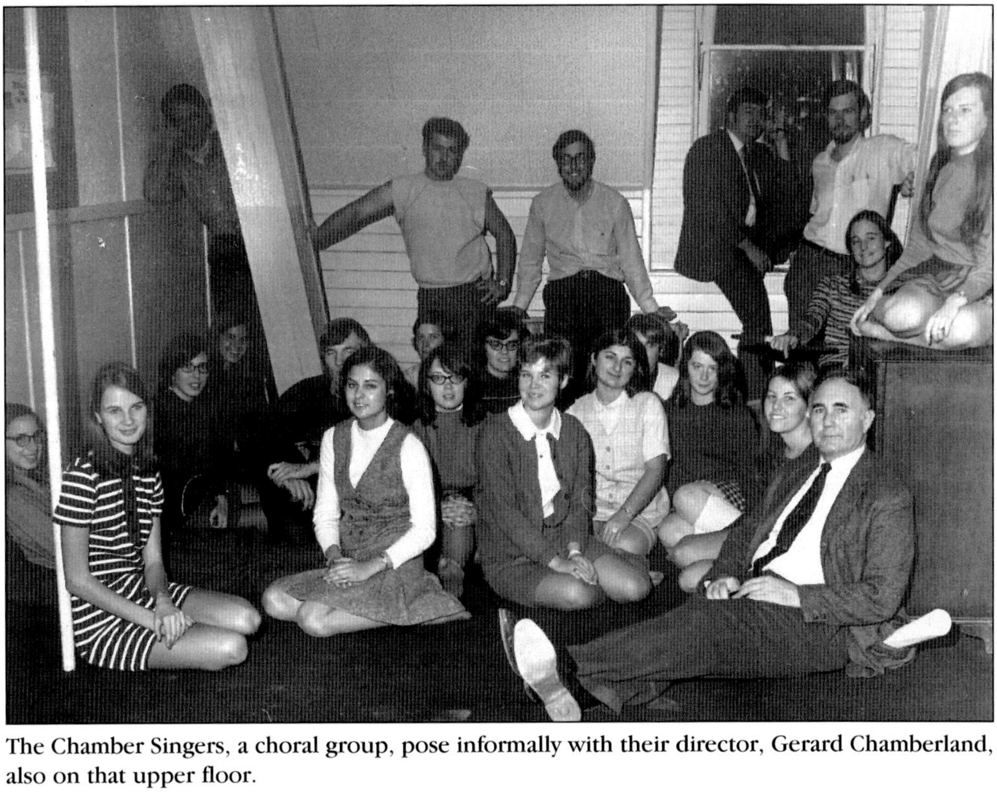

The Chamber Singers, a choral group, pose informally with their director, Gerard Chamberland, also on that upper floor.

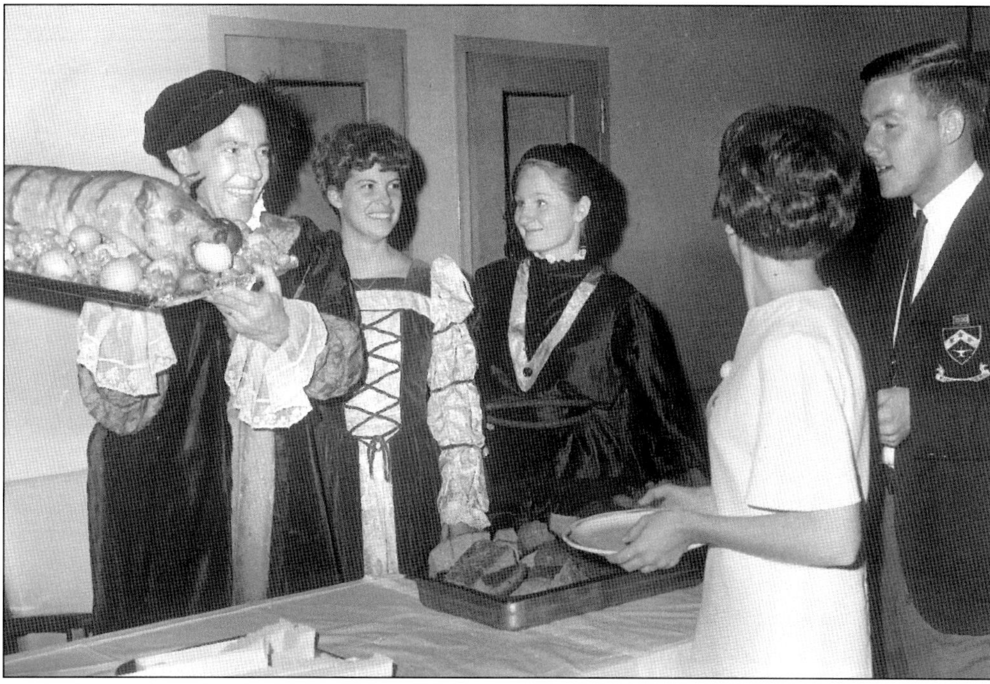

For some years, the music department sponsored a Medieval Feast in the dining room, at which guests dined on appropriate foods and were entertained with period music.

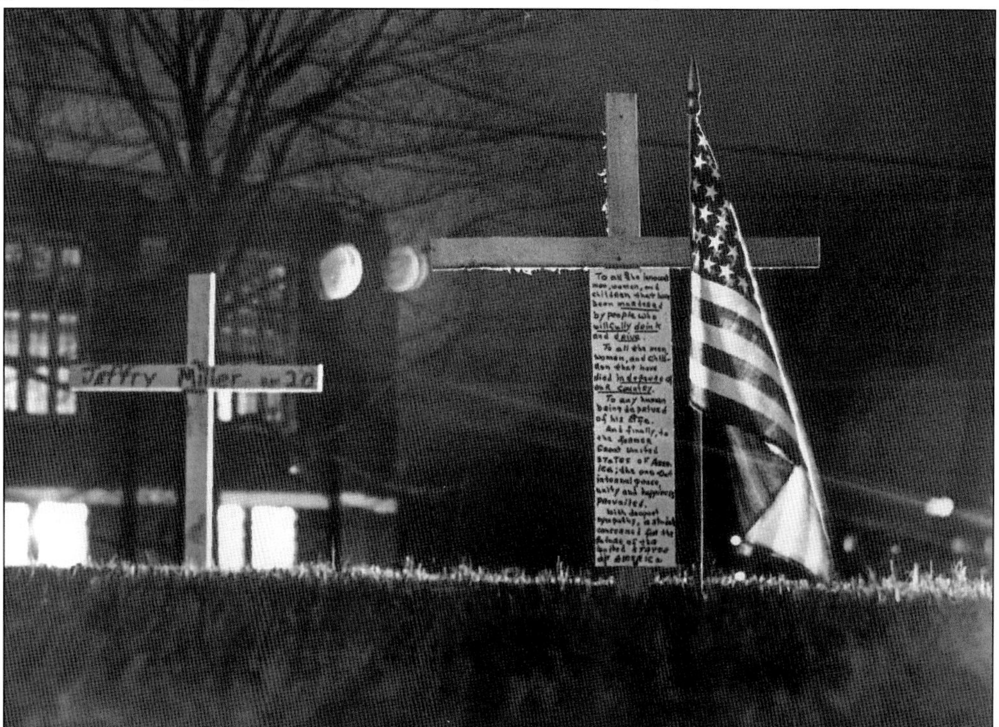

The shootings at Kent State in May 1970 led to demonstrations nationwide. Gorham students erected these signs of grief and protest.

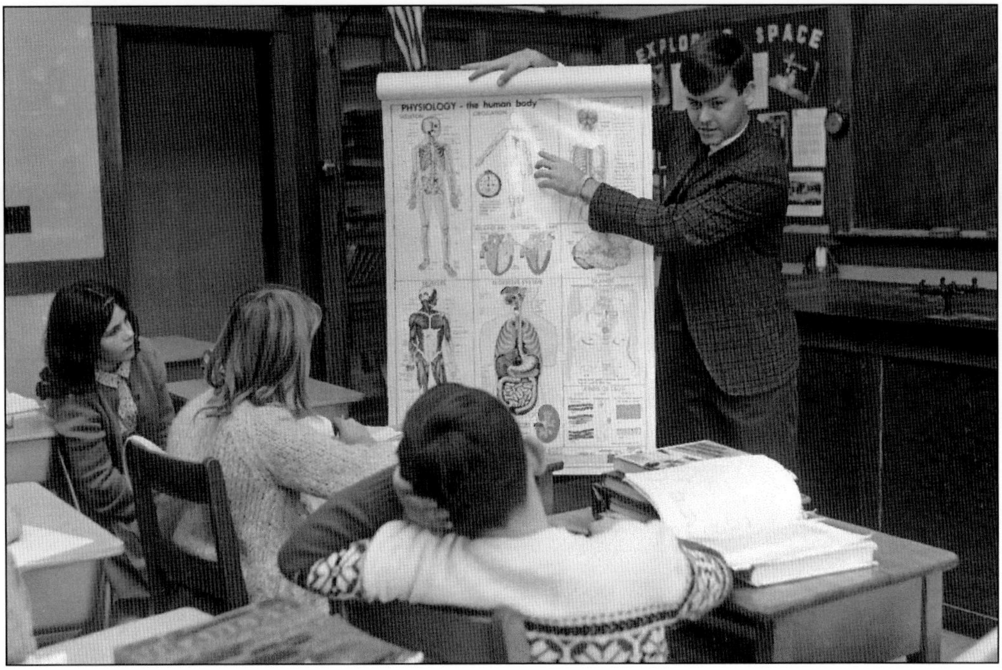

Practice teaching remained part of the program in education, as students spent a semester in a school. This image suggests that topics as well as techniques would have changed.

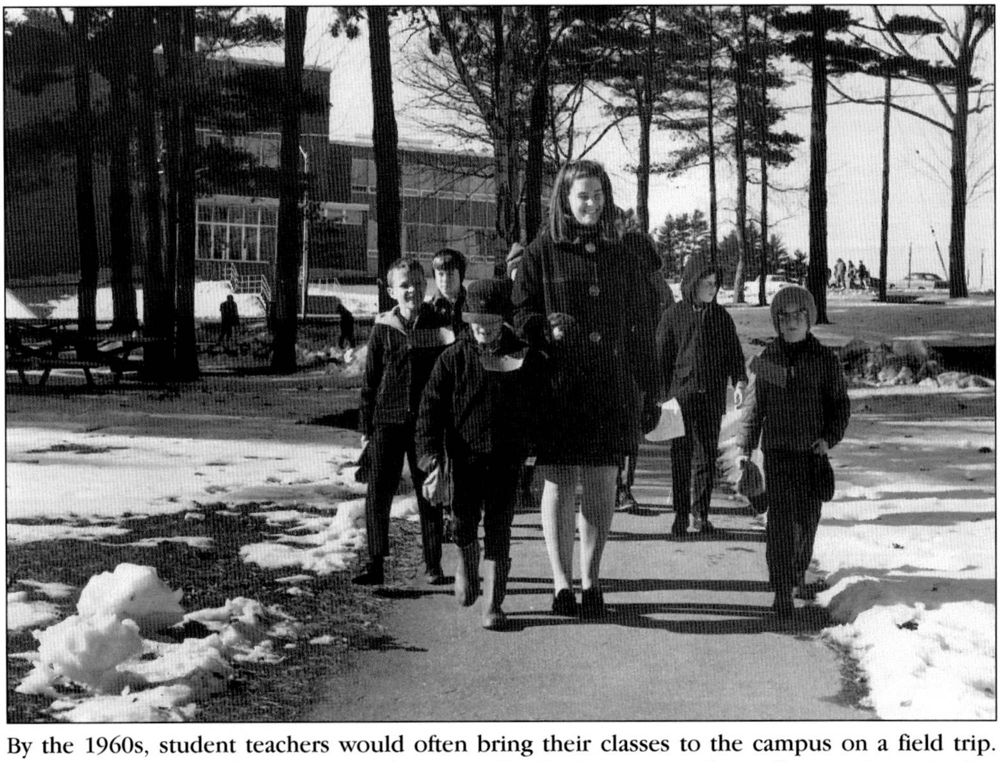

By the 1960s, student teachers would often bring their classes to the campus on a field trip. One attraction was the Museum of Man, with displays set up by college anthropologists and geographers.

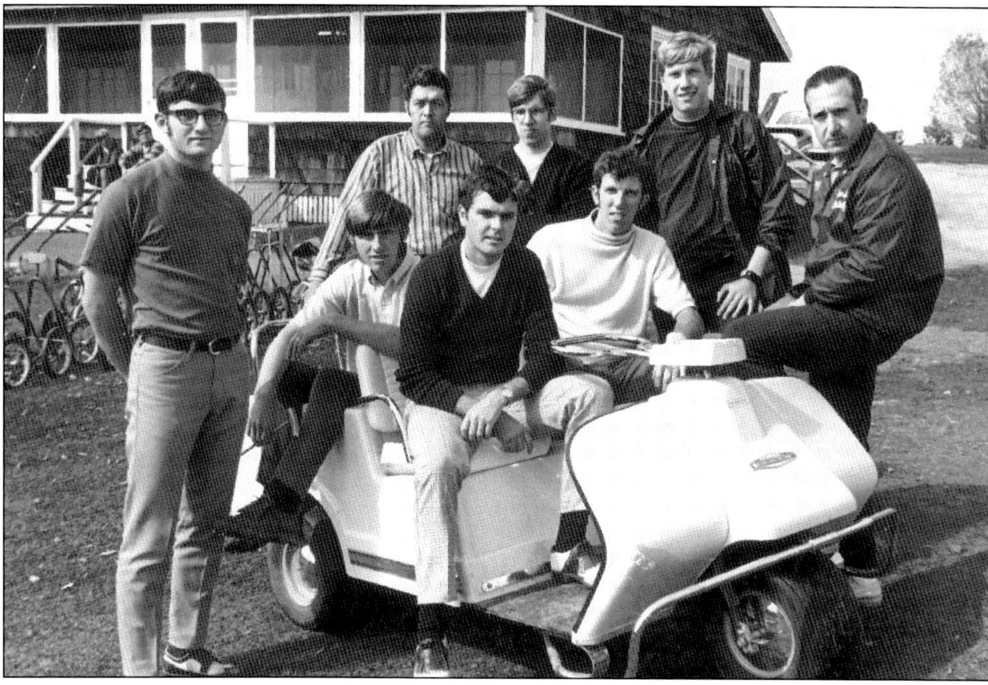

Competitive athletics took many forms. Coach Richard Costello (right) poses with the 1969–1970 golf team. They are, from left to right, as follows: (front row) George Kouloungis, Don Holden, Tim Flanagan, and Robert Blanchette; (back row) Dick Crosby, Rick Shea, and Jay Saurman.

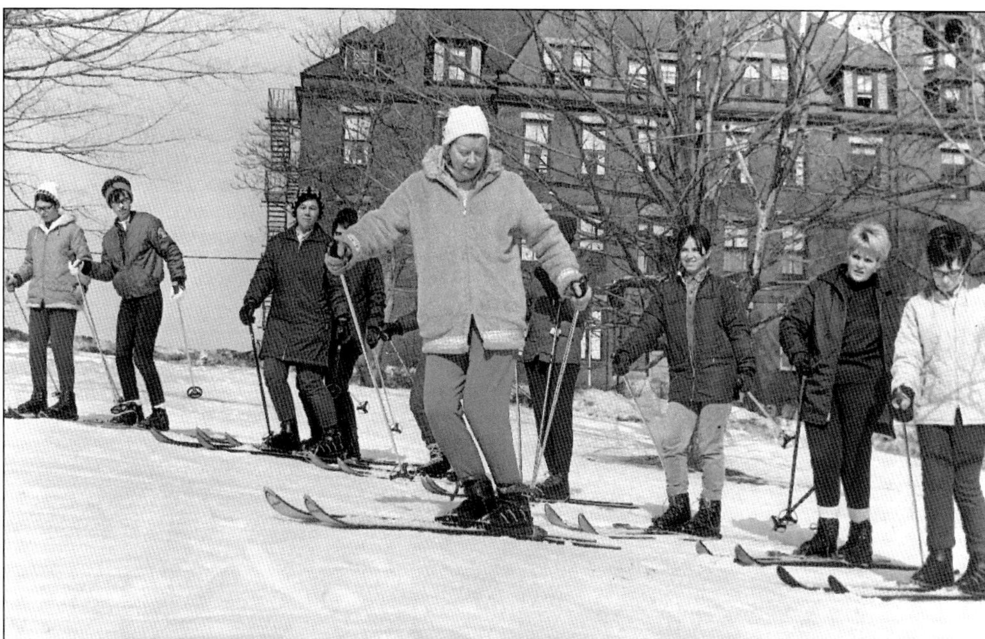

Numerous sports classes flourished. Until a planting of shrubbery was installed there, the sloping lawn near Robie Hall was used by Jeanette Goodwin for beginning ski classes and by neighboring children for sledding.

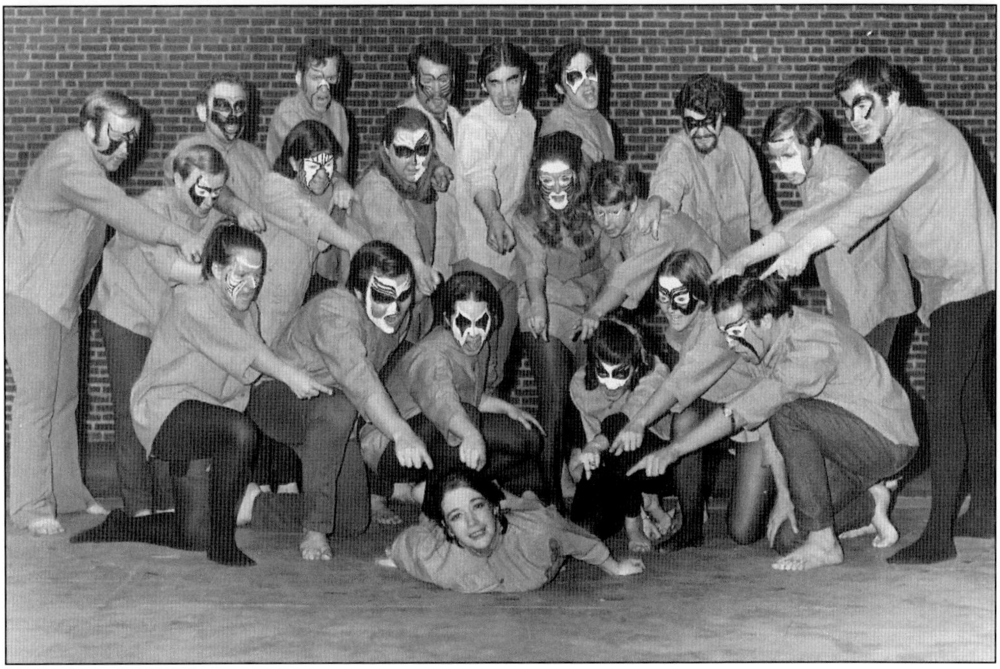

With the addition of specialized courses, theatrical performances were polished. In 1969, Susan Pickett (center, front) starred in *The Good Woman of Setsuan*, a production that incorporated music and varied visuals, including the painted faces of the rest of the cast. (One Chinese theater convention left faces of innocents unpainted.) Face designs were by Alan Bray '71.

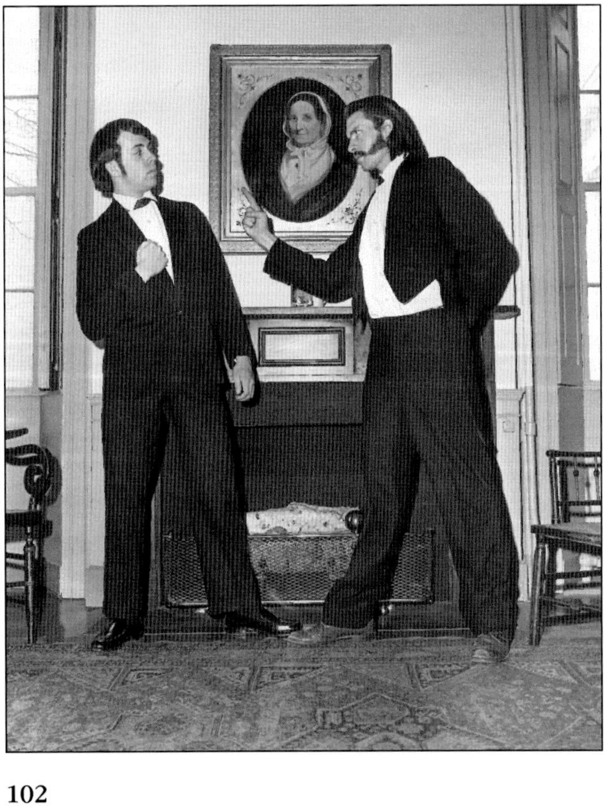

Louis Clark II (left) and Timothy Wooten faced off in *The Poor of Portland*, a play adapted from the 19th-century melodrama *The Poor of London*. Publicity pictures for this early 1970 presentation were taken in the McLellan Mansion in Portland.

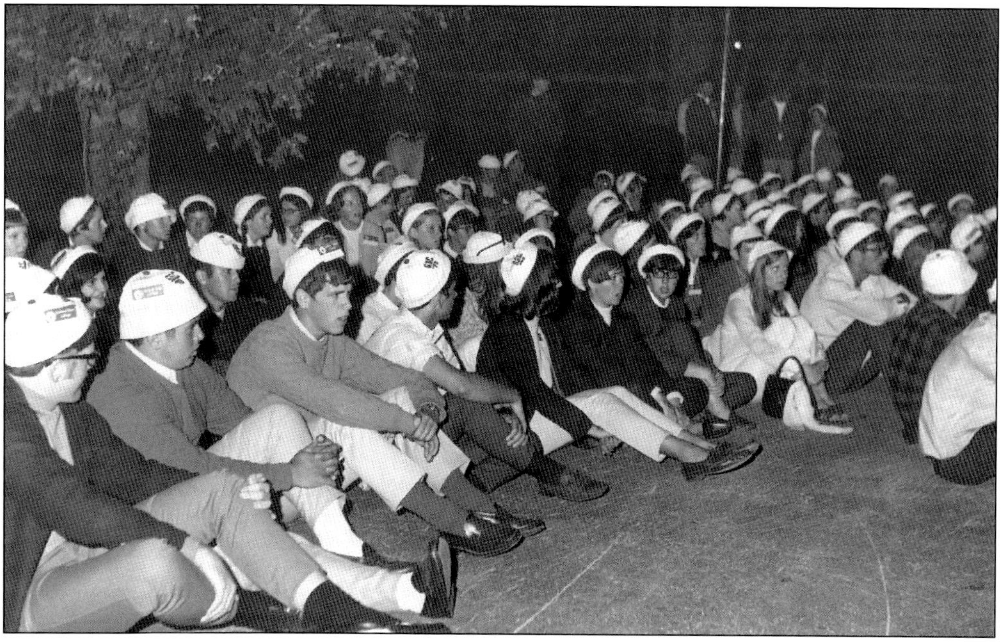

Freshmen at Gorham did not have to undergo wearing mandatory beanies for their first weeks, but did for a few years have special caps at orientation. This group—gathering in the grove and wearing hats with "GSC '73"—would have been unaware that by 1973, there would no longer be a "GSC."

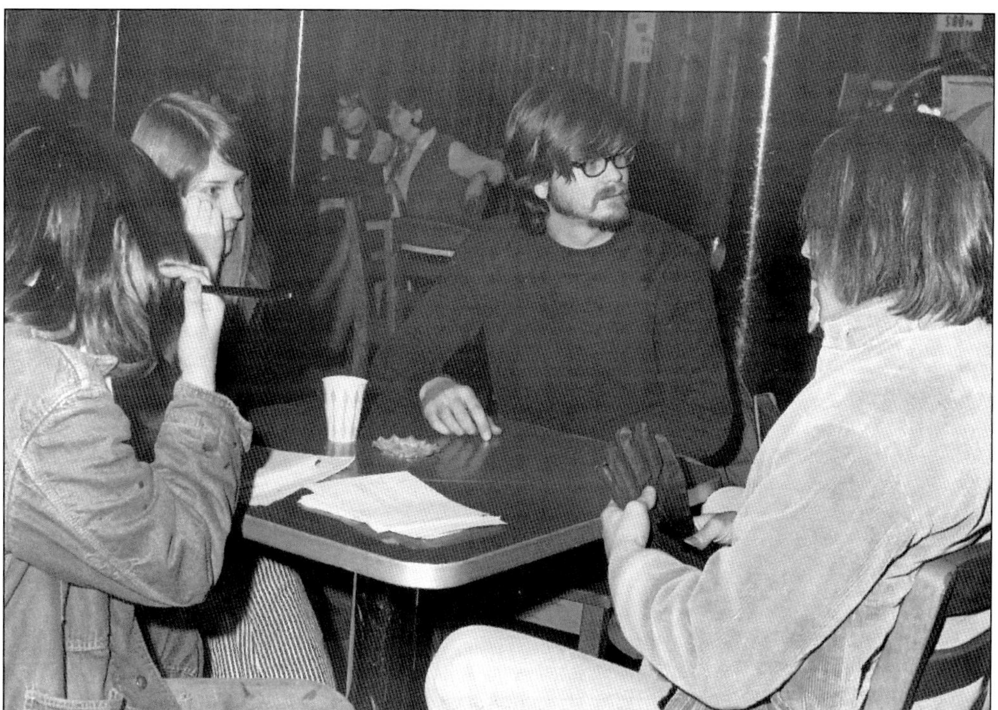

For years before 1970, a social center on campus was the old cafeteria located in the basement of Corthell Hall.

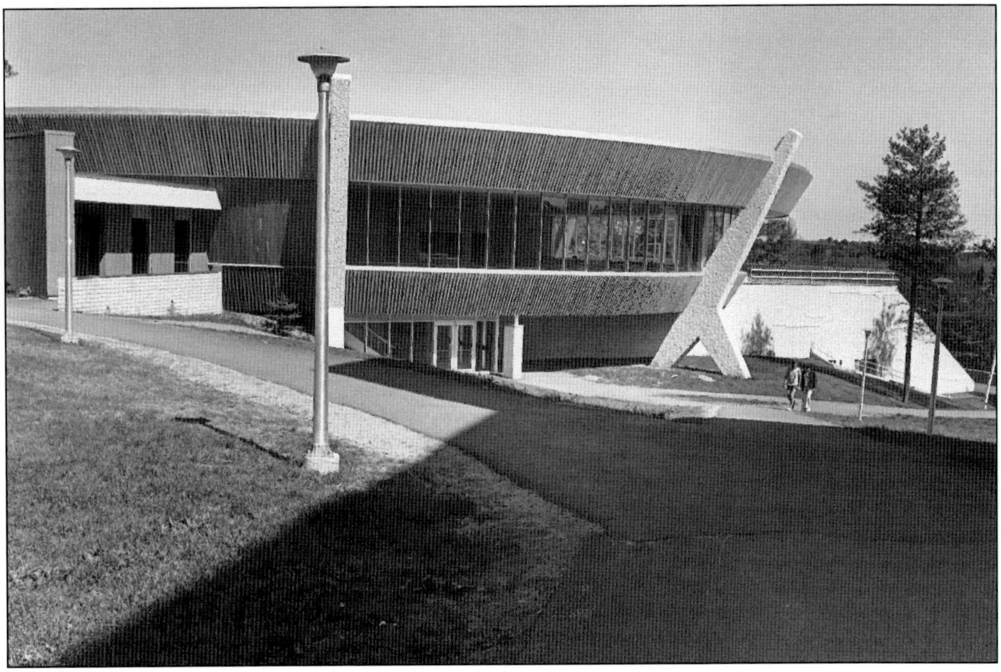

In the late 1960s, work began on a dining facility/student center constructed in an unusual round shape. It sat on a hillside so that both upper-level dining rooms and lower-level student center (snack bar, bookstore, meeting rooms, and open space) could be entered from the ground level.

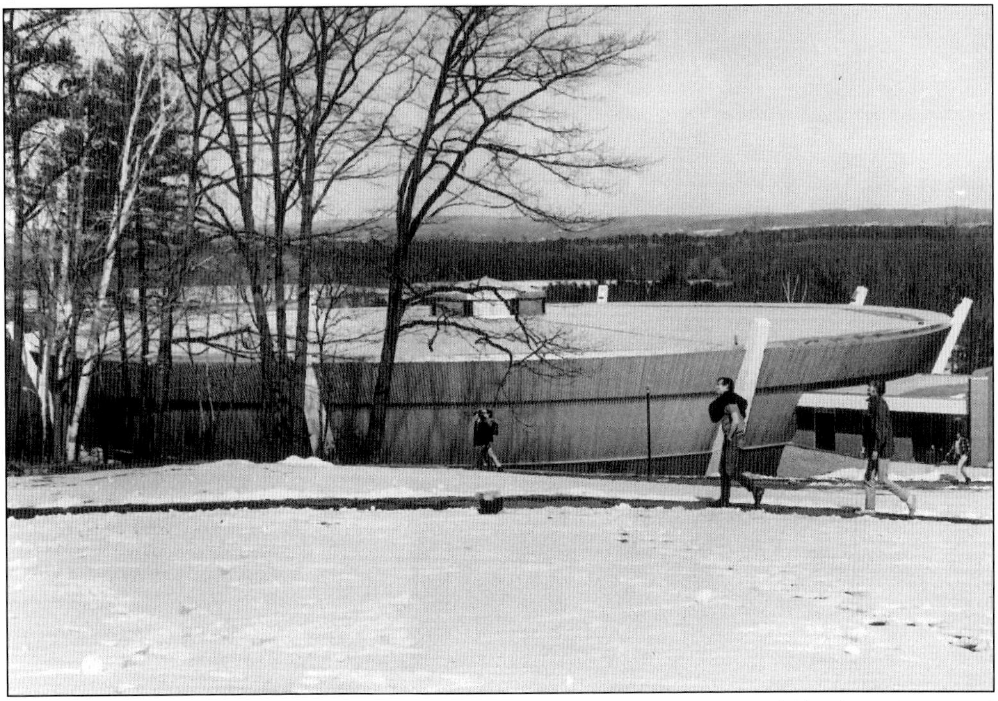

Completed in 1970, the building (called "the Spaceship" for its shape) would be formally named the Kenneth T.H. Brooks Student Center in 1992 to honor the fourth and last chief administrator of the Gorham campus. (See page 106.)

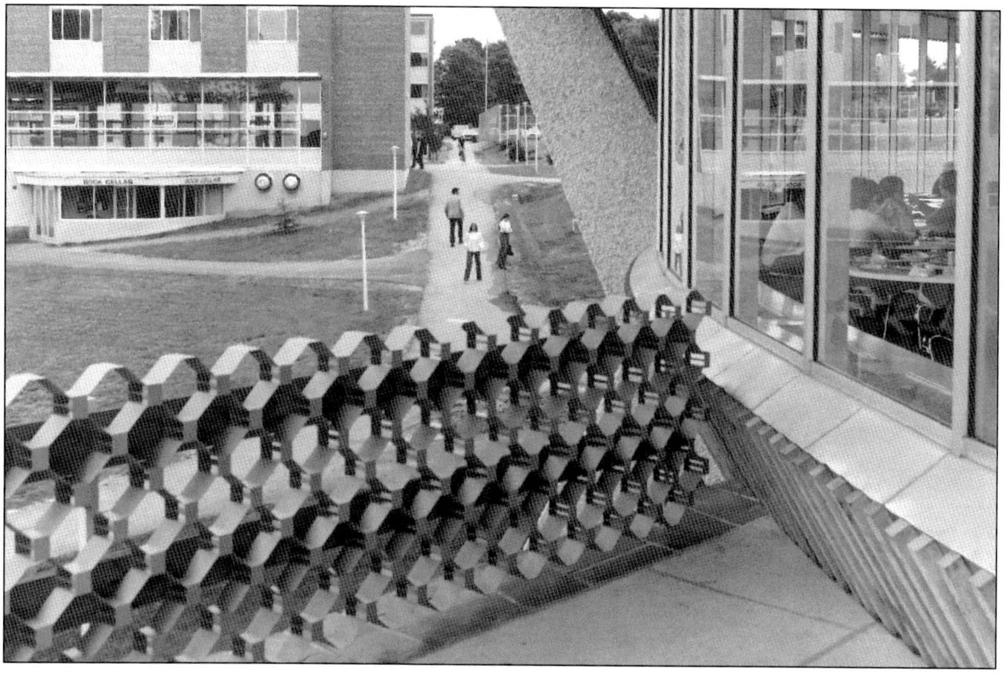

From the balcony outside the dining room, this view looks toward Upton Hall, showing some students walking from their meal. On the left is the Bookcellar, located in the lower level of Upton below the old dining space. The store would soon move to the student center.

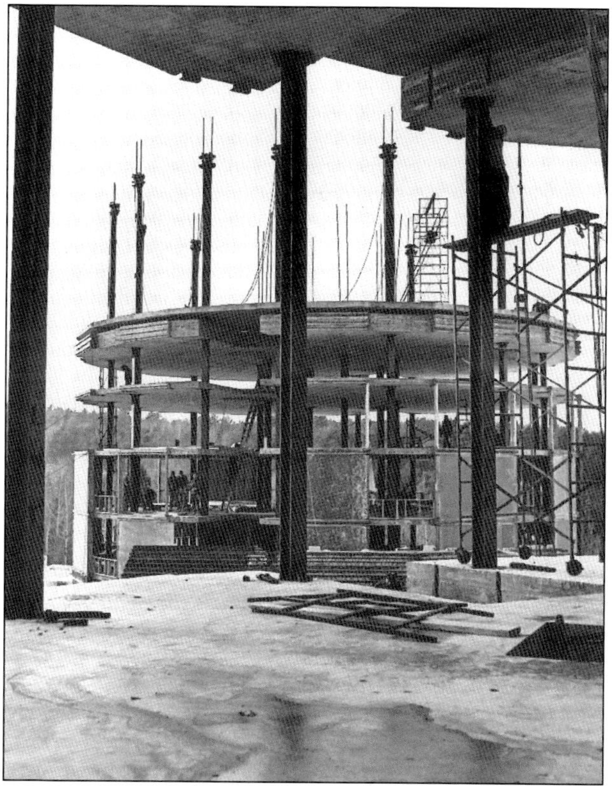

The two dormitories erected in 1969–1970 were also round, built that way to employ a construction technique in which the floors were poured, one after the other, at ground level, and then lifted into position, with solid blocks of wall set between. Here, some lower floors are already in place, with others being lifted.

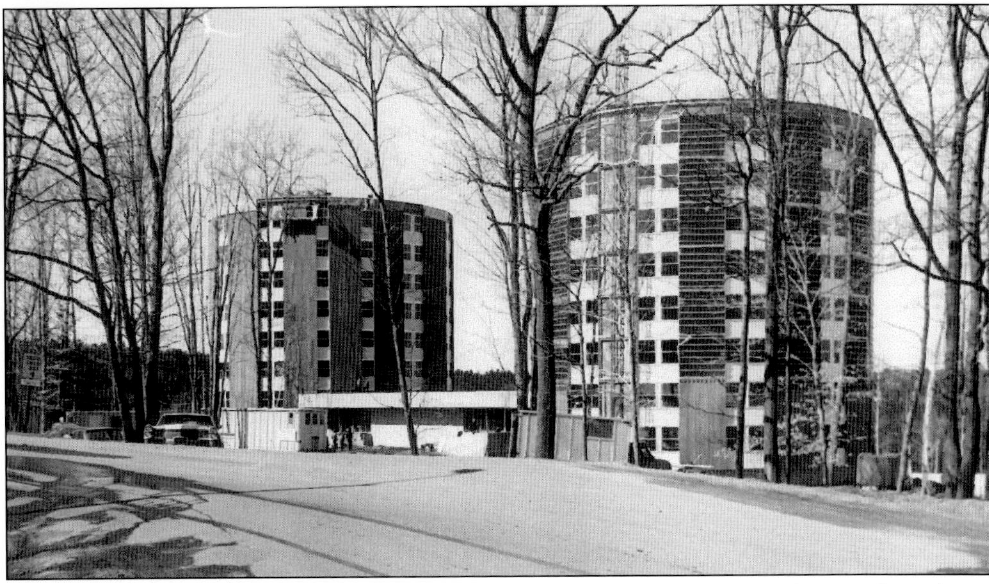

The wooden skins on the finished buildings were largely for looks. Breaking with tradition, these were not designated as either women's or men's dormitories but were expected to serve both groups.

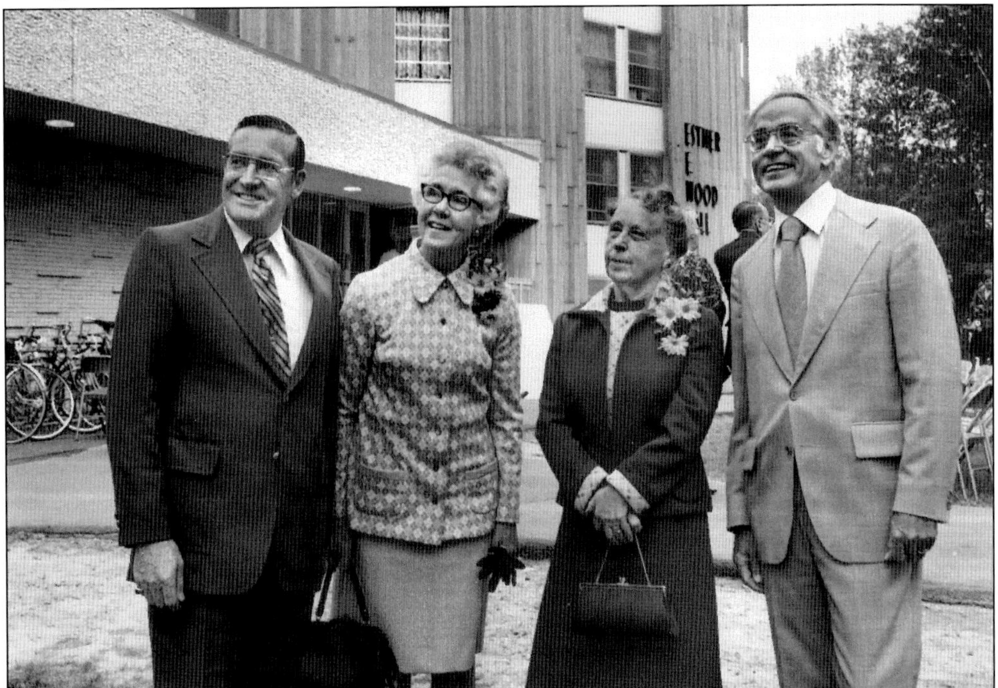

"The Towers" were named for Edna F. Dickey and Esther E. Wood, both of whom taught history and served as dean of women. (Dickey was dean for a much longer period, and Wood is best remembered for her enjoyable classes.) Shown at the 1973 dedication are, from left to right, Kenneth T.H. Brooks (former president of Gorham State College), Edna F. Dickey, Esther E. Wood, and Walter Fridinger (interim president of the University of Maine at Portland-Gorham).

Seven

University of Maine at Portland-Gorham, 1970–1977, and University of Southern Maine

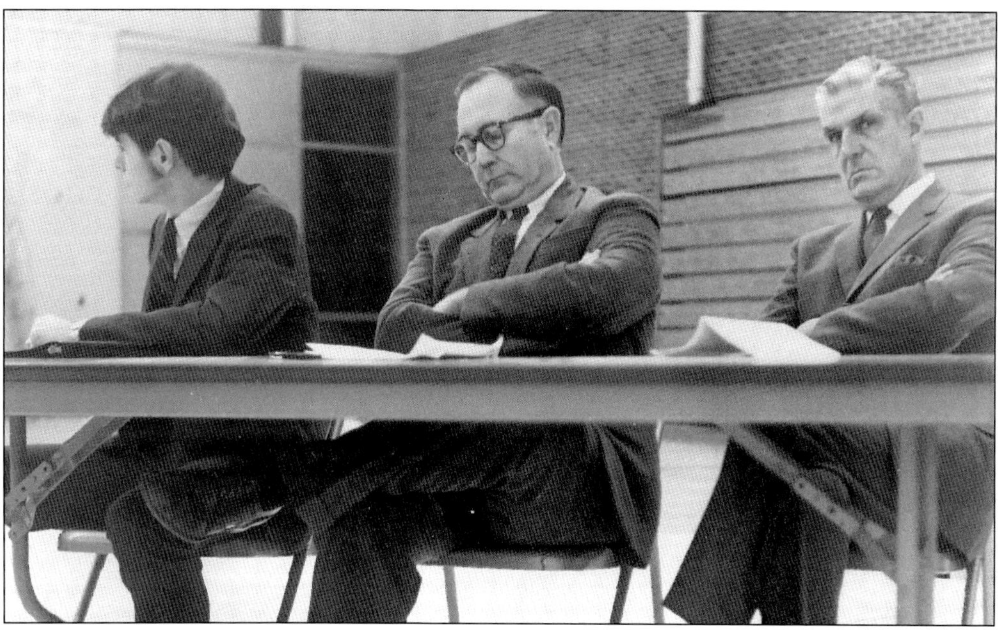

The establishment of a statewide university system was under discussion in Maine for years, the details taking much time to arrange. What should be the relationship of the state colleges to the Orono campus? (The University of Maine administrators suggested all institutions other than that at Orono should be two-year ones.) Gorham and Portland duplicated some offerings, so a merger would probably save money. Hearings were held by the new system chancellor, with differing views presented. Shown at a 1969 hearing in Gorham are Richard Dyer (student), Gerard Chamberland (music faculty), and Audway Treworgy (Gorham resident). The merger occurred in 1970.

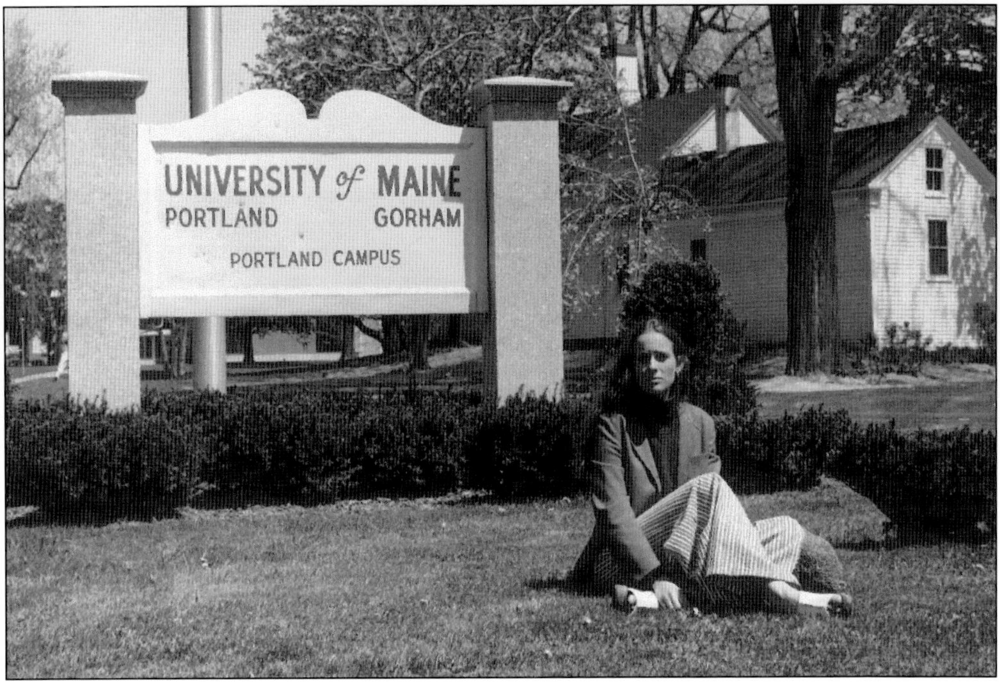

One shortening of "University of Maine at Portland-Gorham" (considering the popularity of Walt Kelly's comic strip) was "PoGo U." Some thought the sports teams should be the Possums. Others insisted the nickname was too undignified. The adoption of "University of Southern Maine" in 1977 provided dignity and stressed unity.

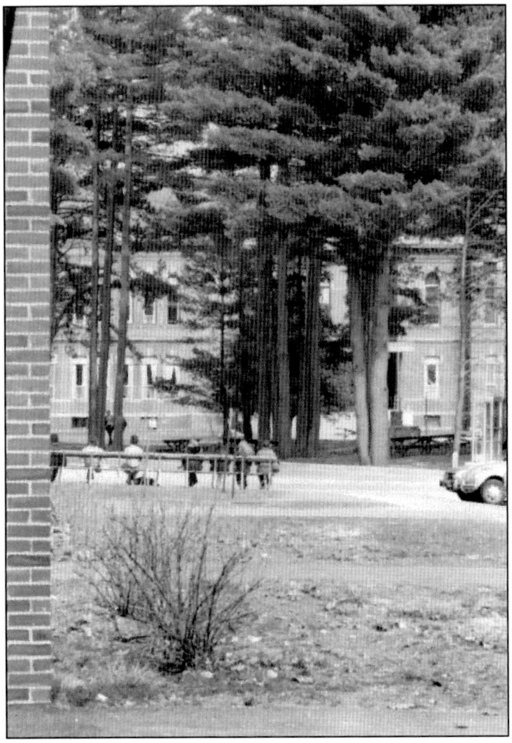

Bus service had to be established to connect the campuses, and students lining up to board or patiently sitting on outside benches became common sights. From a ground-level entry to Bailey Hall, this view looks past a bench toward Corthell Hall.

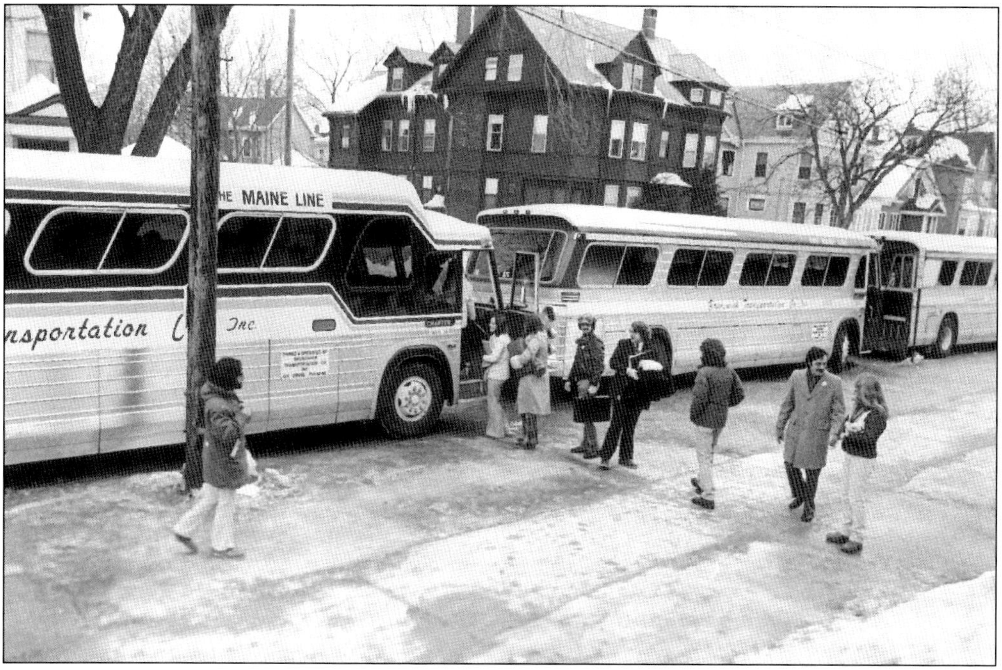

The original bus stop in Portland was outside Payson Smith, where students boarded vehicles to travel to the Gorham campus for courses not offered in Portland. (Usually only one bus arrived at a time. The number of vehicles in this photograph suggests a special occasion.)

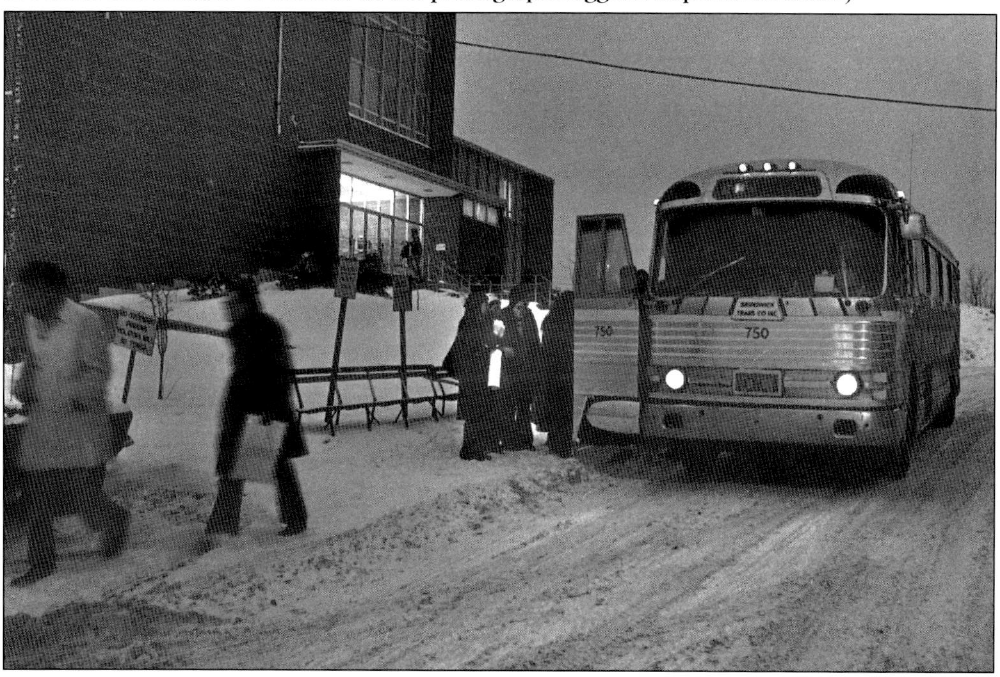

The buses served both day and evening classes, increasingly important when the Continuing Education Division was abolished and both part-time and full-time students could take classes either at night or during the day. Here, students climb aboard while others leave the bus outside Bailey Hall.

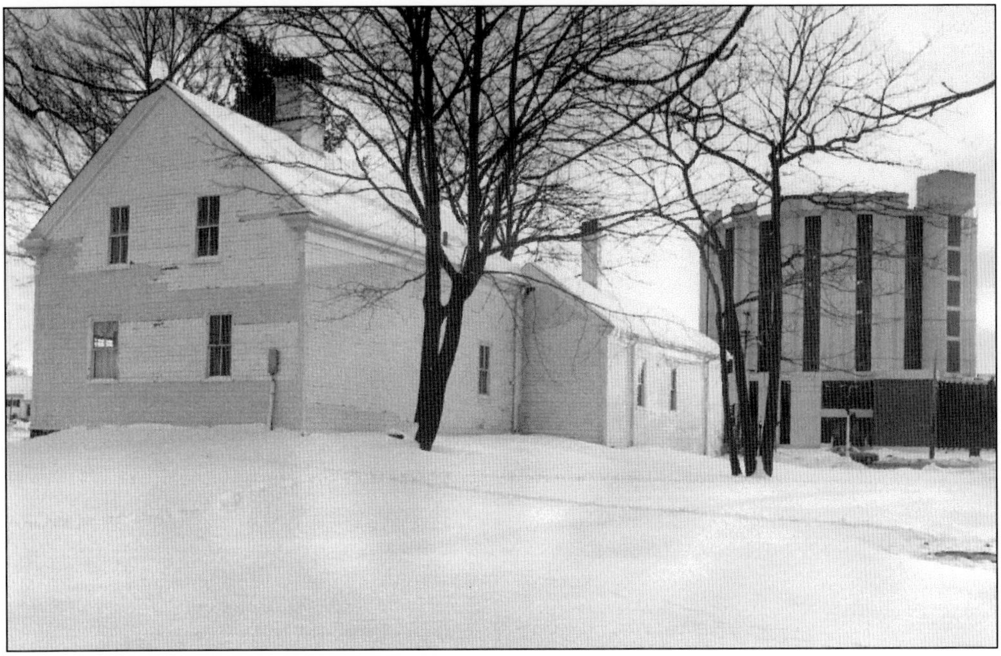

On property across Brighton and Deering Avenues from the Portland campus, another round tower was erected for the School of Law to share with the Center for Research and Advanced Study. Opened in 1972, the building (right) came also to hold the offices of the university president. This view juxtaposes the newest building with the campus's oldest, the old farmhouse, restored to hold alumni offices.

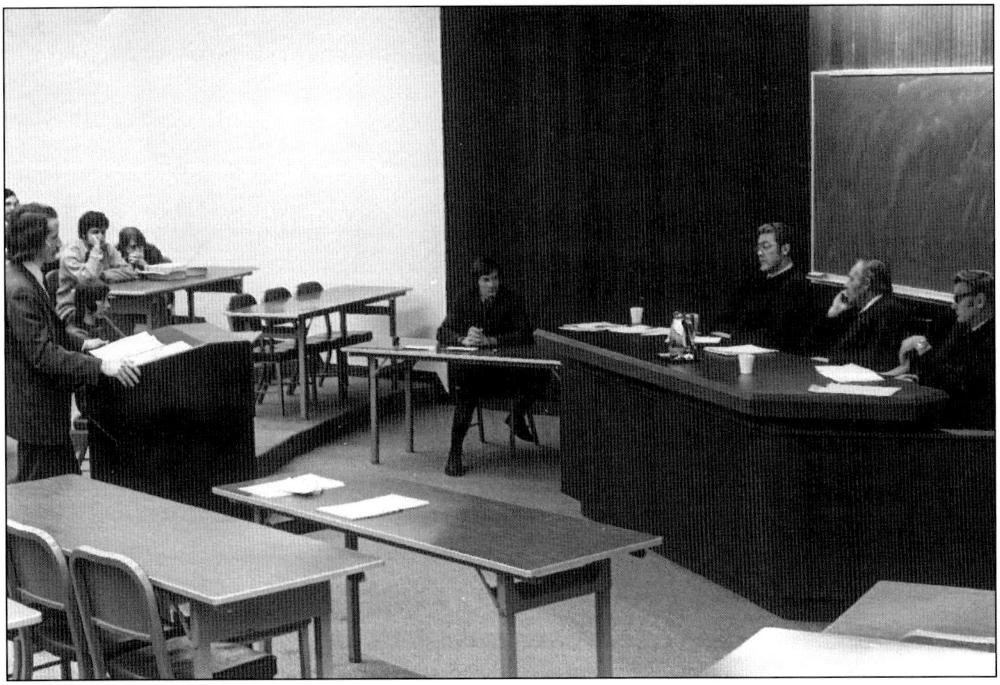

The new building included a "courtroom," in which a Moot Court competition was being held at the time of this picture.

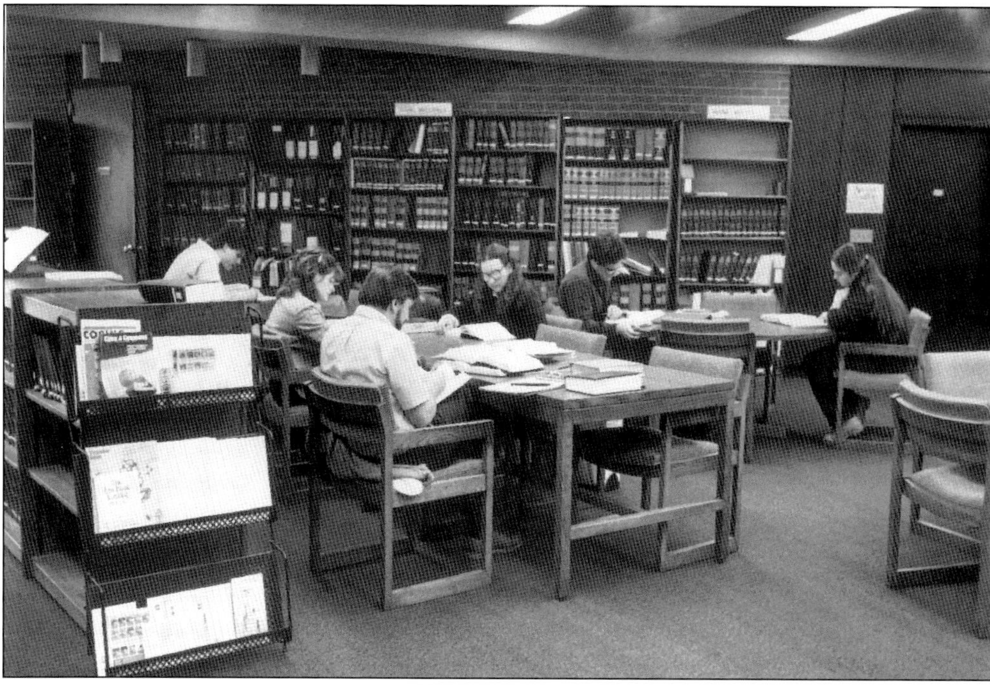

One floor was given over to the law library, dedicated to Donald Garbrecht, its longtime librarian (page 32).

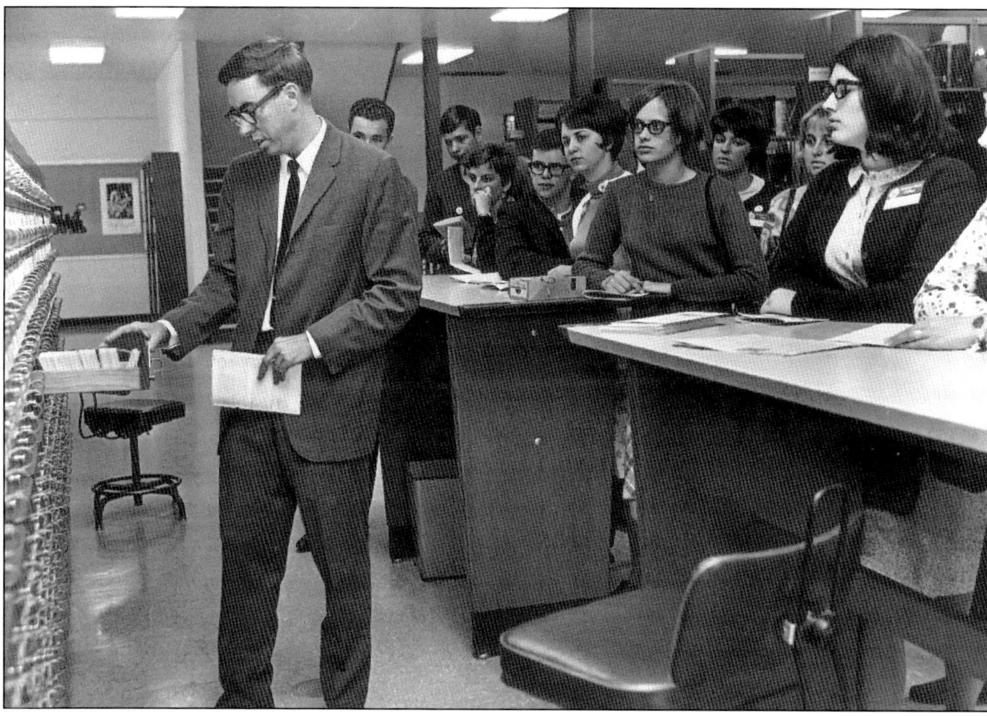

In the Bailey Hall library, Ronald McDougall explains to incoming classes how to use the card catalog. McDougall sometimes repeated such lectures for special research courses. Those card files can no longer be found, having given way to computers.

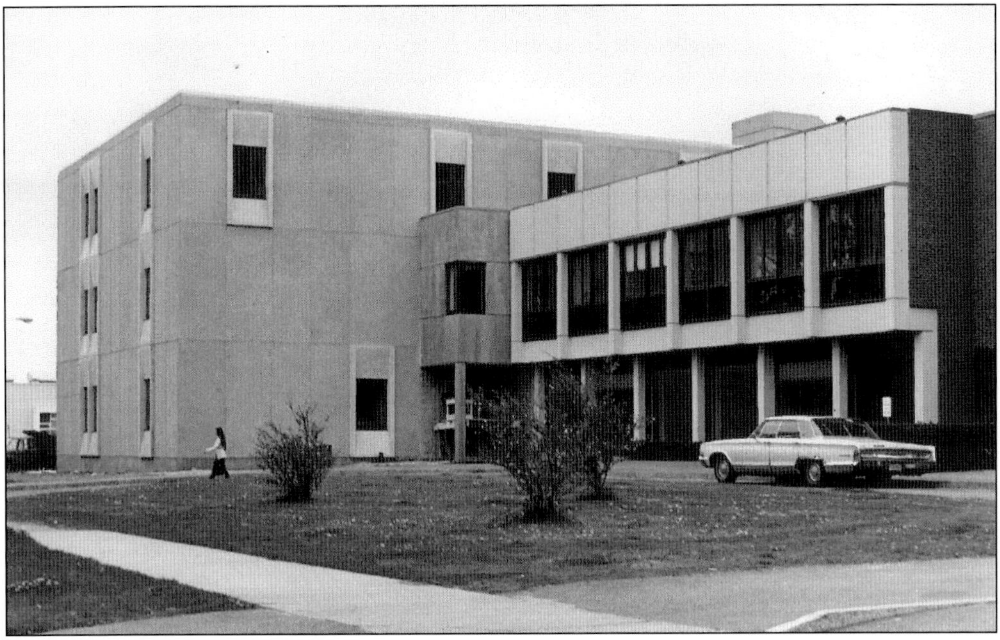

Although there was supposed to be a moratorium on all new construction on either campus until academic priorities and locations could be agreed on by faculty, a second science building was approved and begun on the Portland campus. It was completed in 1975. The departure from agreements was unsettling.

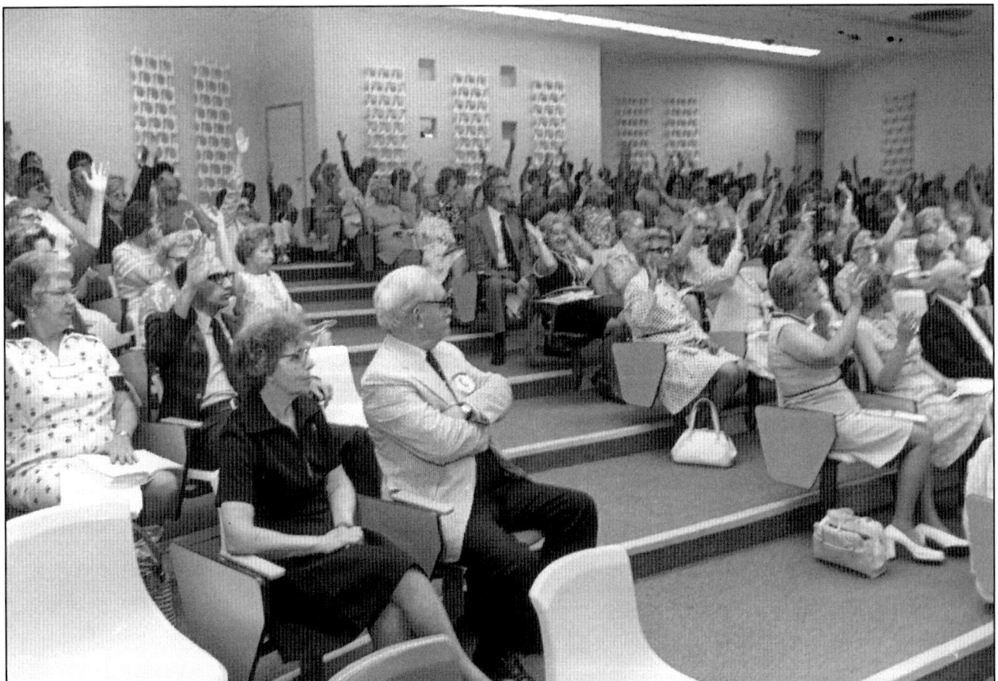

Questions of cooperation extended beyond faculty, staff, and students. When the Gorham Alumni Association voted in 1975 to merge with other alumni groups, there was, as can be seen in facial expressions and body language, real opposition. Supporters of the idea stressed unity.

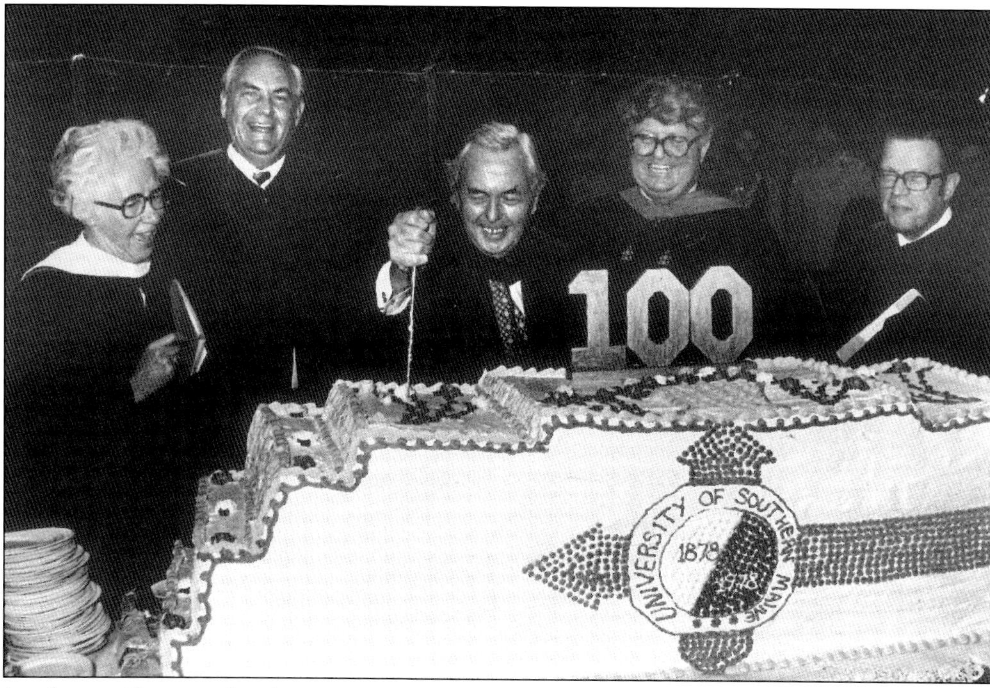

Another unifying undertaking was a centennial celebration in 1978, involving convocations, concerts, exhibitions, and a party with a huge cake. Former British Prime Minister Harold Wilson, a keynote speaker, cut the first piece, with Edna Dickey (Centennial Committee chairman), Kenneth Allen (acting president), Patrick McCarthy (chancellor), and Francis Brown (trustee chairman) looking on.

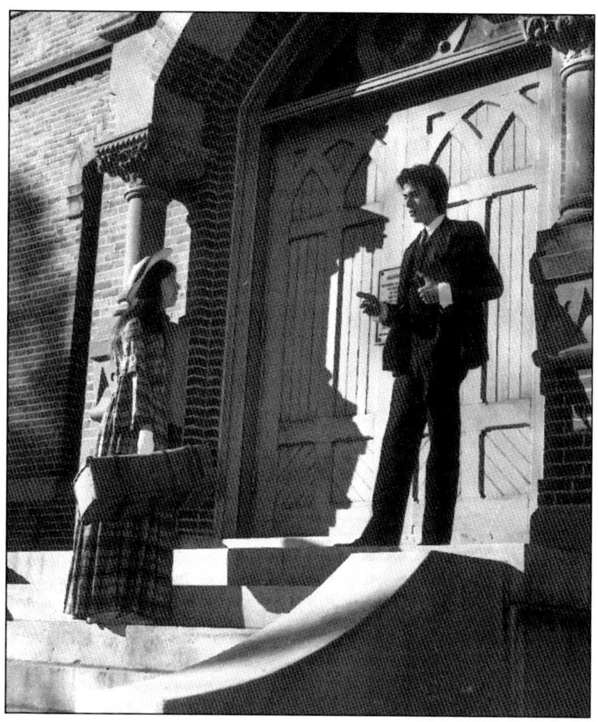

Written by theater major Carole Bohannon, *Strawberries on the Hill* was performed by the department for the occasion. Standing at the south doorway of Corthell Hall, Todd Collard (as Mr. Corthell) greets an unidentified incoming student.

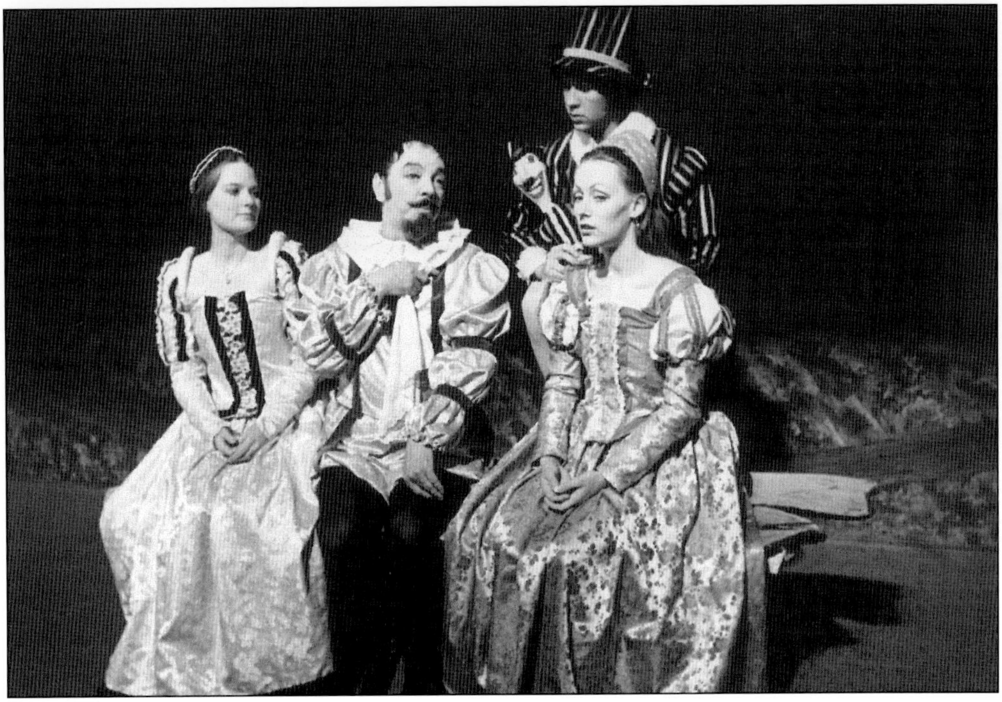

Theatrical presentations were given on both campuses. The cast members of a 1975 performance of *As You Like It* are, from left to right, Diane Whiton, Albert Duclos (drama professor), and Marianne Owen, with Edward Romanoff standing behind them.

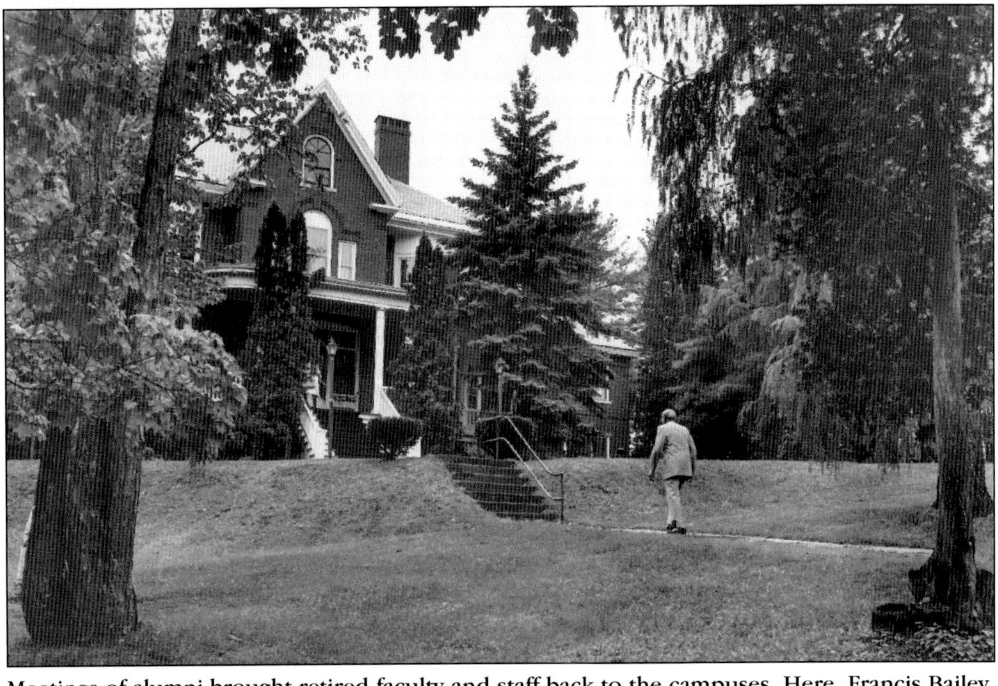

Meetings of alumni brought retired faculty and staff back to the campuses. Here, Francis Bailey, principal of the Gorham Normal School and later president of Gorham State Teachers College, walks to a gathering at the house in which he had lived on campus.

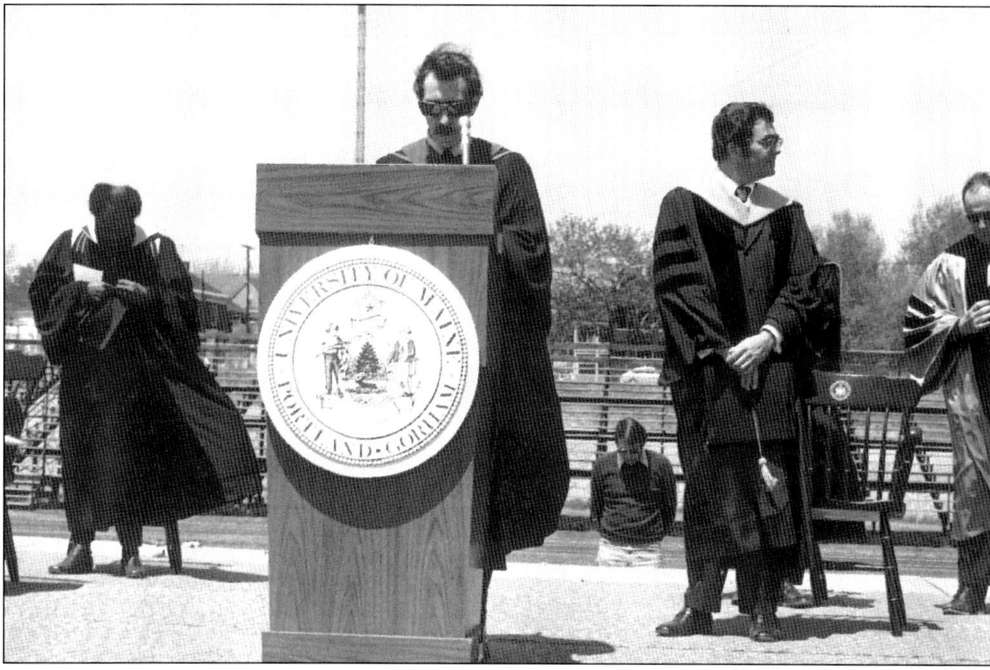

Because neither gym was large enough, early commencement ceremonies of the University of Maine at Portland-Gorham (UMPG) were held at Portland Stadium. Windblown robes on the stage in 1972 indicate how unsuited that location was for serious ceremonies. To the left of the unidentified speaker is Rev. Russell J. Peppe. To the right stands Louis Calisti, UMPG's first president, and Robert Estes, interim dean of arts and sciences. The opening of the Cumberland County Civic Center in 1977 (see cover) was welcomed.

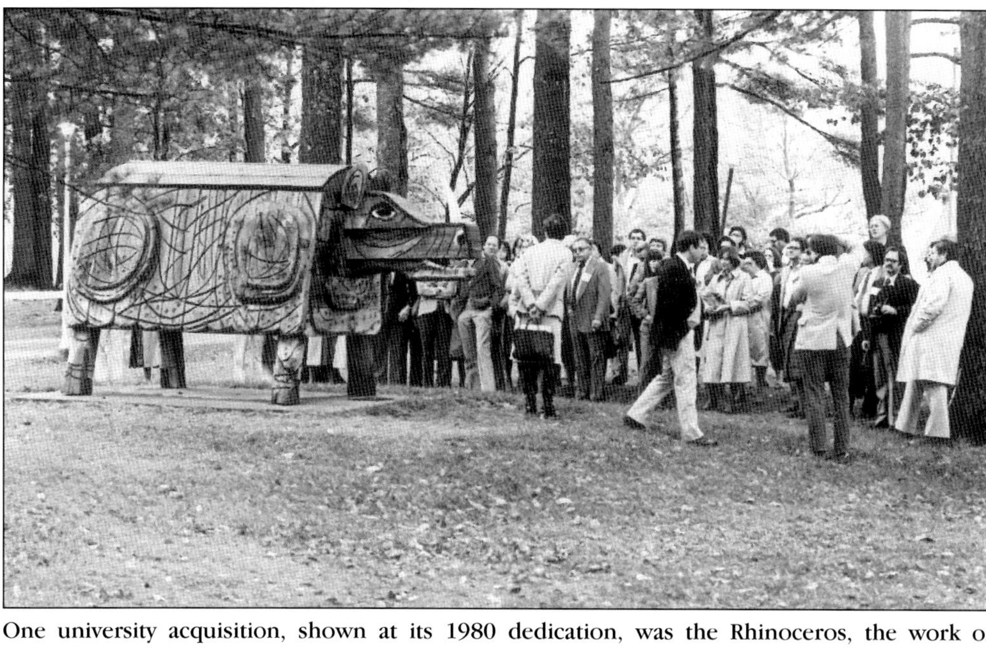

One university acquisition, shown at its 1980 dedication, was the Rhinoceros, the work of sculptor Bernard Langlais and acquired by the state as part of the taxes on his estate. Designed to stand out-of-doors, it was placed in the grove at Gorham.

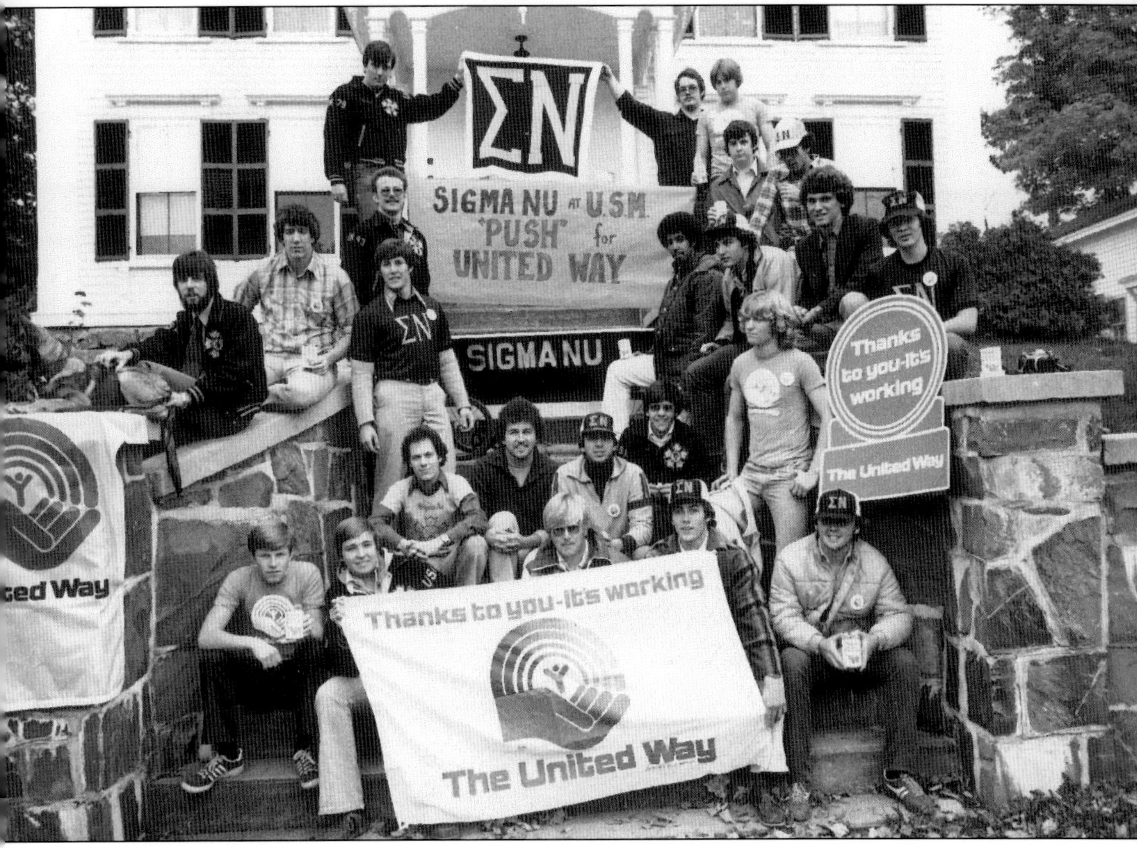

Fraternities date from Gorham's first "male club" of 1925–1926. At first, they were largely organizations of men who shared off-campus housing, adopted a Greek name, and sponsored on-campus activities, earning prominent coverage in yearbooks. Two existed in 1948, three in the late 1950s. The groups then sought national affiliations, and six fraternities were in existence by the 1990s. Some acquired their own houses. In this 1979 photograph, brothers of Sigma Nu, founded locally in 1975, pose on the steps of their historic house, with the old bathtub (mounted on wheels) that they pushed from Gorham to Portland, collecting money for the United Way. Seated in front are unidentified, Alan Robitaille, Charles Hupper, Jeffrey Hill, and Kurt Elkanich, with James Handy, John Plante, Kim Lufkin, and Marc Poulin just behind. On the steps to the left of the tub stand Dennis Curran and Douglas Bell. At the other end are Carlos Franco and Mark Tibbits. The others, clockwise from the left, are Robert Levin, Dennis Creeden, Michael Martel, Michael Ashley, unidentified, unidentified, Mark Maroon, John Gilmer, Davis Chung, David Pease, and Robert Levin.

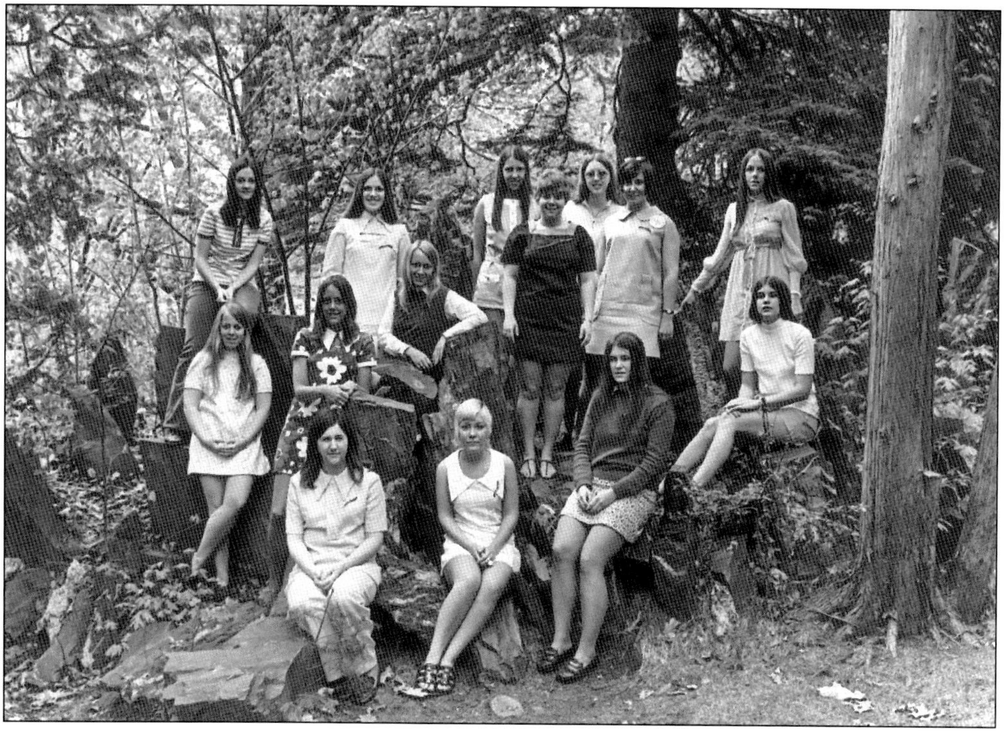

Sororities developed later. The first was Kappa Delta Epsilon, an academic sorority for women in education that was organized in 1966–1967. Here, members pose in the rock garden in 1971.

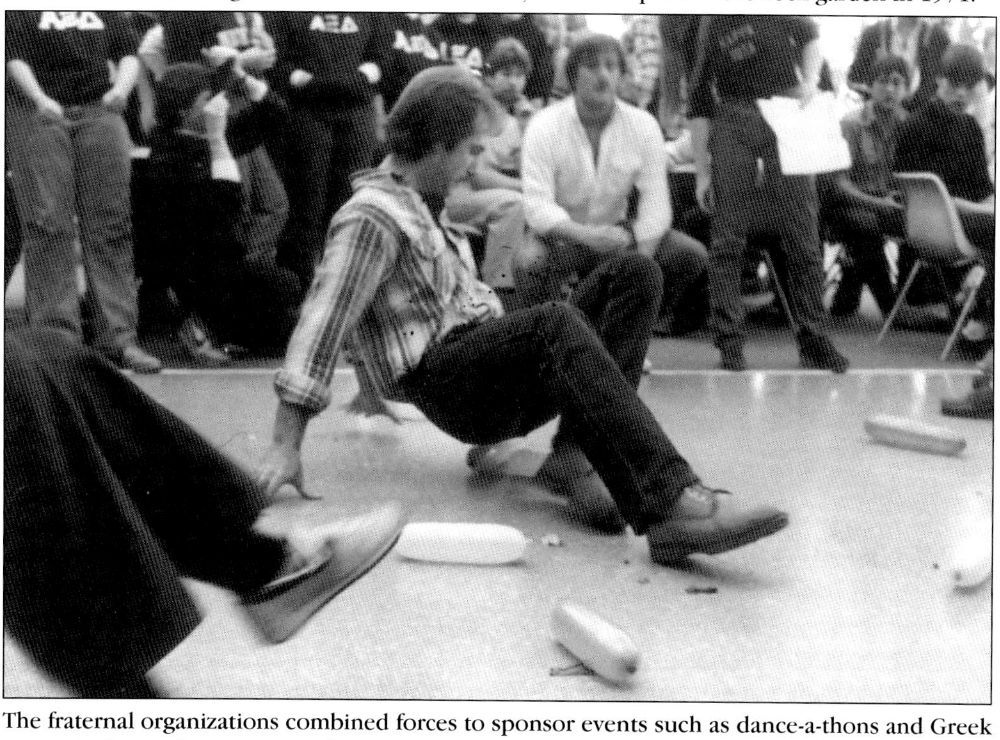

The fraternal organizations combined forces to sponsor events such as dance-a-thons and Greek games in the student centers. The 1983 games included a "balloon sit."

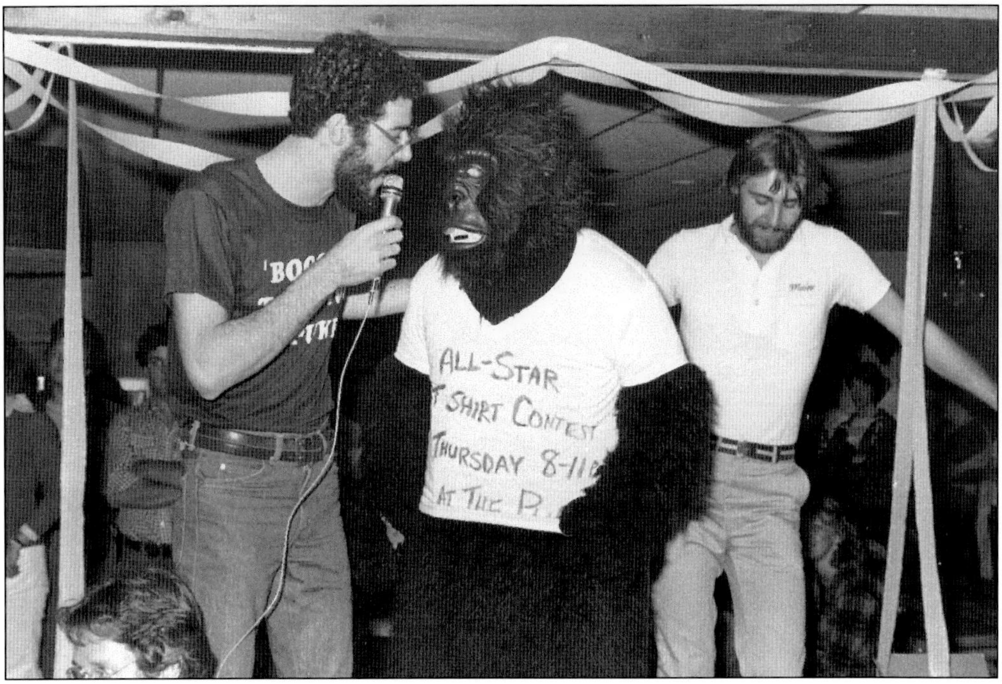

Dormitories also planned parties, such as the Anderson T-shirt night at the Pub, advertised by a visiting gorilla.

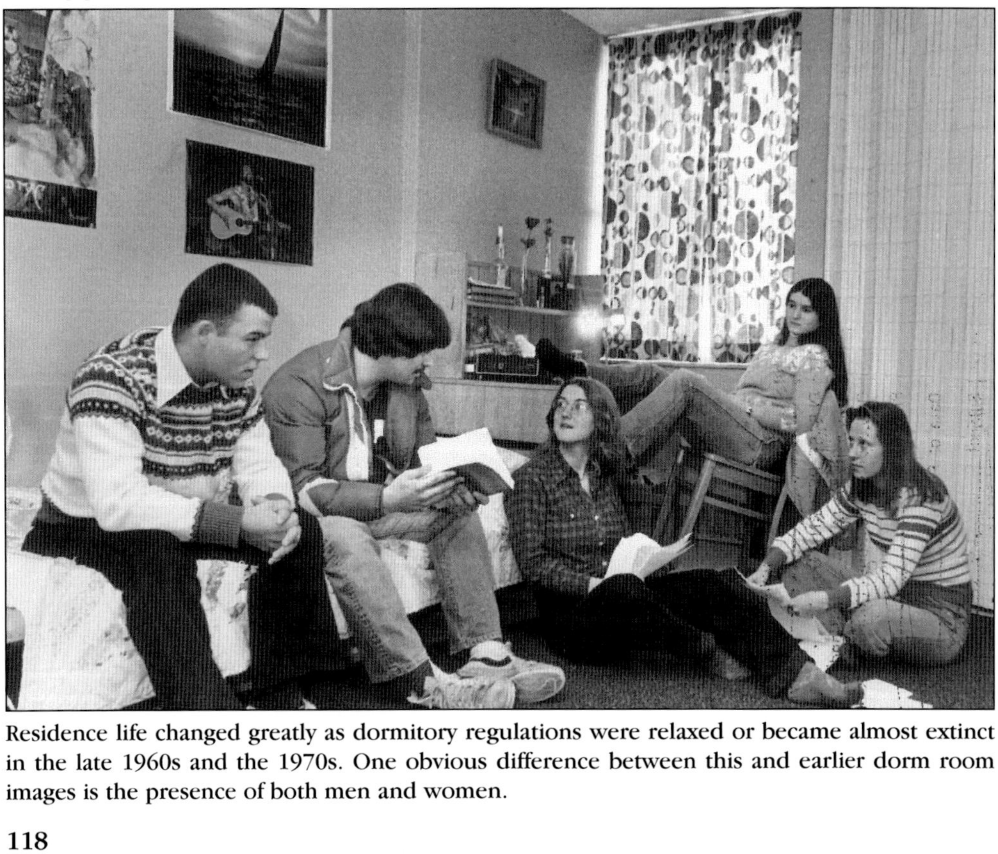

Residence life changed greatly as dormitory regulations were relaxed or became almost extinct in the late 1960s and the 1970s. One obvious difference between this and earlier dorm room images is the presence of both men and women.

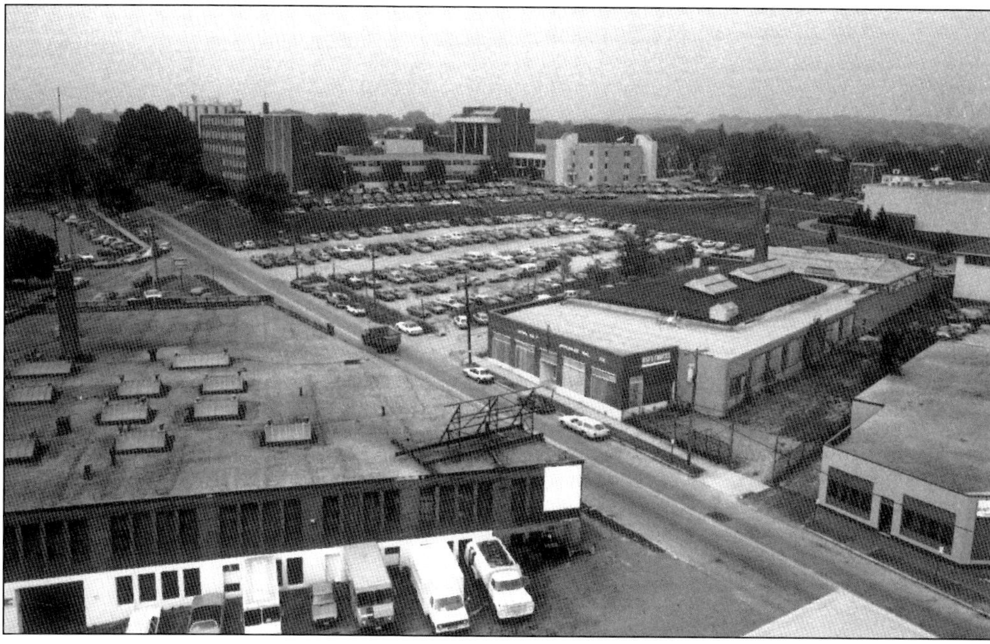

The commercial structure abutting a Portland campus parking lot in the center of this photograph (probably taken from what was later the library) was in 1985 remodeled to hold a larger cafeteria, a new bookstore, meeting rooms, and open space for activities. It would become the Robert S. Woodbury Student Center in honor of the 1979–1986 University of Southern Maine president (later chancellor of the University of Maine System).

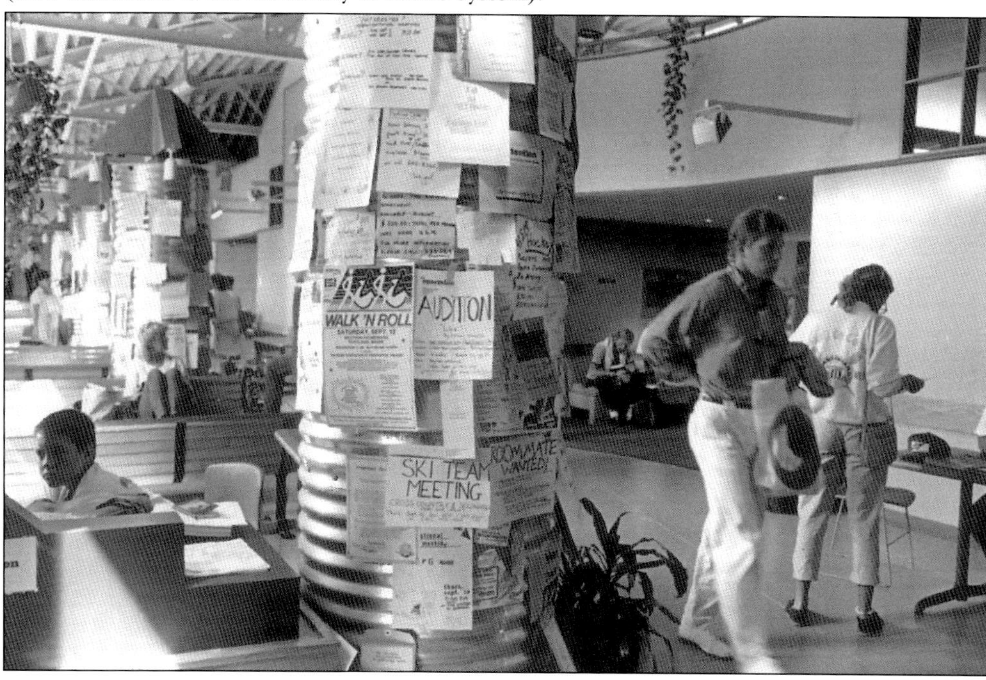

A brightly lit corridor connects the cafeteria end of the Student Center with the bookstore at the other end. It also gives access to meeting spaces and serves as a locale for dissemination of campus information—from kiosks or booths.

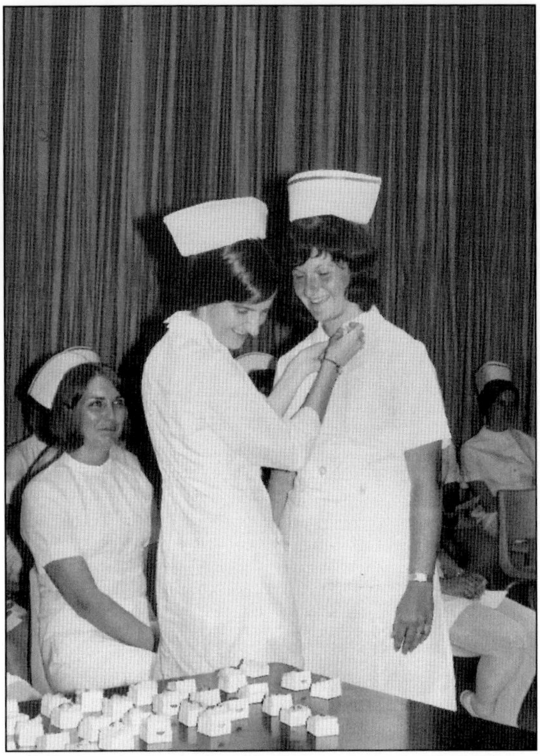

Students of the School of Nursing take their "core" of liberal arts classes, but necessarily maintain a degree of separation, with special courses as well as practical hospital work. They also have their own ceremonies, like this traditional pinning of graduating seniors.

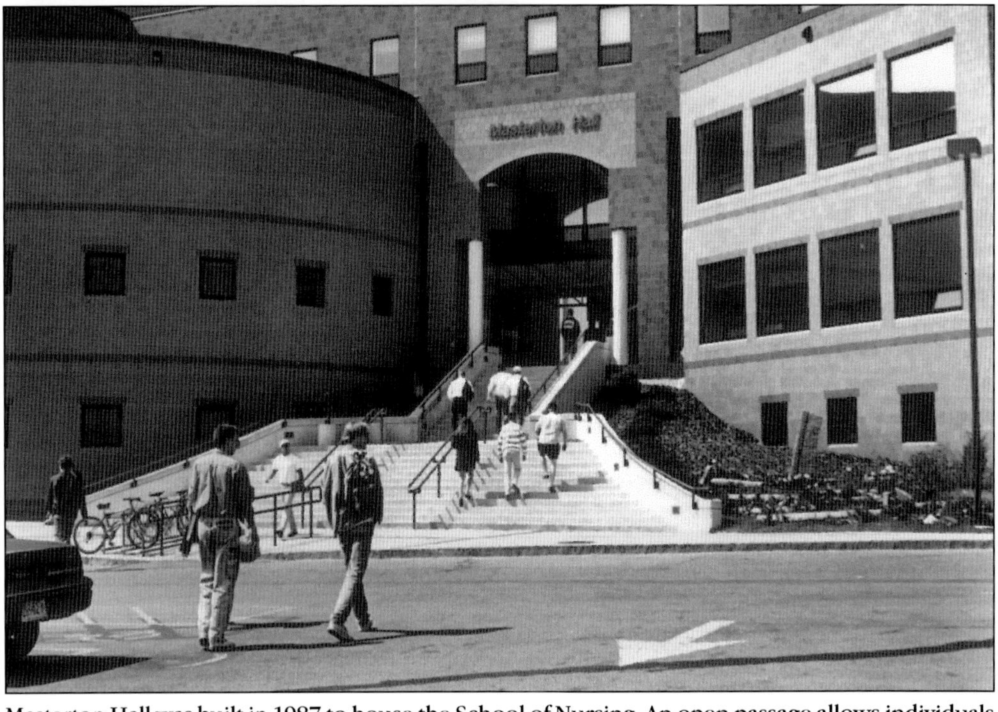

Masterton Hall was built in 1987 to house the School of Nursing. An open passage allows individuals to move from the level of the original campus and then down broad steps to a parking lot and the Student Center. The building was named for civic leaders Robert and Nancy Masterton.

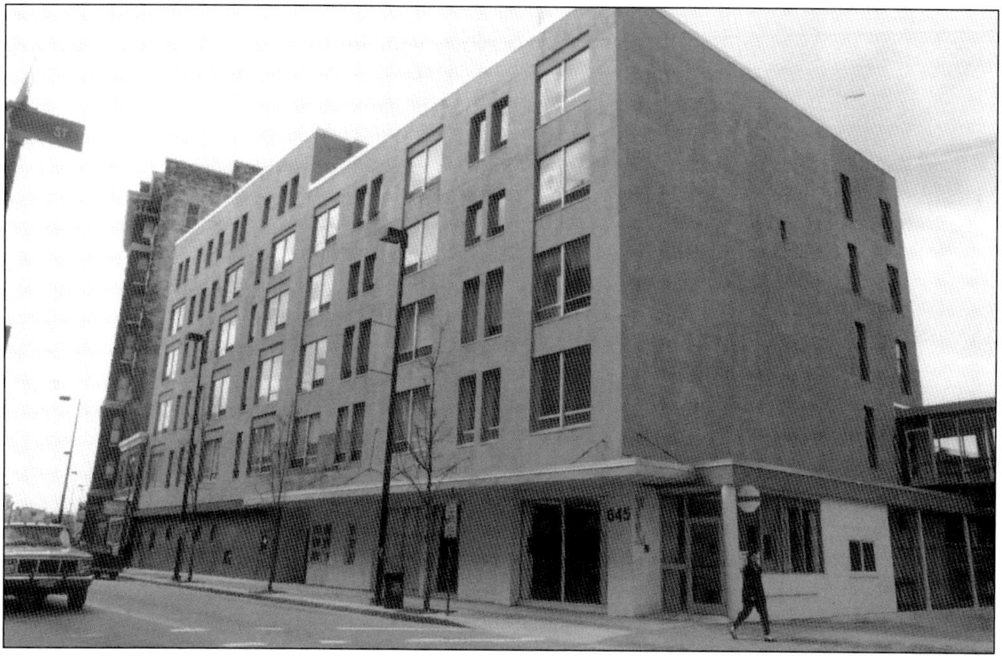

In 1987, the one-time Columbia Hotel (later the Portlander) on Congress Street was leased for use as a downtown dormitory. A year later, it was purchased and has become Portland Hall and has its own bus line to campus.

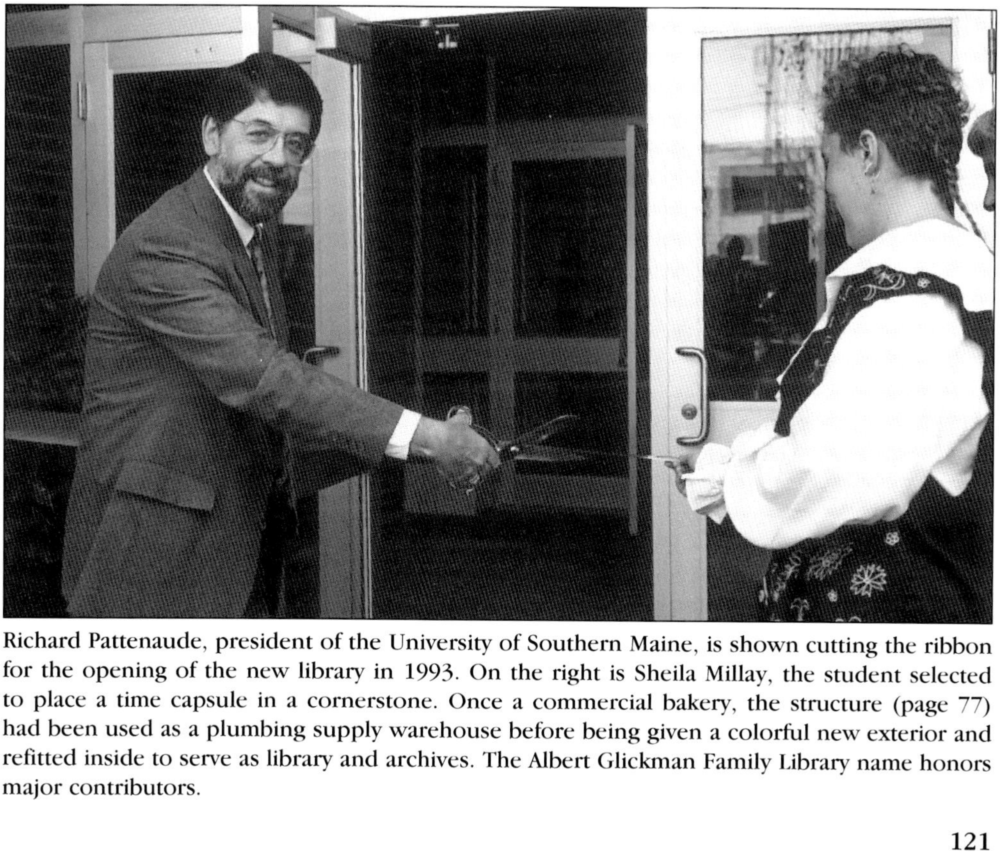

Richard Pattenaude, president of the University of Southern Maine, is shown cutting the ribbon for the opening of the new library in 1993. On the right is Sheila Millay, the student selected to place a time capsule in a cornerstone. Once a commercial bakery, the structure (page 77) had been used as a plumbing supply warehouse before being given a colorful new exterior and refitted inside to serve as library and archives. The Albert Glickman Family Library name honors major contributors.

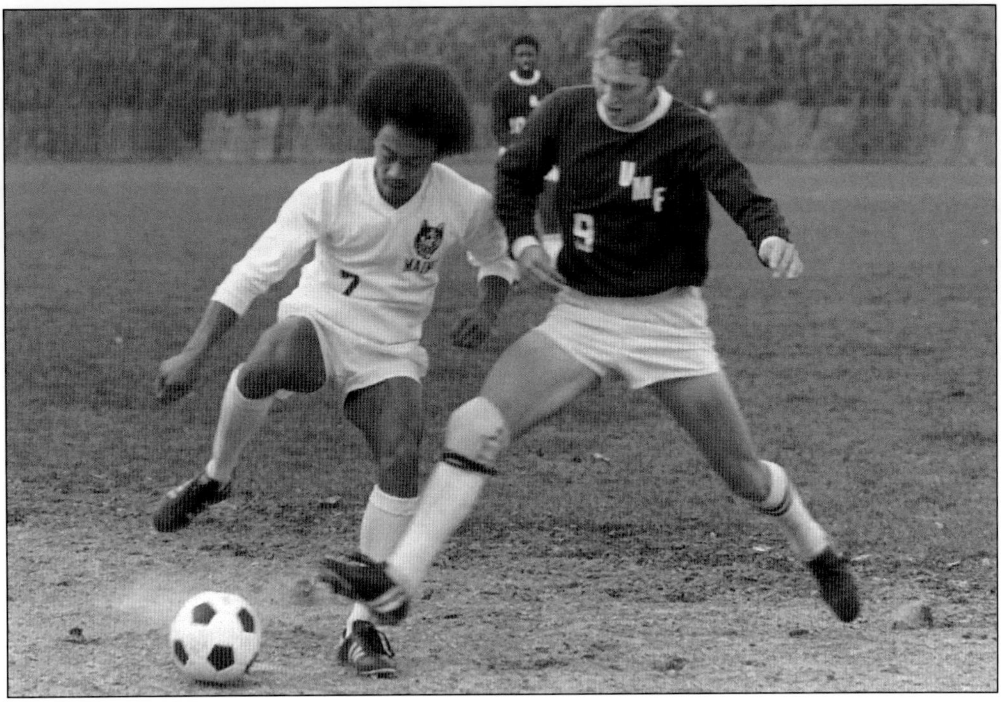

Soccer was not new (see page 25), but it became a popular competitive sport only in recent decades. The University of Maine at Portland-Gorham team was helped by the recruiting of students from the Caribbean. Andrew Whittaker (in the Huskies shirt, No. 7) helped lead the team to defeat the University of Maine at Farmington in 1975.

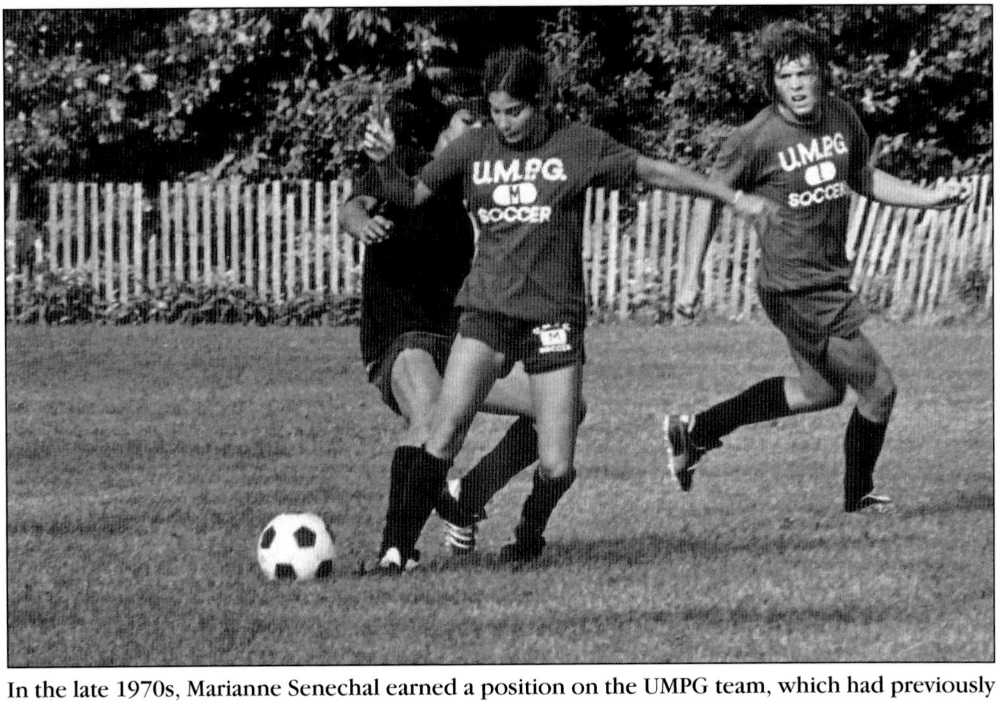

In the late 1970s, Marianne Senechal earned a position on the UMPG team, which had previously been all male.

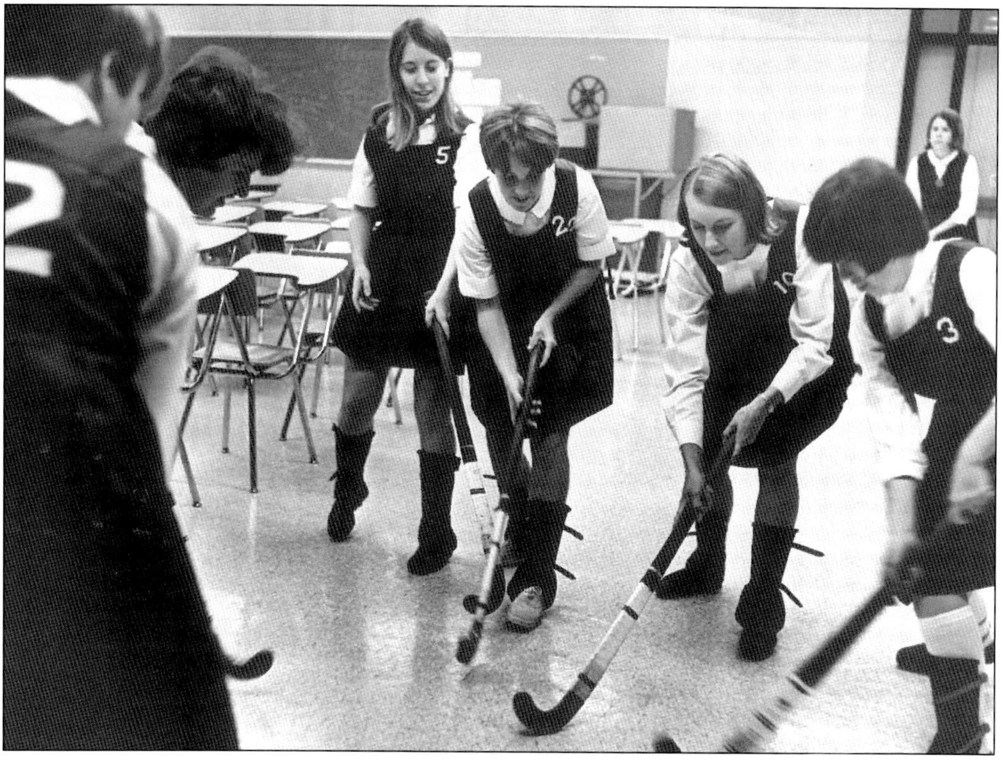

Sports programs continue to expand, especially those for women. Field hockey was only one of the many classes offered in the gym classrooms.

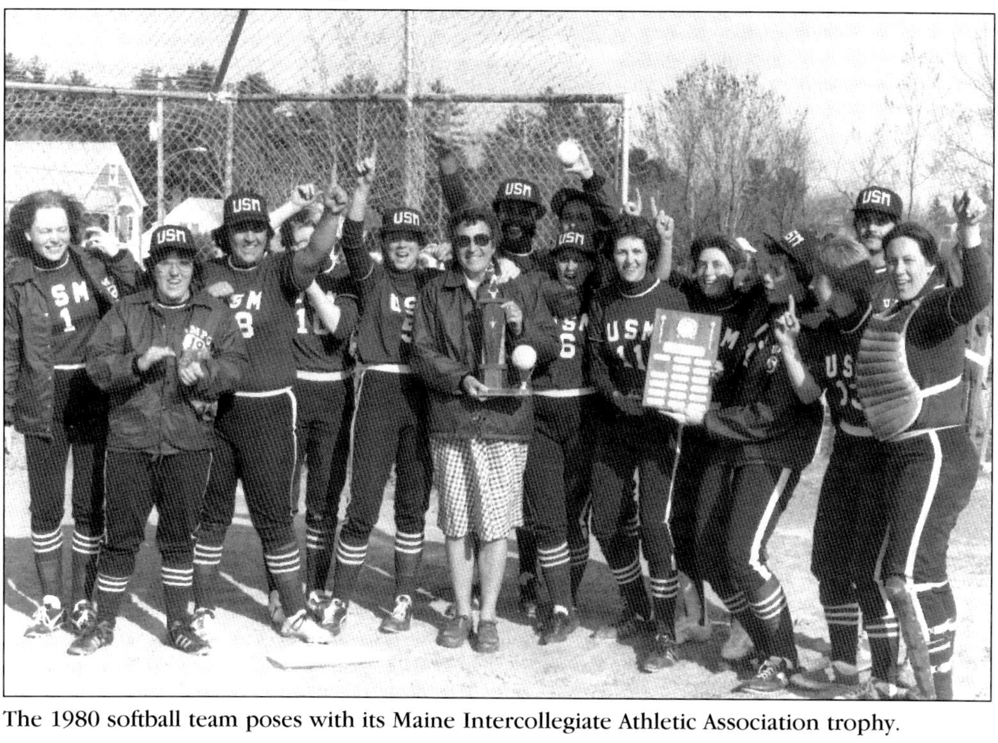

The 1980 softball team poses with its Maine Intercollegiate Athletic Association trophy.

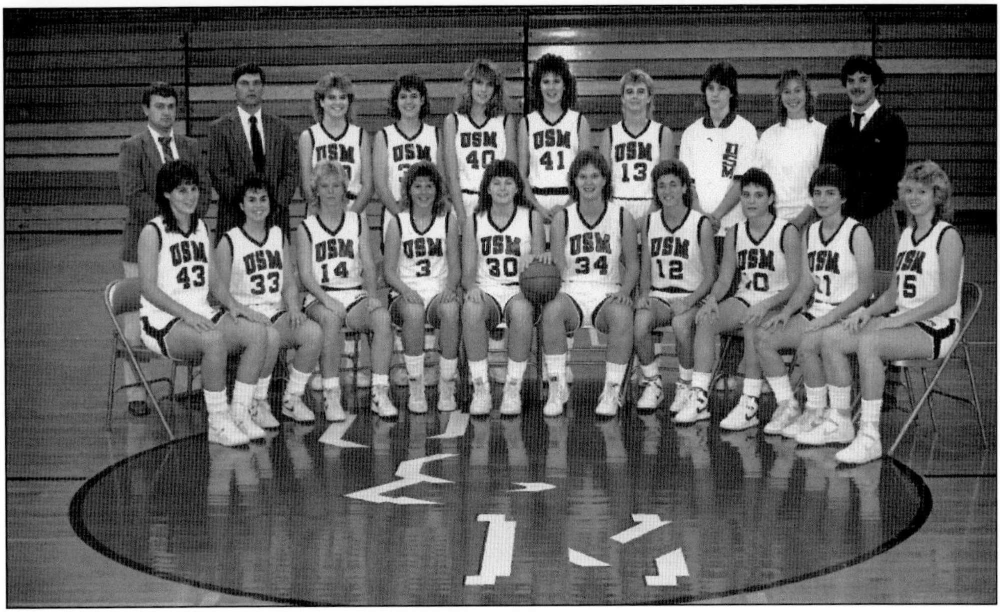

Some women's basketball teams have reached the Final Four. The members of the 1987–1988 team are shown, from left to right, as follows: (front row) Gina LeBlanc, Trudi Nelson, Tammy Knowles, Chrissie Mellor, Diana Duff (captain), Mary Harrigan (captain), Kristen Potito, Kris Littlefield, Jen Allen, and Julie Cooper; (back row) Gary Fifield (head coach), Tom Murphy (assistant coach), Sue Bernier, Janet Whitney, Nancy Love, Amy Johnson, Erica Swenson, Julie Fabian, Chrissie Schmidt (manager), and Greg Sands (student assistant coach).

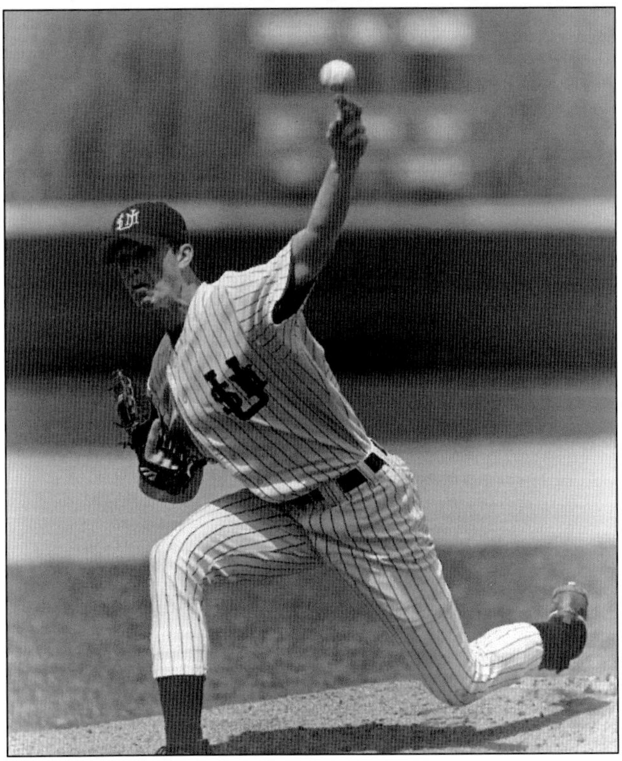

When the 1997 University of Southern Maine baseball team won the National Division Three Championship, Jason Jensen was a star pitcher.

Not all sports are competitive. James Sullivan, athletic director, was particularly interested in activities for the handicapped and helped institute a program in recreational therapy.

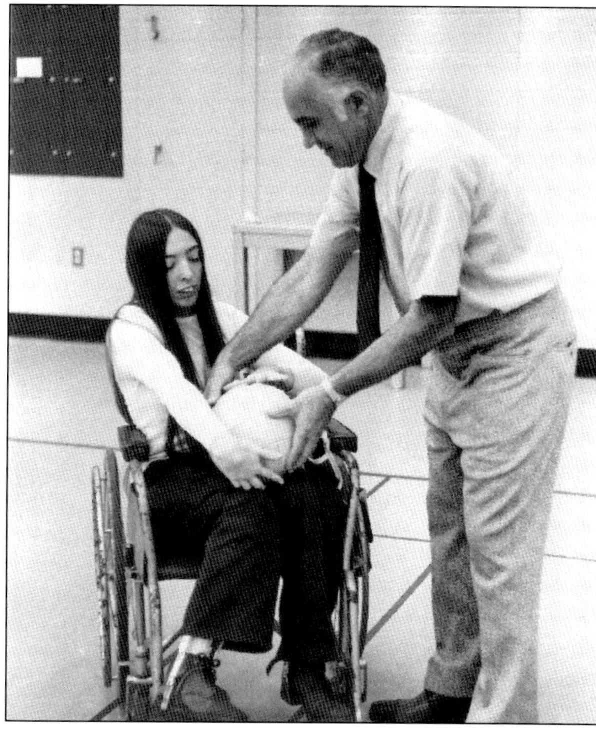

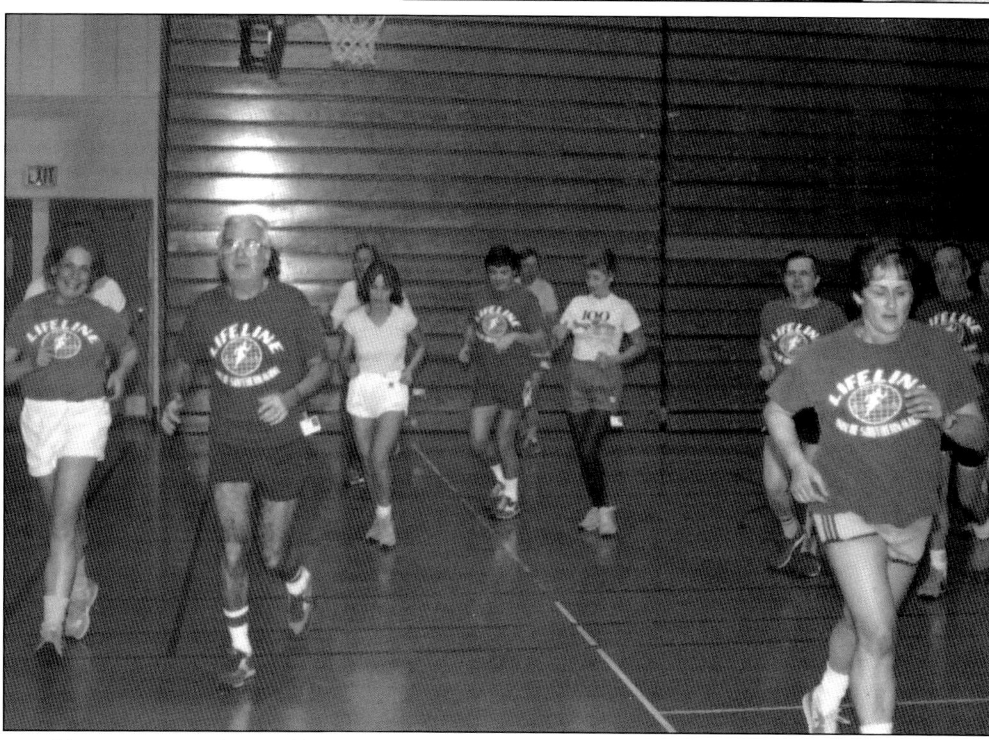

In addition to providing college courses (as well as non-credit enrichment programs) for the community, the university has long opened its gyms to non-students, in a Lifeline program for fitness. Some classes jog.

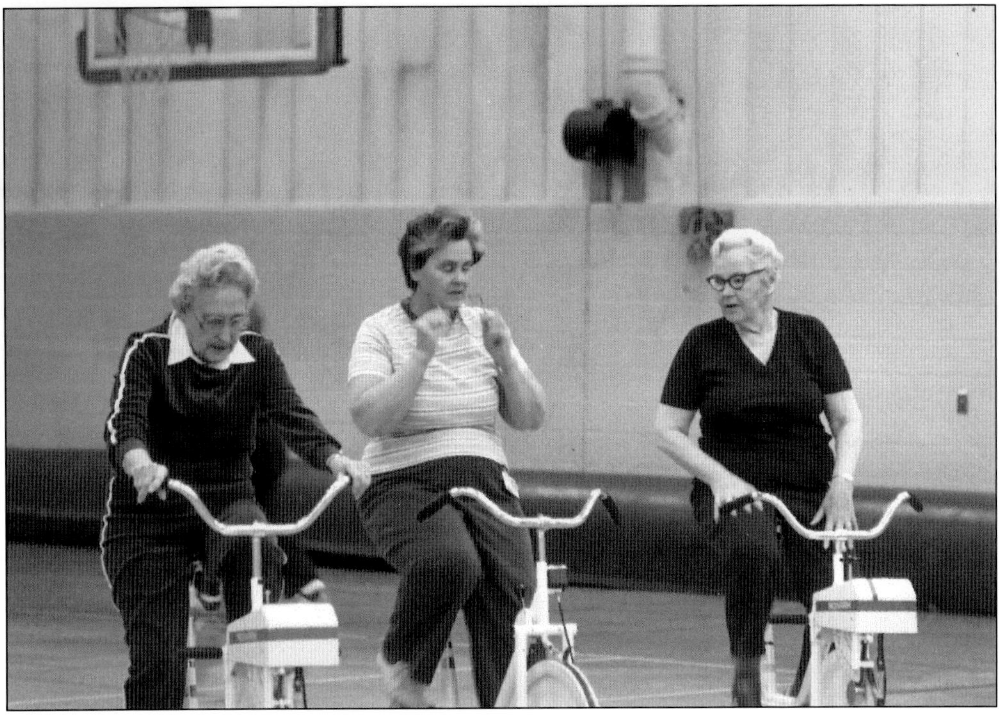

Others use stationary bikes.

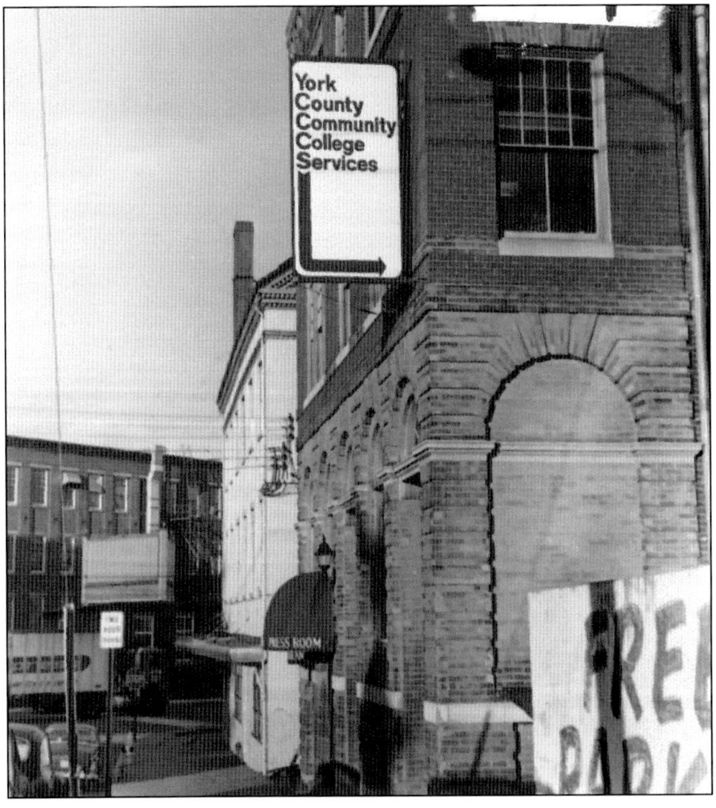

York County Community College Services (YCCCS) was an outreach program begun in 1973 with an office in Sanford and lasting about a decade before being reorganized. University faculty members continue to give courses in the present Sanford Center, and some full-time students find it easier to attend those classes as part of their programs.

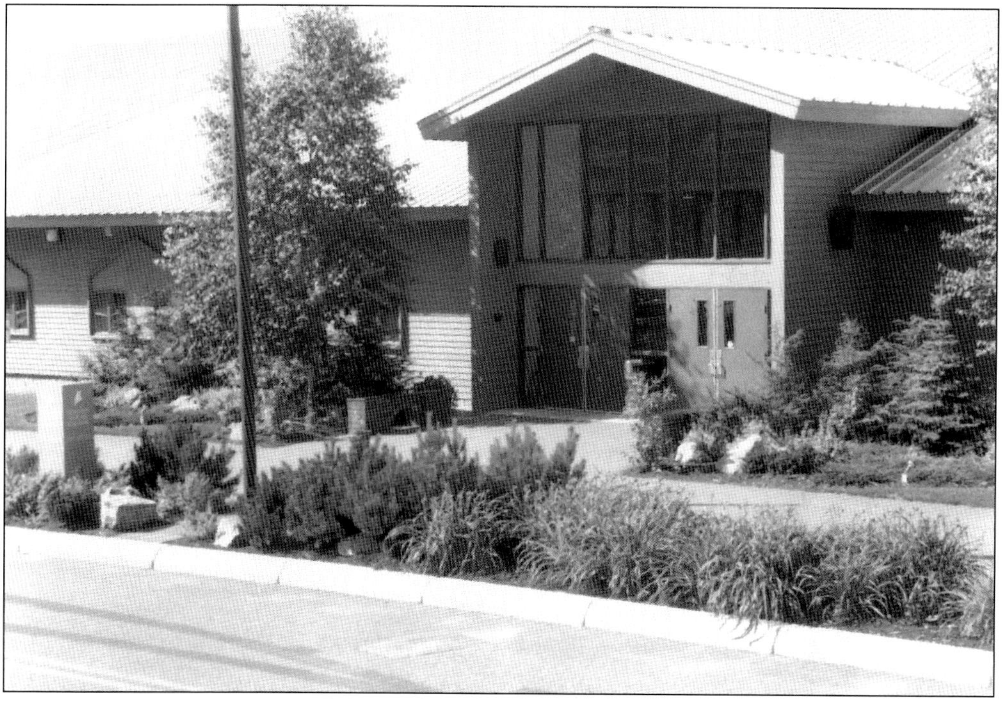

At the behest of its community, Lewiston-Auburn College was established in 1988, with quarters in a remodeled industrial building. Although with its own administration, programs, and some faculty, it is a part of the University of Southern Maine and frequently uses the university's faculty for certain courses.

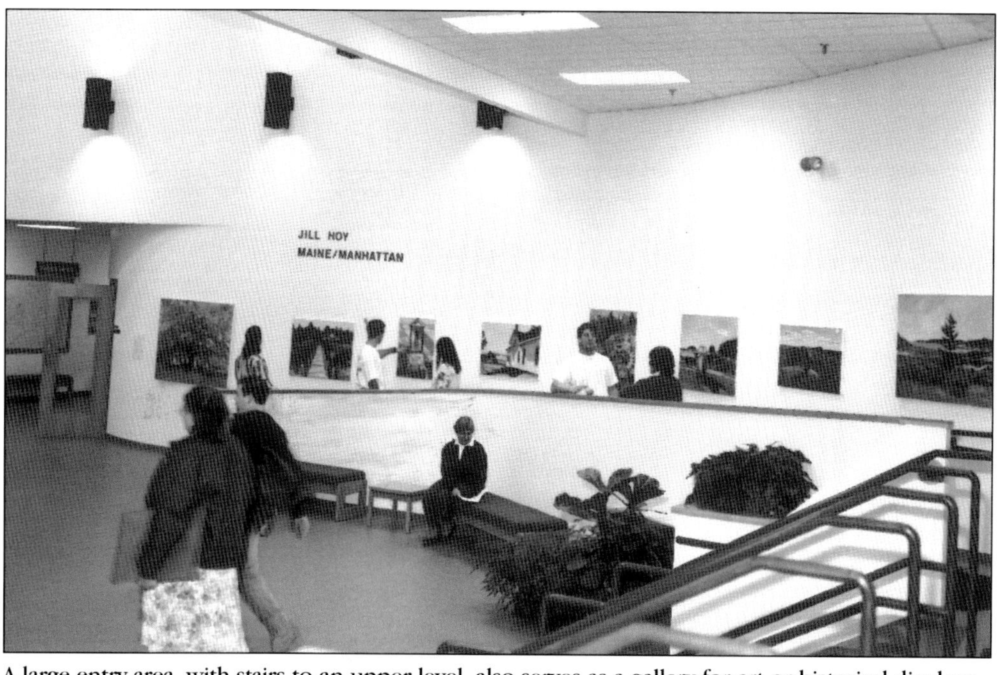

A large entry area, with stairs to an upper level, also serves as a gallery for art or historical displays.

ACKNOWLEDGMENTS

Most of these photographs are from the University Archives Special Collections at the University of Southern Maine library, where Susie Bock, archivist, and Mary Madden, assistant archivist, were of incalculable assistance. Additional images came from collections of the Maine Historic Preservation Commission (pp. 9, 14 top, 29, 33); the Maine Historical Society (p. 36 bottom); Greater Portland Landmarks (pp. 31, 121 top); the Gorham Historical Society (pp. 11 bottom, 14 bottom, 19 top, 20 top); Maine Medical Center (p. 30 bottom); and the University of Southern Maine offices of publications (pp. 119 bottom, 120 bottom, 121 bottom), athletics (p. 124), and Lewiston-Auburn College (p. 127). The Portland Press Herald permitted use of photographs (pp. 50 bottom, 85 bottom). Alumnae who responded to a request in the spring issue of *Mainestream* and shared their snapshots were Janis Rand (pp. 53 top, 56 bottom, 57 bottom, 58, 59), Virginia Foster (pp. 52 top, 55, 56 top), Doris Whitten (pp. 22 bottom), and Philippa Nice (pp. 62 top, 64 top). Most photographers are unidentified, but credit should be given to Don Johnson (p. 50 bottom), Sam Brocato (p. 55), and Libby Barrett (p. 121 bottom).

Also assisting my searches were Earle Shettleworth Jr. of the Maine Historic Preservation Commission; Cally Gurley and Roberta Gray of New England College's Westbrook Campus, who helped me document the PJC-WJC connection; Ursula Baier; George Watson of GHS; Cynthia Tibbetts of the MMC Media Center; Roger Philippon of LAC; and, at MHS, Stephanie Philbrick, William Barry, and Nicholas Noyes. The latter contributed an image from his family album (p. 39 bottom). Betty Huntley, the University of Southern Maine alumni director, lent me books and shared other documents. This book also owes much to Pres. Richard Pattenaude, who was supportive from the start, and to the many retirees, faculty, and staff of the University of Southern Maine, on whom I called for suggestions and data. Particularly helpful were Dick Costello, Walter Stump, Minor Rootes, and John Plante. Unfortunately, all ideas could not be accommodated; any remaining errors are my responsibility.